The Myrtle Reed Cook Book

Myrtle Reed

[ZHINGOORA BOOKS]

This edition is published by
Zhingoora Books.

CONTENTS

THE PHILOSOPHY OF BREAKFAST

The breakfast habit is of antique origin. Presumably the primeval man arose from troubled dreams, in the first gray light of dawn, and set forth upon devious forest trails, seeking that which he might devour, while the primeval woman still slumbered in her cave. Nowadays, it is the lady herself who rises while the day is yet young, slips into a kimono, and patters out into the kitchen to light the gas flame under the breakfast food.

In this matter of breaking the fast, each house is law unto itself. There are some who demand a dinner at seven or eight in the morning, and others who consider breakfast utterly useless. The Englishman, who is still mighty on the face of the earth, eats a breakfast which would seriously tax the digestive apparatus of an ostrich or a goat, and goes on his way rejoicing.

In an English cook-book only seven years old, menus for "ideal" breakfasts are given, which run as follows:

"Devilled Drum-sticks and Eggs on the dish, Pigs Feet, Buttered Toast, Dry Toast, Brown and White Bread and Butter, Marmalade and Porridge."

"Bloaters on Toast, Collared Tongue, Hot Buttered Toast, Dry Toast, Marmalade, Brown and White Bread and Butter, Bread and Milk."

"Pigeon Pie, Stewed Kidney, Milk Rolls, Dry Toast, Brown and White Bread and Butter, Mustard and Cress, Milk Porridge."

And for a "simple breakfast,"—in August, mind you!—this is especially recommended:

"Bloaters on Toast, Corned Beef, Muffins, Brown and White Bread and Butter, Marmalade, and Boiled Hominy."

An American who ate a breakfast like that in August probably would not send his collars to the laundry more than once or twice more, but it takes all kinds of people to make up a world.

Across the Channel from the brawny Briton is the Frenchman, who, with infinitely more wisdom, begins his day with a cup of coffee and a roll. So far, so good, but his *déjeuner à la fourchette* at eleven or twelve is not always unobjectionable from a hygienic standpoint. The "uniform breakfast," which is cheerfully advocated by some, may be hygienic but it is not exciting. Before the weary mental vision stretches an endless procession of breakfasts, all exactly alike, year in and year out. It is quite possible that the "no-breakfast" theory was first formulated by some one who had been, was, or was about to be a victim of this system.

The "no-breakfast" plan has much to recommend it, however. In the first place, it saves a deal of trouble. The family rises, bathes itself, puts on its spotless raiment in leisurely and untroubled fashion, and proceeds to the particular business of the day. There are no burnt toast, soggy waffles, muddy coffee, heavy muffins, or pasty breakfast food to be reckoned with. Theoretically, the energy supplied by last night's dinner is "on tap," waiting to be called upon. And, moreover, one is seldom hungry in the morning, and what is the use of feeding a person who is not hungry?

It has been often said, and justly, that Americans eat too much. Considering the English breakfast, however, we may metaphorically pat ourselves upon the back, for there is no one of us, surely, who taxes the Department of the Interior thus.

"What is one man's meat is another man's poison" has been held pointedly to refer to breakfast, for here, as nowhere else, is the individual a law unto himself. Fruit is the satisfaction of one and the distress of another; cereal is a life-giving food to one and a soggy mass of indigestibility to some one else; and coffee, which is really most innocent when properly made, has lately taken much blame for sins not its own.

Quite often the discomfort caused by the ill-advised combination of acid fruit with a starchy cereal has been attributed to the clear, amber beverage which probably was the much-vaunted "nectar of the gods." Coffee with cream in it may be wrong for some people who could use boiling milk with impunity.

For a woman who spends the early part of the day at home, the omission of breakfast may be salutary. When hunger seizes her, she is within reach of her own kitchen, where proper foods may be properly cooked, but for a business woman or man the plan is little less than suicidal. Mr. Man may, indeed, go down town in comfort, with no thought of food, but, no later than noon, he is keenly desirous of interior decoration. Within his reach there is, usually, but the lunch counter, where, in company with other hapless humans, he sustains himself with leathery pie, coffee which never met the coffee bean, and the durable doughnut of commerce. The result is—to put it mildly—discontent, which seemingly has no adequate cause.

It is better, by far, for Mr. Man to eat a breakfast which shall contain the proteids, carbohydrates, phosphates, and starches that he will require during the day, and omit the noon luncheon entirely, except, perhaps, for a bit of fruit. Moreover, a dainty breakfast, daintily served, has a distinct æsthetic value. The temper of the individual escorted to the front door by a devoted spouse has more than a little to do with the temper of the selfsame individual who is let in at night by the aforesaid D. S.

Many a man is confronted in the morning by an untidy, ill-cooked breakfast, a frowsy woman and a still frowsier baby, and, too often, by querulous whinings and complaints.

The ancient Britons had a pleasing arrangement which they called "The Truce of God." By this, there was no fighting whatever, no matter what the provocation, between sunset on Wednesday and sunrise on Monday. This gave time for other affairs, and for the exercise of patience, toleration, and other virtues of the same ilk.

Many a household might take a leaf from this book to good advantage. Settle all differences after dinner, since at no time of the day is man in more reasonable mood, and ordain a "Truce of God" from dawn until after dinner.

No dinner, however beautifully cooked and served, no fine raiment, however costly and becoming, can ever atone, in the memory of a man, for the wild and untamed morning which too often prevails in the American household. His mind, distraught with business cares, harks back to his home—with pleasure? None too often, more's the pity.

Some one has said that, in order to make a gentleman, one must begin with the grandfather. It is equally true that a good and proper breakfast begins the night before—or, better yet, the morning before.

Careful, systematic planning in advance lightens immeasurably the burden of housekeeping, and, many a time, makes the actual work nothing but fun. Those who have tried the experiment of planning meals for the entire week are enthusiastic in praise of the system. It secures variety, simplifies marketing, arranges for left-overs, and gives many an hour of peace and comfort which could not be had otherwise.

Even if a woman be her own maid, as, according to statistics, eighty-five per cent. of us are, a dainty, hygienic, satisfying breakfast is hers and her lord's for little more than the asking. By careful preparation in advance, the morning labor is reduced to a minimum; by the intelligent use of lists and memoranda, the weary and reluctant body is saved many an unnecessary step.

An alarm clock of the "intermittent" sort insures early rising, a dash of cold water on the face is a physical and mental tonic of the most agreeable kind, and one hour in the morning is worth two at night, as the grandmothers of all of us have often said.

Fruit, usually, may be prepared for serving the night before, and will be improved by a few hours in the refrigerator. Cereals should be soaked over night in the water in which they are to be cooked, and a few hours' cooking in the afternoon will injure very few cereals destined for the breakfast table the next morning. Codfish balls and many other things will be none the worse for a night's waiting; the table can be set, and everything made ready for a perfect breakfast, which half an hour of intelligent effort in the morning will readily evolve.

A plea is made for the use of the chafing-dish, which is fully as attractive at the breakfast table as in the "wee sma' hours" in which it usually shines; for a white apron instead of a gingham one when "my lady" is also the cook; for a crisp, clean shirt-waist instead of an abominable dressing-sack; for smooth, tidy hair, instead of unkempt locks; for a collar and a belt, and a persistent, if determined, cheerfulness.

In the long run, these things pay, and with compound interest at that. They involve a certain amount of labor, a great deal of careful planning, eternal getting-up when it is far more pleasant to abide in dreamland, quite often a despairing weariness, if not a headache, and no small draft upon one's power of self-denial and self-sacrifice.

But he who goes in the morning from a quiet, comfortable, well-ordered house, with a pleasant memory of the presiding genius of his hearthstone, is twice the man that his fellow may be, whose wife breakfasts at ten in her bed, or, frowsy and unkempt, whines at him from across a miserable breakfast—twice as well fitted for the ceaseless grind of an exhausting day in the business arena, whence he returns at night, footsore, weary, and depressed, to the four walls wherein he abides.

"How far that little candle throws its beams! So shines a good deed in a naughty world."

To some, this may seem an undue stress laid upon the material side of existence, but the human animal needs animal comforts even more than his brother of forest and field, and from such humble beginnings great things may come, not the least of which is the fine, spiritual essence of a happy home.

HOW TO SET THE TABLE

Having said so much, we proceed, not to our mutton, as the French have it, but to our breakfast, in which the table plays no small nor unimportant part.

There are rumors that the pretty and sensible fashion of doilies on the bare table is on the wane, but let us hope these are untrue, or, if not, that some of us may have the courage of our convictions and continue to adhere to a custom which has everything in its favor and nothing against it.

In the absence of handsome top of oak or mahogany, the breakfast cloths, fringed or not, as one likes, which are about a yard and a quarter square, are the next best thing. Asbestos mats, under the cloth, protect the table from the hot dishes. Failing these, fairly satisfactory substitutes are made from thin white oil-cloth, between two layers of canton flannel, "fur side outside," and quilted on the machine. Grass table-mats are also used, but always under cloth or doily. Canton flannel, quilted, three layers to a mat, is easily washed, and furnishes a great deal of protection.

Breakfast, most assuredly, is not dinner, and there should be a distinct difference in the laying of the table. The small doilies are easily washed, and fresh ones are possible every morning—an assured gain in the way of daintiness.

Let us suppose that we have a handsome table-top, and an unlimited supply of doilies, tray-cloths and centrepieces. First the centrepiece goes on, exactly in the centre, by the way, and not with a prejudiced leaning to one side or the other. On this belongs the pot of growing fern, the low jar containing a few simple flowers, or a bowl of fruit, decorated with green leaves, if green leaves are to be had.

At each place the breakfast doily, nine or twelve inches square, a small doily for the coffee cup, and another for the glass of water. At the right of the plate, the small silver knife, sharp edge toward the plate, the spoons for fruit and cereal; at the left, one fork, or two, as needed, and the coffee spoon.

In front of the master of the house the small platter containing the *pièce de résistance* will eventually be placed; in front of the mistress of the mansion, the silver tray bearing the coffee service—coffee-pot, hot-water pitcher, cream jug, milk pitcher, and sugar bowl.

Breakfast napkins are smaller than dinner napkins, and the small fringed napkins are not out of place. "Costly thy habit as thy purse will buy" might well refer to linen, for it is the one thing in which price is a direct guarantee of quality.

Satisfactory breakfast cloths and napkins are made of linen sheeting, fringed, hemstitched, or carefully hemmed by hand, and in this way a pretty cloth can be had for less money than in any other. The linen wears well, washes beautifully, and acquires a finer sheen with every tubbing. Insertions and borders of torchon or other heavy lace make a breakfast cloth suitable for the most elaborate occasion, and separate doilies may easily be made to match. The heavy white embroidery which has recently come into favor is unusually attractive here.

Finger-bowls wait on the sideboard, to be placed after the fruit course, or after breakfast. The rose-water, slice of lemon, geranium leaves, and other finger-bowl refinements in favor for dinners are out of place at breakfast. Clear, cool water is in better taste.

The china used at the breakfast table should be different from that used at dinner. Heavier ware is permissible, and more latitude in the way of decoration is given. Much of the breakfast china one sees in the shops is distinctly cheerful in tone, and one must take care to select the more quiet patterns. It is not pleasant to go to breakfast with a fickle appetite, and be greeted by a trumpet-toned "Good Morning" from the china.

Endless difference is allowed, however, and all the quaint, pretty jugs, pitchers, and plates may properly be used at breakfast. One is wise, however, to have a particular color scheme in mind and to buy all china to blend with it. Blue and white is a good combination, and is, perhaps, more suitable for the morning meal than anything else. As a certain philosopher says: "The blue and white look so pretty with the eggs!"

The carafe, muffin plate, platter, and all other bowls, platters, plates, and pitchers not on the individual cover have each a separate doily, with the protecting mat always under hot dishes. A well-set table is governed by a simple law—that of precision. Dishes arranged in an order little less than military, all angles either right or acute, will, for some occult reason, always look well. Informality may be given by the arrangement of the flowers, or by a flower or two laid carelessly on the table. But one must be careful not to trifle too much with this law of precision. Knives, forks, and spoons must all be laid straight, but not near enough together to touch, and napkins and dishes must be precisely placed, else confusion and riot will result.

The breakfast selected as a type consists of fruit, a cereal, salt fish, or salt meat, or eggs, or omelets, hot bread of some kind, and pancakes or waffles, or coffee cake, one dish from each group, and coffee. Six dishes in all, which may be less if desired, but never more. All six form a breakfast sufficiently hearty for a stone mason or a piano mover; one or two give a breakfast light enough to tempt those who eat no breakfast at all. For serving it are required small and medium-sized plates, knives, forks, spoons, egg cups, platters, service plates, cups and saucers, glasses, coffee-pot, pitchers, sugar bowl, and cream jug, syrup pitcher, and fruit bowl.

Fruit is said to be "gold in the morning," and it is a poor breakfast, indeed, from which it is omitted. Even in winter it is not hard to secure variety, if time and thought be taken, for the dried fruits are always in the market and by careful cooking may be made acceptable to the most uncertain appetite.

Medical authorities recommend a glass of water taken the first thing upon rising, either hot or cold as suits one best. A little lemon-juice takes the "flat" taste from plain hot water, and clear, cool water, not iced, needs nothing at all. This simple observance of a very obvious hygienic rule will temper the tempestuous morning for any one. One washes his face, his hands, his body—then why not his stomach, which has worked hard a large part of the night, and is earnestly desirous of the soothing refreshment of a bath?

To those carping critics who cavil at the appearance of the stomach in a chapter entitled "How to Set the Table," we need only say that the table is set for the stomach, and the stomach should be set for the table, and anyway, it comes very near being a table of contents, *n'est-ce pas*?

THE KITCHEN RUBAIYAT

Wake, for the Alarm Clock scatters into FlightThe variegated Nightmares of the Night;Allures the Gas into the Kitchen RangeAnd pleads for Rolls and Muffins that are Light.

Before the Splendor of the last Dream diedMethought a Voice from out my Doorway cried:"When all the Breakfast is Prepared for himWhy doth my lord within his Crib abide?"

And, as the cat Purred, she who was BeforeWithin the Kitchen shouted: "Guard the Door!Else this new Bridget will have Flown the CoopAnd, once Departed, will Return no More!"

All maids in sight the Wise One gladly HiresAnd one of them she Presently acquires,Yet toward the Bureau does not fail to LookBecause all Maids, as well as Men, are liars.

For Mary Ann has gone, with all her Woes,And Dinah, too, has fled—where, no one knows,But still a Bridget from the Bureau comesAnd many a Tekla of her Reference blows.

Come, fill the Cup, and let the Kettle Sing!The Cream and Sugar and Hot Water bring!Methinks this fragrant liquid amber hereWithin the Pot, is pretty much the Thing.

Each Morn a thousand Cereals brings, you say?Yes, but where leaves the Food of Yesterday?And this same Grocer man that sells us NerveShall take Pa's Wheat and Mother's Oats away.

For lo, my small Back Yard is thickly StrownWith Ki-Tee-Munch, Chew-Chew, and Postman's OwnWhere Apple-Nuts and Strength have been Forgot—Ah, how these Papers by the Winds are Blown!

The tender Waffle hearts are Set uponIs either Crisp or Soggy, and AnonLike Maple Syrup made of corn and CobsLasts but a scant Five Minutes, and is Gone.

I often think that never gets so RedMy flower-like Nose as when I've just been FedAnd after Breakfast, in the Glass I look,And never Fail to Wish that I were dead.

And this faint Sallow Place upon my Mien—How came it There? From that fair Coffee Bean?Ah, take the Glass away! Make Haste unlessYou want to see my Whole Complexion green.

When I was Younger, I did oft FrequentThe Married Bunch, and heard Great ArgumentAbout the Fearful Price of Eggs, and HowTo get a Dollar's Work out of a Cent.

And when I asked them of their Recompense,What did they Get for Keeping Down Expense—Oh, many a cup of Coffee, Steaming Hot,Must drown the Memory of their Insolence!

If I were Married 't would be my DesireTo get up Every Morn and Build the FireFor fear my Husband should use Kerosene,And, without warning, be transported Higher.

Ah, with the Coffee all my Years provide!Its chemicals may turn me green Inside,But all my Fears are Scattered to the WindsWhen o'er the fragrant Pot I can Preside.

I blame our Mother Eve, who did mistakeHer Job, and flirted Somewhat with the Snake,For all the Errors of the Flaky Roll,For all the Terrors of the Buckwheat Cake.

A glass of Creamy Milk just from the Cow,Or Buttermilk, drawn from the Goat, I trow,And thou across the Festal Board from Me,A Six-Room Flat were Paradise enow!

Some for a Patent Bread that will not Crumb,And nary Bite of Cereal for Some—Ah, take the Coffee! Let all else go byNor heed the Thick White Fur upon the Tongue.

Look to the Human Wrecks about us: lo,About their Indigestion how they Blow,And lay the Blame on Coffee, crystal Clear,Or say the Crisp Hot Muffin is their Foe!

And those who chew and chew upon the Grain,Have got so used to Chewing, they are FainTo Dwell upon their Health Food in their TalkAnd presently their Neighbors go Insane.

FOOT-NOTES

1. The author began with the intention of adapting the entire Rubaiyat to kitchen purposes, but thought better of it just in time to head off the Lyric Muse, who was coming at full gallop, with her trunk.

2. Those who do not like The Kitchen Rubaiyat will doubtless be glad there is no more of it.

3. Those who do like it can begin at the beginning and read it again. The rest of it would be about like this installment, anyway.

P. S. If the demand is great enough, the rest of it may appear in another book.

P. S. 2. The publisher of this book has an unalterable prejudice against printing poetry, but he allowed The Kitchen Rubaiyat to slip by without question.

P. S. 3. ?

FRUITS IN SEASON

Apples	All the year.
Apricots	July 20 to August 20.
Bananas	All the year.
Blackberries	July 1 to August 15.
Cherries	June 1 to July 15.
Currants, Red and White	July 1 to August 15.

Figs, dried	All the year.
Figs, bag	October and November.
Gooseberries	July.
Grapes, Concord	August 20 to November 15.
" Malaga	November to March.
" California	December to March.
Grapefruit	October to July.
Green Gage Plums	August 1 to September 15.
Huckleberries	July and August.
Melons, Musk, Water, Cantaloupe	July 15 to October 15.
Oranges	December to May.

Peaches	August and September.
Pears	August and September.
Pineapples	June to September.
Plums, Blue	September.
Quinces	September, October, and November.
Rhubarb	April to September.
Raspberries, Black and Red	July and August.
Strawberries	May and June.
Tangerines	November to February.

The above table, of course, is only a rough outline, as seasons and localities vary so much. The tendency, too, is to extend the season of every fruit indefinitely, as transporting and refrigerating methods improve. Fruit out of season is always expensive, and often unripe and unsatisfactory. Fortunately, when it is at its best it is always abundant and at the lowest price.

Among the dried fruits may be mentioned Prunelles, Apricots, Apples, Blackberries, Cherries, Nectarines, Peaches, peeled and unpeeled, Pears,

Plums, Raspberries, Prunes, Figs, and Dates. Canned fruits which may be used for breakfast, with proper preparation, are Pears, Peaches, Apricots, Cherries, Plums, and Pineapples.

Dried fruits may be soaked over night in the water in which they are to be cooked, and simmered slowly, until they are tender, with little sugar or none at all. They may also be steamed, either with or without sugar, omitting the soaking, until tender enough for a straw to pierce. Combinations of dried fruits are often agreeable, and a few raisins will sometimes add a pleasant flavor.

Canned fruits intended for breakfast should be drained and very thoroughly rinsed in cold water, then allowed to stand for some hours in a cool place.

Many of the fruits, both dried and fresh, combine well with cereals. Care must be taken, however, to follow such acid fruits as Currants, Cherries, Oranges, and Grapefruit, with meat or egg dishes, omitting the cereal, as the starch and acid are very likely to fight with each other when once inside, to the inconvenience of the non-combatant. A fruit which for any reason tastes "flat" can be instantly improved in flavor and tonic quality by a sprinkle of lemon-juice.

Below are given different ways of preparing fruit for the breakfast table.

APPLES

I. When served whole, apples should be carefully washed and rubbed to a high polish with a crash towel. Only perfect fruit should be served in this way, and green leaves in the fruit bowl are especially desirable. Fruit-knives are essential.

II. Pare, quarter, and core good eating apples, removing all imperfections. Serve a few quarters on each plate, with or without sugar. A sprinkle of cinnamon or lemon-juice will improve fruit which has little flavor. A grating of nutmeg may also be used.

III. *À la Condé.*—Pare, quarter, and core good cooking apples. Arrange in rows in an earthen baking-dish, sprinkle with powdered sugar and lemon-juice, pour a little water into the baking-dish, and add a heaping tablespoonful of butter. Bake slowly, basting frequently with the apple-juice and melted butter. When tender, take out, drain, and cool, saving the juice. Serve with boiled rice or other cereal, using the juice instead of milk.

IV. *À la Cherbourg.*—Pare and core good cooking apples; halve or quarter if desired. Cook slowly in a thin syrup flavored with lemon-peel and a bit of ginger-root. Serve separately or with cereal.

V. *À la Fermière.*—Pare and core the apples and arrange in a well-buttered baking-dish. Sprinkle slightly with sugar and cinnamon; baste often with melted butter, and serve with boiled rice or other cereal, using the juice instead of milk.

VI. *À la Française.*—Core and then peel tart apples. Put into cold water from half an inch to an inch in depth, sprinkle with sugar, cover tightly, and cook very slowly on the back part of the range till tender. Flavorings already noted may be added at pleasure. Skim out the apples, reduce the remaining syrup one-half by rapid boiling, pour over the apples, and cool. Serve cold, with or without cereal.

VII. *À la Ninon.*—Sprinkle baked apples with freshly grated cocoanut on taking from the oven. Serve on a mound of boiled rice with the milk of the cocoanut.

VIII. *À la Réligieuse.*—Core cooking apples; score the skin deeply in a circle all around the fruit. Sprinkle a little sugar in the cores, and dissolve a little currant jelly in the water used for the basting. Cook slowly, and baste once with melted butter. The peel is supposed to rise all around the apple, like a veil—hence the name.

IX. *Baked.*—Peel or not, as preferred. Sprinkle with melted butter and sugar, baste now and then with hot water, and serve separately or with cereal.

X. *Baked, with Bananas.*—Core, draw a peeled and scraped banana through each core, trimming the ends off even, and bake slowly, basting with hot water, melted butter, and lemon-juice. The apples may be peeled if desired. Serve separately, or with cereal.

XI. *Baked, with Cereal.*—Pare or not, as preferred, but core. Fill the centres with left-over cooked cereal and bake slowly. Butter, lemon-juice, or any flavoring recommended before can be used to advantage. Any quartered apples, baked or stewed, can be covered with any preferred cereal, and served with sugar and cream.

XII. *Baked, with Cherries.*—Core the apples, fill the centres with pitted cherries, either sour or sweet, bake carefully, basting with syrup and melted butter. The apples may be peeled or not. Take up carefully, and serve separately, or with cereal.

XIII. *Baked, with Currants.*—Fill the centres with currants, red or white, and use plenty of sugar. Baste with hot water or melted butter. May be served with cereal if enough sugar is used in baking.

XIV. *Baked, with Dates.*—Wash and stone dates, fill the cores of apples with them, sprinkle with powdered sugar and bake, basting with butter, lemon-juice, and hot water. The apples may be peeled or not.

XV. *Baked, with Figs.*—Wash the figs carefully, and pack into the cores of apples. Bake, basting with lemon syrup and melted butter. Serve separately or with cereal.

XVI. *Baked, with Gooseberries.*—Cap and stem a handful of gooseberries. Fill the cores of large, firm apples with them, using plenty of sugar. Baste with melted butter and hot water. May be served with cereal if plenty of sugar is used in cooking.

XVII. *Baked, with Prunes.*—Select tart apples, and peel or not, as preferred. Core and fill the centres with stewed prunes, stoned and drained. Bake slowly, basting with the prune-juice, or with lemon-juice, melted butter, spiced syrup, or hot water containing grated lemon-peel and a teaspoonful of sherry. Two or three cloves may be stuck into each apple, and removed after the apples are cold. Serve, very cold, with cream; separately, or with a cereal.

XVIII. *Baked, with Quinces.*—Fill the cores of sweet apples with bits of quince and plenty of sugar. Bake slowly, basting with melted butter and syrup. Serve separately or with cereal.

XIX. *Baked, with Spice.*—Select very sour apples, and peel or not, as preferred. Core, and stuff the cavities with brown sugar, putting two whole cloves into each apple. Baste with hot water containing a bit of grated lemon-peel and a teaspoonful of sherry, putting a teaspoonful of butter into the liquor as it forms in the dish. Bake slowly, covered, until the apples are very tender. Serve separately or with a cereal. Cinnamon, or nutmeg, or a blade of mace may be used instead of the cloves.

XX. *Boiled.*—Boil slowly in a saucepan with as little water as possible. Do not peel. When tender, lift out, add sugar to the water in which they were boiled; reduce half by rapid boiling, pour over the apples, and let cool. Currant-juice, lemon-juice, cinnamon, nutmeg, or a suspicion of clove may be added to the syrup if the apples lack flavor.

XXI. *Coddled.*—Core, cut in halves, but do not peel. Lay in the bottom of an earthen dish, sprinkle lightly with sugar, add a little water, and cook very slowly on the top of the stove until tender.

XXII. *Crusts.*—Cut stale bread in circles, lay half of a peeled and cored apple on each piece. Bake carefully, basting with melted butter and a little lemon-juice if desired. When the apples are done, sprinkle with powdered sugar, and take from the oven. Serve either hot or cold.

XXIII. *Dried.*—Soak over night in water to cover, after washing thoroughly; cook slowly until soft, sweeten, and flavor with lemon. Raisins, dates, figs, or other dried fruits may be added at pleasure.

XXIV. *Fried.*—Core, but do not pare. If very juicy, dredge with flour and fry slowly in hot fat till tender. They are served with pork, or, sprinkled with powdered sugar and cinnamon, with cereals.

XXV. *Glazed.*—Core tart apples. Fill the centres with cinnamon, sugar, bits of butter, and a raisin or two. Bake slowly, basting with lemon-syrup. When nearly done, brush with the beaten white of egg and sprinkle with powdered sugar. Serve separately or with cereal.

XXVI. *In Bloom.*—Cook pared red apples in any preferred way, and stew the skin separately, in a little water, until the color is extracted. The tiniest bit of red vegetable coloring may be needed. Strain this liquid, and pour it over the apples when done. Or, add currant jelly to color the water in which the apples are boiled, or to the water for basting pared baked apples.

XXVII. *In Casserole.*—Arrange good cooking apples in an earthen casserole. Cover with a thin syrup made of brown sugar, add a little spice and a bit of orange- or lemon-peel. Bake, very slowly, tightly covered. Serve cold from the casserole.

XXVIII. *In Crumbs.*—Cut strips of stale bread to fit stone custard-cups. Dip in milk, and arrange in the moulds. Fill the centres with apple sauce, cover with a circle of the bread, and steam thirty minutes. Serve cold, with cream.

XXIX. *In Rice-Cups.*—Line buttered custard cups with cold boiled rice. Fill the centres with apple sauce or cooked quartered apples, mildly tart rather than sweet. Cover with more of the rice. Steam half an hour and let cool in the cups. Turn out on chilled plates and serve with cream. Cream may be used with any cooked apple, if the Secretary of the Interior files no objections. Cereals, other than rice, left over, can be used in the same way. A wreath of cooked apple quarters around the base of each individual mould is a dainty and acceptable garnish.

XXX. *Jellied.*—Cut tart apples in halves, core, place in buttered baking-dish, skin side down, measure the water and add enough barely to cover; add twice as much sugar as water, cover and boil slowly till the apples are tender. Skim out, drain, boil the syrup rapidly till reduced one half; pour over the apples and let cool. Flavorings referred to before can be added to the syrup if desired.

XXXI. *Mock Pineapple.*—Arrange alternate slices of sweet apples and oranges, peeled, on a chilled plate, one above the other. Sprinkle with powdered sugar, pour over the orange-juice and serve immediately.

XXXII. *Sauce.*—Peel, quarter, and core quick-cooking apples. Sweeten slightly, and when very tender, rub through a sieve and let cool. Any flavoring recommended before may be used.

XXXIII. *Snow.*—Peel white-fleshed, firm apples, grate quickly on a coarse grater, and serve in roughly piled heaps on small plates immediately. Use sugar or not.

XXXIV. *Southern, Fried.*—Core and cut in thick slices, but do not peel. Dip in egg and crumbs and fry in ham or bacon fat and serve with those meats.

XXXV. *Stewed.*—Pare, core, and halve large cooking-apples. Put into an earthen dish, cover with water, sprinkle with sugar, cover tightly, and cook slowly. If flat in taste, sprinkle with lemon-juice, cinnamon, or nutmeg.

XXXVI. *Stewed with Dates.*—Add washed and stoned dates to stewed apples when partially cooked, and finish cooking. Dried apricots, fresh or dried cherries, rhubarb, figs, plums, dried peaches, pears, or quinces, may be used in the same way.

XXXVII. *Stewed with Rice.*—Boil rice as usual in boiling water, adding a little salt. When partly done, add pared, cored, and quartered quick-cooking apples. Finish cooking. Serve very cold with cream and sugar. Flavorings noted above may be added at discretion.

APRICOTS

I. Wipe with a dry cloth and serve with fruit-knives. A green leaf on each plate is a dainty fruit doily.

II. *Canned.*—Drain, rinse in cold water, arrange on plates, and let stand several hours before serving. Sugar or not, as desired. Save the syrup to flavor syrup for pancakes, or to use for puddings, fritters, etc.

III. *Dried.*—Soak over night, cook very slowly in the water in which they were soaked, adding very little sugar. Serve with cereal, or separately.

IV. *Sauce.*—Cook as above, and rub the fruit through a sieve. The canned, drained, and freshened fruit may be used in the same way.

BANANAS

I. Serve in the skins with fruit-knives, one to each person.

II. Skin and scrape and serve immediately. People who cannot ordinarily eat bananas usually find them harmless when the tough, stringy pulp is scraped off.

III. *Baked.*—Bake without peeling, basting with hot water and melted butter occasionally. Let cool in the skins.

IV. *Baked.*—Skin, scrape, and bake, basting with lemon-juice and melted butter. Sprinkle with sugar if desired.

V. *Au naturel.*—Slice into saucers, sprinkle with lemon-juice and sugar.

VI. *With Sugar and Cream.*—Slice, sprinkle with powdered sugar, pour cream over, and serve at once.

VII. *With Oranges.*—Slice, add an equal quantity of sliced oranges, and sprinkle with sugar.

VIII. *With Cereal.*—Slice fresh bananas into a saucer, sprinkle with sugar, cover with boiled rice or with any preferred cereal.

IX. Equally good with sliced peaches.

BLACKBERRIES

Serve with powdered sugar, with or without cream. A tablespoonful of cracked ice in a saucer of berries is appreciated on a hot morning.

BLUE PLUMS

See Green Gages.

CHERRIES

I. Serve very cold, with the stems on. A dainty way is to lay the cherries upon a bed of cracked ice, and serve with powdered sugar in individual dishes.

II. Pit the cherries, saving the juice, and serve in saucers with sugar and plenty of cracked ice.

III. *Iced.*—Beat the white of an egg to a foam. Dip each cherry into it, then roll in powdered sugar, and set on a platter in the refrigerator. Must be prepared overnight.

IV. *Crusts.*—Butter rounds of stale bread, spread with pitted cherries and their juice, sprinkle with sugar, and bake. Serve very cold.

CURRANTS

Serve in cracked ice with plenty of sugar. These are also served iced, and on crusts. See Cherries III and IV.

FIGS

May be served from the basket. This, of course, applies only to the more expensive varieties, which are clean. The ordinary dried fig of commerce must be washed many times, and is usually sweet enough without adding more sugar.

II. *Steamed.*—Set a plate of figs in a steamer over boiling water until plump and soft, then set away to cool.

III. *Stewed.*—Clean, soak, and cook slowly till tender in a little water. Skim out, drain, sweeten the syrup slightly, reduce one half, pour over the figs, and cool. A bit of vanilla or wine may be added to the syrup.

IV. *With Cereal.*—Cover a saucer of steamed or stewed figs with any preferred cereal. Serve with cream if desired.

V. *In Rice-Cups.*—See Apples XXIX.

VI. *In Crumbs.*—See Apples XXVIII.

GOOSEBERRIES

These berries must be stewed in order to be acceptable. The fruit, after stewing, may be rubbed through a sieve fine enough to keep back the seeds, or it may be baked on crusts. See Cherries IV.

GRAPES

This luscious fruit is at its best when served fresh from the vines, with the bloom still on. Never wash a bunch of grapes if it can be avoided. Serve with grape scissors to cut the bunches apart. People who fear appendicitis may have the grapes squeezed from the skins and the seeds afterwards removed. They are very nice this way, with sugar and pounded ice.

GRAPEFRUIT

A good grapefruit will have dark spots, a skin which seems thin, will be firm to the touch, and heavy for its size. To serve, cut crosswise, and remove the white, bitter pulp which is in the core, and separate the sections. Fill the core with sugar and serve cold. A little rum or kirsch may be added just before serving, but, as George Ade said, "A good girl needs no help," and it is equally true of a good grapefruit. If anybody knows why it is called grapefruit, please write to the author of this book in care of the publishers.

GREEN GAGES

Serve as they come, with the bloom on, or peel, pit, and serve with cracked ice and powdered sugar.

HUCKLEBERRIES

Look the fruit over carefully. Nothing pleases a fly so much as to die and be mistaken for a huckleberry. Serve with cracked ice, with sugar or cream, or both.

MUSKMELONS

Keep on ice till the last moment. Cut crosswise, take out the seeds with a spoon, and put a cube of ice in each half. Green leaves on the plate are a dainty touch.

ORANGES

Serve with fruit-knives, or in halves with spoons—either the orange-spoon which comes for that purpose, or a very heavy teaspoon. Another way is to remove the peel, except a strip an inch wide at the equator, cut at a division line and straighten out the peel, taking care not to break off the sections. Or, the fruit may be peeled, sliced, and served on plates with sugar.

PEACHES

Wipe with a dry cloth and serve with fruit-knives. Or, if you think much of your breakfast napkins, peel and cut just before serving, as they discolor quickly. Serve with cracked ice, or with cream. Hard peaches may be baked, as apples are, and served cold with cream. Stewed peaches may be served on crusts.

PEARS

Serve as they come, with fruit-knives. Hard pears may be baked or stewed according to directions previously given.

PINEAPPLE

Peel, cut out the eyes, and shred from the core with a silver fork. Sprinkle with sugar and keep on ice some hours before serving. Pineapple is the only fruit known to have a distinct digestive value, and it works most readily on starches. It combines pleasantly with bananas.

PRUNELLES

These are soaked, and boiled in the water in in which they are soaked, with the addition of a very little sugar. Dried apricots, blackberries, cherries, nectarines, and prunes are cooked in the same way. They may also be steamed and afterwards sprinkled with sugar.

PRUNES

These are no longer despised since the price has gone up, and the more expensive kinds are well worth having. A bit of lemon-peel or spice may flavor the syrup acceptably, and they are especially healthful in combination with cereals, according to recipes previously given.

QUINCES

Peel, stuff the cores with sugar, and bake according to directions given for apples. A little lemon may be used in the syrup for basting.

RASPBERRIES AND STRAWBERRIES

These delicious berries should not be washed unless absolutely necessary, nor should they be insulted with sugar and cream. If very sour, strawberries may be dipped in powdered sugar. Large, fine ones are served with the stems and hulls on. Raspberries, if ripe, seldom need sugar. Cracked ice is a pleasing accompaniment.

RHUBARB

I. Peel, cut into inch-lengths, and stew with plenty of sugar. Serve cold.

II. Cut, but do not peel, boil five minutes, then change the water and cook slowly with plenty of sugar till done.

III. *Baked.*—Do not peel. Cut into inch-pieces, put into a buttered baking-dish or stone jar, sprinkle plentifully with sugar, and bake slowly. It will be a rich red in color.

IV. Cook on crusts. See Cherries IV.

V. Add a handful of seeded raisins to rhubarb cooked in any of the above ways when it is about half done. Figs, dates, and other dried fruits, used with rhubarb, make a combination pleasing to some.

TANGERINES

See Oranges.

WATERMELON

Like muskmelon, watermelon must be very thoroughly chilled. Serve in slices from a platter or on individual plates, removing the rind before serving, if desired; or cut the melon in half, slice off the lower end so that it may stand firmly, and serve the pulp from the shell with a silver spoon. Ice pounded to snow is a pleasant addition to any fruit, when the thermometer is ninety-five or six in the shade.

CEREALS

So many breakfast foods are upon the market that it would be impossible to enumerate all of them, especially as new ones are appearing continually. Full and complete directions for cooking all of them are printed upon the packages in which they are sold. It may not be amiss to add, however, that in almost every instance, twice or three times the time allowed for cooking would improve the cereal in taste and digestibility.

The uncooked cereals are many. A wise housekeeper will use the uncooked cereals when she has no maid. "A word to the wise is unnecessary."

Pleasing variety in the daily menu is secured by getting a different cereal each time. In this way, it takes about a year to get back to the beginning again, and there is no chance to tire of any of them.

Cereals should always be cooked in a double boiler; and soaking over night in the water in which they are to be cooked, where it is not possible to secure the necessary time for long cooking, will prove a distinct advantage. Leftover cereals should be covered with cold water immediately, in the double boiler, and kept in a cool place until the next day. Bring slowly to a boil, and cook as usual. In the hot weather, cereals may be cooked the day before using, moulded in custard-cups, and kept in the ice-box over night. They are very acceptable when served ice-cold, and, if moulded with fruit, or served with fruit on the same plate, so much the better.

Pearled wheat, pearled barley, and coarse hominy require five cupfuls of water to each cup of cereal, and need from four to six hours' cooking. Coarse oatmeal and fine hominy must be cooked from four to six hours, but need only four cupfuls of water to each cup of cereal. Rolled wheat and rolled barley are cooked two hours in three times as much water as cereal; rice and rolled oats, with three times as much water, will cook in one hour. Farina, with six cupfuls of water to each cupful of cereal, also cooks in an hour; cerealine flakes cook in thirty minutes, equal parts of water and cereal being used.

Salt must be added just before cooking begins. All cereals are richer if a little milk is added to the water in which they are cooked.

To cook cereals in a double boiler, put the water into the inner kettle, the outer vessel being from half to two thirds full, and when it is boiling furiously, sprinkle in the cereal, a few grains at a time, and not so rapidly as to stop the boiling. When cereals are eaten cold, they require a little more liquid.

BOILED BARLEY

Wash the barley in several waters, cover with cold water; bring to a boil, drain, cover with fresh boiling water, add a little salt, and cook slowly for four hours.

BARLEY GRUEL

Wash half a cupful of pearled barley in several waters; put it into a double boiler with eight cupfuls of water and half an inch of stick cinnamon. Boil for two hours, strain, sweeten, and add two wine glasses of port. Keep in a cool place and reheat when required. An invaluable breakfast cereal for a convalescent.

STEAMED BARLEY

Cooked one cupful of pearled barley in a double boiler four hours, with four cupfuls of water and a little salt. In the morning, add a cupful of boiling water or milk, stir occasionally, reheat thoroughly, and serve.

BREWIS

Dry bread in the oven so slowly that it is a light brown in color. Crush into crumbs with the rolling-pin and sift through the frying-basket. Measure the milk, salt it slightly, and bring to a boil. Put in half as much of the dried crumbs. Boil five or ten minutes, season with butter, pepper, and salt, and serve at once with cream. It must be stirred all the time it is cooking. By omitting the butter, it may be served with sugar. Brown, rye, graham, or corn bread may be mixed with the white bread to advantage. The dried and sifted crumbs of brown bread, when served cold with cream, taste surprisingly like a popular cereal which etiquette forbids us to mention. This is a good way to use up accumulated crumbs.

CORN-MEAL MUSH

The best meal comes from the South. It is white, moist, and coarse, and is called "water ground." It is a very different proposition from the dry, yellow powder sold in Northern groceries. For mush, use four times as much water as meal. Salt the water, and sprinkle in the meal very slowly when it is at a galloping boil. Boil an hour or more, stirring frequently. A better mush is made by using half milk and half water. Serve hot or cold with cream, or milk, and sugar. If wanted for frying, wet a pan in cold water, pour in the hot mush, and let cool.

CORN AND WHEAT PORRIDGE

Half a cupful of corn-meal and half a cupful of flour. Make into a batter with cold water and put into two cupfuls of boiling water. Stir often and cook half an hour or more, then add four cupfuls of boiling milk. Cook half an hour longer, stirring often. Serve hot or cold, with cream and sugar.

CORN MUSH OR HASTY PUDDING

One cupful of corn-meal and one cupful of cold water. Mix and stir into two cupfuls of salted boiling water. One half cupful of white flour may be mixed with the meal. When the mush becomes thick, place in a steamer and steam six hours. Rinse a pan with cold water, pour in the mush, smooth the top with hand or spoon wet in cold water, and let stand in a cold place twelve hours. This is used for frying. Other cereals may be used in the same way. The sliced mush should be dredged in flour and cooked in salt pork, ham, or bacon fat in the spider, or in lard or butter if it is to be served with syrup.

HULLED CORN

This can occasionally be found in city markets, and is a delicious cereal, eaten hot or cold with milk or cream or sugar.

COLD CEREAL WITH FRUIT

Pack left-over cereal into buttered custard cups, scoop out the inside, fill with any sort of stewed or fresh fruit cut fine and sweetened, cover the top with more cereal, and let stand some hours in a cold place. At serving time turn out and dust with powdered sugar. Cream may be used if it harmonizes with the fruit.

FRIED CREAM

Bring two cupfuls of milk to the boil, add two tablespoonfuls of cornstarch rubbed smooth in a little cold milk, and half a teaspoonful of salt. Take from the fire and add one egg, well beaten, then pour into a mould to cool. When cold, cut into slices, dredge with flour, and fry.

FARINA

Soak over night. In the morning add boiling salted water to cover, and cook half an hour, stirring constantly. Serve hot or cold with cream and sugar, or with sugar and fruit.

APPLE FARINA

Stir one half cupful of farina into one quart of boiling salted water. As soon as mush forms, stir in four tart apples, peeled, cored, and sliced, and cook until the apples are soft. If the apples lack flavor, a bit of orange- or lemon-peel, or any preferred spice may be added. Serve hot or cold with cream or sugar. This will mould well.

FARINA BALLS

Half a cupful of farina, two cupfuls of milk, half a teaspoonful of salt, a sprinkle of paprika, six drops of onion-juice, and the yolk of one egg. Cook the farina in the salted milk for half an hour in a double boiler. When it is stiff, add the egg and the seasoning. Reheat, pour into a dish, and let cool. When cold, make into small flat cakes, dip in egg, then in crumbs, and fry. These can be made ready for frying the day before.

FAIRY FARINA

Mix three tablespoonfuls of farina with three quarters of a teaspoonful of salt and half a cupful of milk, taken from two cupfuls. Bring the rest of the milk to a boil with two cupfuls of water and stir in the farina mixture. Cook slowly half an hour, turn into individual moulds, and serve cold with sugar and cream.

JELLIED FARINA

One cupful of farina, sprinkled into two and a half cupfuls of boiled salted milk. Stir till it thickens, then boil half an hour without stirring. Serve hot or cold with sugar and cream. This will mould nicely, and may be used with fruit.

FARINA MUSH

Boil one quart of salted milk, and, when boiling, add half a cupful of farina, stirring constantly. Add a lump of butter and serve with cream and sugar.

FLUMMERY

One and a half cupfuls of pinhead oatmeal, a saltspoonful of salt, a tablespoonful of white sugar, two tablespoonfuls of orange-flower water. Cover the oatmeal with cold water and let it soak twenty-four hours, then drain off the water, cover again, and let steep twenty-four hours longer. Strain through a fine sieve, add the salt, and boil till as thick as mush, stirring constantly. Add the sugar and the orange-flower water, pour into saucers, and serve hot or cold with cream and sugar. This recipe dates back to the time of Queen Elizabeth.

GRITS

One cupful of well-washed grits is slowly added to two cupfuls of boiling water, and boiled one hour. Soaking over night is an advantage. If the porridge is too thick, it may be thinned with milk. Serve hot or cold with cream and sugar.

FRIED GRITS

Pack left-over grits into a wet mould. Turn out, slice, dredge in flour, and fry.

OATMEAL GRUEL

Mix one tablespoonful of oatmeal in half a cupful of cold water, add three cupfuls of milk, or of water, or of milk and water, and a little salt. Cook half an hour in a double boiler, stirring often. Strain if desired, and serve hot or cold. May be flavored with a bit of lemon-peel, spice, or orange-flower water. For children and convalescents.

OATMEAL GRUEL WITH EGG

One cupful of oatmeal and one teaspoonful of salt stirred into four cupfuls of boiling water. Boil one hour, strain, and pour on to two eggs well beaten. Reheat until it thickens, and serve with cream and sugar.

WHEAT GRUEL

Mix one teaspoonful of salt with half a cupful of flour, make into a paste with a little cold water and cook in a double boiler till smooth and thick. Thin with milk, if necessary. Strain and sweeten; serve either hot or cold. May be flavored with spice, lemon-peel, or wine.

BOILED HOMINY

Stir one cupful of well-washed hominy into two quarts of boiling water. Cook one hour. Use half milk and half water if preferred.

HOMINY BALLS

To a cupful of cold hominy add one tablespoonful of melted butter, stir well, add enough milk to rub the hominy to a paste, add a teaspoonful of sugar and one egg, unbeaten. Shape into small flat balls, dredge with flour, dip in beaten egg, then in crumbs, and fry. These may be prepared beforehand and kept in a cool place till ready to fry.

FRIED HOMINY

Pack left-over hominy into a mould. When cold, slice, dredge with flour, and fry, or dip in egg and crumbs and fry.

HOMINY WITH MILK

Soak hominy all night. In the morning cover with boiling salted water and boil until very tender. Drain off the water, cover with milk, boil up once more, and serve.

STEAMED HOMINY

Soak hominy over night in an equal measure of cold water. In the morning add twice as much boiling salted water and boil fifteen minutes, then put into a steamer and steam six hours.

HOMINY PORRIDGE

Soak a cupful of granulated hominy in four cupfuls of water over night. Add a teaspoonful of salt, one cupful of milk, and boil one hour in the morning.

CRACKED WHEAT MUSH

Butter a double boiler inside, put in four cupfuls of water and a little salt. When boiling add one cupful of cracked wheat which has been washed in several waters. Boil ten minutes, then simmer three hours. Serve with sugar and cream.

GRAHAM FLOUR MUSH

Mix one cupful of graham flour with a teaspoonful of salt, and make it into a paste with cold water. Mix gradually with four cupfuls of boiling water. Boil half an hour, stirring constantly. Serve with cream and sugar.

OATMEAL MUSH

Mix one cupful of coarse oatmeal with a little salt, sprinkle into four cupfuls of boiling water. Boil fifteen minutes, stirring constantly, in the double boiler. Cover and cook slowly three hours longer.

RYE MUSH

One quart of boiling water, one teaspoonful of salt, five heaping tablespoonfuls of rye meal. Sprinkle the meal into the boiling water, stirring constantly, add the salt, bring to the boil once more, cover, and cook slowly in the double boiler one hour and a half. Serve with sugar and cream.

FRIED OATMEAL MUSH

Wet a pan or mould in cold water and pack into it left-over oatmeal. Twelve hours later, turn out, cut into slices, dredge with flour and fry, serving with a simple syrup if desired. Any left-over cereal which does not contain fruit may be used in the same way.

GRAHAM MUSH WITH APPLES

Slice peeled and cored tart apples into graham mush prepared according to the recipe previously given, as soon as it begins to boil.

MUSH CAKES

Season two cupfuls of left-over cereal with salt and pepper and a few drops of onion-juice. Shape into small flat cakes with floured hands and dredge with flour. Fry in ham or bacon fat and serve with those meats.

MUSH BALLS

Add a tablespoonful of melted butter and two unbeaten eggs to two cupfuls of hot corn-meal mush. Cool. Shape into small flat cakes, dredge with flour, and fry brown. These may be prepared the day before using.

VELVET MUSH

Melt two tablespoonfuls of butter in a double boiler, add two cupfuls of flour, and stir until it leaves the sides of the kettle; add five cupfuls of milk, stirring constantly and bringing to the boil at each cupful. Add a teaspoonful of salt, mix thoroughly, and serve with sugar and cream.

COLD GRAHAM MUSH WITH FRUIT

Stir chopped dates or figs into graham mush made according to previous directions, turn into a mould, and cool. The next morning, slice, and serve with sugar and cream.

STEAMED OATMEAL

Add a quart of cold water and a teaspoonful of salt to a cupful of oatmeal. Put in a steamer over a kettle of cold water, bring to the boil gradually, and steam two hours after it begins to cook.

OATMEAL JELLY

Soak one cupful of oatmeal over night in cold water to cover deeply. Add boiling salted water in the morning and boil several hours, adding more water as needed. Do not stir any more than necessary. When every grain is transparent and jelly-like, it is done. It is delicious served cold, with fruit and sugar, or with sugar and cream.

CREAMED OATMEAL

Boil oatmeal for an hour and a half according to recipes previously given. Rub through a sieve, cover with hot milk, and cook very slowly half an hour longer. Serve with sugar and cream.

OATMEAL BLANC MANGE

Bring one quart of milk to the boil, add a teaspoonful of salt, and stir in one cupful of oatmeal. Boil forty-five minutes, then add two eggs well beaten just before removing from the fire. Serve hot or cold with cream and sugar. A bit of grated lemon- or orange-peel, wine, or spice may be added to the milk.

LIGHT OATMEAL

Cook oatmeal twenty-five minutes according to directions previously given, then set the dish in a moderate oven for half an hour. The grains will swell.

BAKED OATMEAL

The day before using, stir two cupfuls of oatmeal into two quarts of boiling water, salted, and boil ten minutes. Turn into a buttered earthen dish, cover, and bake slowly two hours. In the morning set the dish into a pan of boiling water and put in the oven for forty-five minutes.

MILK PORRIDGE

One tablespoonful of flour rubbed smooth with half a cupful or more of water. Add a cupful of boiling milk, a little salt and spice, and cook ten minutes or more in the double boiler.

RICE PORRIDGE

One cupful of rice, washed in several waters, and one cupful of oatmeal. Cook one hour in plenty of boiling salted water, and add a heaping tablespoonful of butter before serving.

WHEATLET PORRIDGE

One cupful of wheatlet, two cupfuls of boiling water, and one teaspoonful of salt. Cook slowly for an hour.

CREAMED OAT PORRIDGE

Soak two cupfuls of oatmeal in four cupfuls of water over night. In the morning, strain and boil the water thirty minutes. Scald a pint and a half of rich milk, thicken with a tablespoonful of flour rubbed smooth in a little cold milk, add to the water, with a teaspoonful of butter and a half teaspoonful of salt. Boil up well and serve with cream and sugar.

BOILED   RICE

(Hop Sing's Recipe)

"Washee lice in cold water bellee muchee. Water boil all ready muchee quick. Water shakee lice—no burn. Boil till one lice all rub away in fingers. Put in pan all holee, pour over cold water bellee muchee, set in hot oven, make dry, eatee all up."

BOILED RICE

(American Recipe)

Wash one cupful of rice in several waters. Sprinkle it, a little at a time, into eight quarts of slightly salted water at a galloping boil. Boil steadily for twenty minutes. Drain, toss carefully with a fork, and dry ten minutes in a hot oven.

BOILED RICE WITH MILK

Cook as above until it has boiled ten minutes, then drain, cover with boiling milk, and cook slowly ten minutes longer in a covered double boiler. Uncover, and stand in a hot oven for a few minutes, stirring occasionally with a fork.

RICE BALLS

One cupful of boiled rice, one half cupful of milk, one egg, one tablespoonful of sugar, a pinch of salt, and a slight grating of nutmeg or a sprinkle of cinnamon. Put the milk on to boil, add the rice and seasoning. When it boils, add the egg, cook till thick, take from the fire, and cool. Form in to small flat cakes, dip in egg and crumbs, and fry. These may be prepared beforehand.

STEAMED RICE

Wash a small cupful of rice and put into a double boiler with three cupfuls of milk and a pinch of salt. Cook until creamy, add a teaspoonful of butter and three tablespoonfuls of sugar. Fruit may be added.

SAMP

Cover the samp with boiling water, boil ten minutes, then drain, rinse in cold water, cover with fresh boiling water and a little salt. Cook slowly six hours, adding fresh boiling water as needed. Serve hot or cold with cream and sugar.

CREAM TOAST

Dip slices of toast in boiling water and set into the oven. Stir one heaping tablespoonful of corn-meal into four cupfuls of boiling salted milk, and add two tablespoonfuls of butter. When the milk thickens, stir in the whites of three eggs beaten to a stiff froth, boil up again, pour over the toast, keep in the oven five minutes longer and serve.

MILK TOAST

Lay slices of toast in cereal bowls, spread with butter, sprinkle with salt and pepper, pour boiling milk over and serve immediately.

SOFT TOAST

Dip crisp slices of toast for a moment in boiling salted water, pour over melted butter, set in the oven a moment and serve with cream.

CRUSHED WHEAT WITH RAISINS

Add a handful of stoned and cleaned raisins to crushed wheat mush made according to recipe previously given, and as soon as it begins to boil. Raisins are a healthful and agreeable addition to almost any cereal.

COLD CRACKED WHEAT

Add half a teaspoonful of salt to three cupfuls of boiling water, stir in half a cupful of cracked wheat. Cook uncovered till the water has almost disappeared, then add three cupfuls of hot milk. Cover and cook until the wheat is soft, then uncover and cook until the wheat is almost dry. Stir carefully now and then while cooking. Turn into individual moulds to harden, and serve cold with sugar and cream.

SALT FISH

With very, very few exceptions, fish and meats other than salt are not suitable for breakfast. So many delicious preparations of these are possible, however, that no one need lament the restriction which general use has made. The humble and lowly codfish may be made into many a dainty tidbit,—to make no invidious distinction,—and, for some occult reason, the taste craves salt in the morning.

BROILED BLOATERS

Scrape and clean the fish, wipe dry and split, laying flat upon a buttered gridiron. Broil about six minutes, turning frequently. When brown, pour over melted butter. Serve with lemon quarters and parsley.

YARMOUTH BLOATERS

See Potomac Herring.

CODFISH BALLS

Cut into inch pieces a heaping cupful of salt codfish. Remove the bones, skin, and put into an earthen dish. Pour boiling water on and keep hot two hours. Pour off the water, cool, and shred the fish with the fingers. Add a heaping cupful of hot mashed potatoes. Mix a teaspoonful of flour with a heaping tablespoonful of butter, add three tablespoonfuls of boiling water, and cook until thick. Season with salt and pepper, mix with the fish and potato, and with floured hands form into eight small flat cakes. Dredge with flour and set away to be fried the following morning.

CODFISH BALLS—II

Two cupfuls of freshened and shredded fish, two cupfuls of sliced raw potatoes, one tablespoonful of butter, half a cupful of cream or milk, two eggs, and a sprinkle of white pepper. Put the potatoes in a pan, spread the fish on top, cover with cold water, and boil until the potatoes are done. Drain, mash together, then add the butter, pepper, milk, and beaten egg. Beat until very light. Shape into round balls the size of small apples, dredge in flour, and fry until brown in deep fat.

CODFISH BALLS—III

Prepare as Codfish Balls II, but use twice as much potato as fish.

CODFISH BALLS À LA BURNS

Make codfish balls into flat cakes and just before serving, put a poached egg on each.

PICKED-UP CODFISH

Pour boiling water on a cupful of salt codfish which has been shredded and had the bones removed. When the water cools, pour it off and cover with fresh boiling water. Drain again when the second water cools. Blend a tablespoonful of butter with a tablespoonful of flour, add a cupful of milk, and cook, stirring constantly, until thick. Add the codfish and a teaspoonful of finely minced parsley. Serve on toast and garnish with hard-boiled egg cut in slices. Sprinkle with black pepper.

CREAMED CODFISH

Two cupfuls of shredded codfish, three cupfuls of milk, yolk of one egg, one tablespoonful of butter, two tablespoonfuls of flour, two quarts of water, pepper, and salt. Cover the fish with the water and set it over a slow fire. When it boils, drain it and cover with the milk. Bring to a boil again. Have the butter and flour rubbed smooth with a little cold milk and add to the boiling milk. Stir steadily till it thickens, then add the beaten yolk of the egg, and cook five minutes longer. Season with pepper. A little minced parsley may be added. Half an hour before the fish is shredded it should be put to soak in cold water, unless it is preferred very salt.

CREAMED ROAST CODFISH

Brush the salt from a whole salted cod with a stiff brush. Place in a baking-pan and put in a hot oven until brown and crisp. Take out, lay on a board, and pound with a potato-masher till thoroughly bruised and broken. Place in the baking-pan, cover with boiling water, and soak twenty minutes. Drain, place on a platter, dot with butter, and put back into the oven till the butter sizzles. Take from the oven, pour over a cupful of cream, garnish with parsley, and serve.

CODFISH À LA MODE

Pick up a cupful of salt cod very fine, and freshen it. Mix with two cupfuls of mashed potato, two cupfuls of cream or milk, and two well-beaten eggs. Add half a cupful of melted butter and a little black pepper. Mix thoroughly, pile roughly in an earthen baking-dish or casserole, and bake twenty-five minutes in a hot oven. If it does not brown readily, brush the top with melted butter for the last five minutes of cooking.

NEW ENGLAND SALT COD

Cut the fish in squares and soak over night. In the morning drain and rinse, cover with fresh boiling water, and simmer till tender. Spread on a platter and put in the oven. Make a drawn-butter sauce of one tablespoonful of butter and two tablespoonfuls of flour cooked till the mixture leaves the pan. Add one cupful of cold water, and stir constantly till the sauce is thick and smooth and free from lumps. Pour over the cod and serve. Minced parsley, a squeeze of lemon-juice, or a hard-boiled egg chopped fine may be added to the sauce.

BOILED SALTED COD WITH EGG SAUCE

Chop fine a pound of salted cod that has been freshened, boiled, and cooled. Mix a heaping teaspoonful of corn-meal with one cupful of milk, and stir over the fire until it thickens, then add one cupful of mashed potatoes, two heaping tablespoonfuls of butter, a teaspoonful of minced parsley, and two well-beaten eggs. Let it get very hot. Make the drawn-butter sauce with the egg in it, given in the recipe for New England Salt Cod, and serve with the sauce poured over.

SALTED COD WITH BROWN BUTTER

Freshen the fish for twenty-four hours. Place over the fire in cold water and bring slowly to a boil. Put a little butter and a few sprigs of parsley in a frying-pan. Skim out the fish and put on a platter in the oven. When the butter is brown, pour over the fish and serve with lemon-quarters and fresh parsley.

CODFISH CUTLETS

Use the mixture for Codfish Balls II. Shape into cutlet form,—small tin moulds come for the purpose,—dip in egg and crumbs, and fry in deep fat. Stick a piece of macaroni in the small end of the cutlet, and garnish with a paper frill. Serve with lemon and parsley.

BOILED SALT CODFISH

Select a piece of cod that has been boned. Brush the salt from it with a stiff brush and broil under the gas flame until brown. Lay in a baking-pan and pour over boiling water to cover. Let stand ten minutes, drain, and repeat the process. Drain, put on a hot platter, pour over melted butter, sprinkle with pepper and minced parsley.

FLAKED SALT CODFISH

Soak two pounds of fish over night. In the morning scrub it well, cover with slices of onion, pour boiling water over, and let it soak till the water is cool. Skim out, wipe, and broil. Put into a platter, break with a fork, and pour over a drawn-butter sauce seasoned with pepper, parsley, and lemon-juice. Keep in a hot oven five minutes before serving.

CODFISH PUFF

Make the mixture for Codfish Balls II. Add the whites of two eggs beaten to a stiff froth, folding them in lightly. Butter a stoneware platter, spread the puff upon it, and bake in a hot oven till well puffed and browned. Or, cook in a buttered frying-pan till a brown crust has formed, then fold like an omelet.

CREAMED COD WITH EGG SAUCE

Freshen, boil, and drain, according to directions previously given. Arrange on a platter and cover with cream sauce, which has minced parsley and chopped hard-boiled eggs mixed with it.

ESCALLOPED CODFISH

Make a Codfish Puff, sprinkle with grated cheese, and bake brown.

FINNAN HADDIE À LA DELMONICO

Make a cream sauce, using two tablespoonfuls of butter and two of flour; cook till they bubble, add a pint of milk, and stir till thick and smooth. Add a pound of Finnan Haddie flaked, and the yolks of two eggs, well beaten, three hard-boiled eggs cut fine, and a tablespoonful of strong cheese, grated. Season with black pepper, heat thoroughly, and serve.

FINNAN HADDIE À LA MARTIN

Make the cream sauce, add the flaked Finnan Haddie, according to the recipe for Finnan Haddie à la Delmonico, add one half-cupful of shredded green peppers, let boil up once, and serve on toast.

FINNAN HADDIE FISH BALLS

Prepare as Codfish Balls II.

BROILED FINNAN HADDIE

Parboil, drain, wipe, then skin. Broil, pour over melted butter, sprinkle with pepper and minced parsley. Serve with lemon quarters.

PICKED-UP FINNAN HADDIE

Cut the fish in convenient pieces for serving. Cover with boiling water, boil five minutes, drain, and rinse in fresh boiling water. Arrange on a platter, dot with butter, put in the oven, and when the butter sizzles, serve.

CREAMED ROAST FINNAN HADDIE

See Creamed Roast Codfish.

BROILED FINNAN HADDIE—II

Soak in cold water half an hour, and in boiling water ten minutes. Wipe dry, marinade in oil and lemon-juice, and broil as usual.

BAKED SMOKED HADDOCK

Put the haddock into a baking-pan, cover with boiling water, drain, dot with butter, sprinkle with black pepper, and bake in a hot oven for ten minutes. Serve very hot.

BROILED SMOKED HADDOCK

Rub with butter, dredge with flour, and broil over clear coals, or under a gas flame.

FRIED SMOKED HADDOCK

Cover with olive oil and soak over night. Skim out and fry brown in the oil. Pepper well and serve at once with lemon quarters and a garnish of parsley.

HERRING BALLS

Partly boil bloaters or herrings, skin, add an equal bulk of mashed potatoes made from baked potatoes. Add a lump of butter and enough cream to soften it. Form into balls, dip in egg and crumbs, and fry in deep fat.

POTOMAC HERRING

Those having roe are preferable. Put into a frying-pan with boiling water to cover, boil five minutes, drain, add a lump of butter, and return to the fire. When it melts, and the fish is well covered with it, serve.

KIPPERED HERRING

See Potomac Herring.

BROILED SMOKED HERRING

Soak over night. Pour boiling water over it in the morning; when the water cools, plunge it into ice water for five minutes, wipe dry, and broil under a gas flame.

BROILED SALT MACKEREL

Wash in several waters, remove the head and part of the tail. Scrape the thin black skin from the inside. Put the fish in a pan of cold water, skin side up, over night at least, and, if very salt, by four o'clock in the afternoon. In the morning wash in fresh cold water, wipe dry on a clean cloth, rub with melted butter, sprinkle with pepper, and broil carefully. It must be watched every moment, as it burns easily. When brown, serve on a hot platter, dot the fish with bits of butter, and garnish with parsley and lemon quarters.

CREAMED SALT MACKEREL

Freshen according to directions previously given. Put in cold water, bring to a boil, then drain. Pour over it half a cupful of cream. Roll a piece of butter the size of an egg in flour and add to the cream. Let boil up once and serve.

BOILED SALT MACKEREL

Freshen according to directions previously given, rinse thoroughly. Tie in a cloth, put into a kettle of cold water, bring slowly to the boil, and cook half an hour. Remove the cloth, take out the backbone, and pour over melted butter and half a cupful of cream. Sprinkle with black pepper and garnish with parsley.

BOILED SALT MACKEREL, CREAMED

Prepare as above. Heat a cupful of milk to the boil. Stir into it a teaspoonful of cornstarch made smooth with a little cold milk. When it thickens, add two tablespoonfuls of butter, and a little pepper, salt and minced parsley. Beat an egg very light, pour the sauce gradually over it, reheat for about a minute. Pour over the fish and garnish with slices of hard-boiled eggs.

BAKED SALT MACKEREL

Freshen according to directions previously given. Put into a baking-pan and pour on boiling water to cover. When the water cools, drain. Cover the fish with dots of butter, pour over half a cupful of cream or milk, and bake till brown.

FRIED SALT MACKEREL

Freshen according to directions previously given, soaking a full twenty-four hours and changing the water frequently. In the morning, drain, wipe dry, dredge with flour, and fry brown in butter. Garnish with lemon quarters and parsley.

BOILED SALT MACKEREL—II

Freshen, and boil in water made very acid with lemon-juice. Serve with melted or drawn butter.

BROILED SALT MACKEREL—II

Freshen, wipe dry, and soak for an hour in French dressing, made of three tablespoonfuls of olive oil, and one of lemon-juice or tarragon vinegar. Broil as usual.

BROILED SALT SALMON

Soak the salmon twenty-four hours in cold water, changing the water frequently. Drain, wipe dry, rub with butter, and broil over a clear fire. Serve with melted butter. Garnish with lemon quarters and parsley.

BROILED SMOKED SALMON

Rub with butter and broil with the flesh side nearest the fire. Serve on a hot platter with lemon quarters, melted butter, and parsley.

BROILED KIPPERED SALMON

Cut the salmon into strips, rub very lightly with butter, sprinkle with pepper, and broil as usual.

FRIED KIPPERED SALMON

See Fried Smoked Haddock.

BROILED SMOKED SALMON

Wash a piece of smoked salmon in three or four waters, parboil fifteen minutes. Skim out, wipe dry, rub with butter, and broil. Cover with melted butter, sprinkle with pepper and minced parsley, and garnish with lemon quarters.

FRIED SMOKED SALMON

Wash and parboil the salmon, drain, wipe, dip in egg and crumbs, and fry. Serve with lemon quarters and parsley.

Roughly speaking, the recipes for salt fish are interchangeable. A method of cooking recommended for one will be found equally good for some of the others.

Salt fish left-overs may be used in hash, scrambles, omelets or ramekin dishes, or reheated, rubbed to a paste, and served on toast, with a poached egg on each slice.

BREAKFAST MEATS

BEEF BALLS

One cupful of cooked chopped beef, one cupful of cold mashed potatoes, half a cupful of milk, two tablespoonfuls of butter, and one egg. Put the milk and butter in the frying-pan; when it boils up, add the beef and potatoes. Season with salt and pepper, then add the egg, well beaten, and take from the fire. Let cool. When stiff, shape into small flat cakes, dip in egg and bread crumbs, and put in a cool place. Fry in hot fat for three minutes. These can be prepared beforehand.

BEEF HASH WITHOUT POTATOES

Mince the beef, season with grated onion, salt, and pepper. Reheat in the beef gravy, or in hot water, adding a little butter. Serve on toast. Shredded green pepper may be added.

FRIZZLED BEEF

Have dried beef cut very thin. Cover with cold water to which a small pinch of soda has been added, and bring gradually to the boil. Drain, add a lump of butter, and cook till the edges of the beef curl. Serve on slices of buttered toast with poached or fried eggs laid over the beef.

BEEF À LA NEWPORT

Prepare Creamed Dried Beef according to recipe elsewhere given, using the egg to thicken. Add half a cupful of stewed and strained tomatoes and a tablespoonful of grated cheese just before taking from the fire. Heat thoroughly and serve at once on toast.

CORNED BEEF HASH

Equal parts of cooked corn beef and cold potatoes, cut fine, or use more potato than meat if desired. Season with grated onion, pepper and salt, and a little butter, and heat thoroughly. A green pepper, shredded, is an invaluable addition to corned beef hash.

CORNED BEEF HASH À LA DELMONICO

Prepare as above, using the green pepper. Spread the hot hash thickly on thin slices of buttered toast, slip a poached egg on to each piece, sprinkle with pepper, salt, and minced parsley.

CREAMED DRIED BEEF

Prepare as directed for Frizzled Beef, having the beef cut into very small pieces. Make a cream sauce of one tablespoonful of butter, two tablespoonfuls of flour, and two cupfuls of milk. Season with salt and pepper, and when smooth and thick add the cooked beef. A well-beaten egg added just before taking from the fire is an improvement. Serve on toast.

BACON AND EGGS

Have the bacon cut very thin. The colder it is, the better. Remove the rind and cook in a hot frying-pan until crisp. Skim out the bacon, break the eggs into the fat one at a time, and cook slowly, dipping the fat over the eggs occasionally with a spoon. Eggs must always be cooked at a moderate temperature. Serve on a hot platter, the eggs in the centre, the bacon for a garnish.

BROILED BACON

Broil on a gridiron, turning constantly. It will cook in three minutes. Perfectly cooked bacon is clear and crisp.

BREADED BACON

Dip slices of bacon in corn-meal and broil or fry. A Southern method.

BACON AND MUSH

Cut slices of cold corn-meal mush, dredge in flour, and fry brown. Serve with a strip of fried or broiled bacon on each slice.

BACON FRAISE

Make a batter of four eggs, half a cupful of milk, and a teaspoonful of flour. Fry some thin slices of bacon till transparent. Dip them in the batter, spread on a stoneware platter, cover with the remaining batter, and put into a moderate oven till a golden brown.

BACON À LA CRÊME

Fry thin slices of bacon as usual, place on a platter, and put into the oven to keep warm. Make a cream sauce, using the fat in the pan instead of butter. Pour over the bacon, sprinkle with minced parsley, and serve at once.

CALF'S BRAINS

Soak in cold water, parboil, remove pipes and membranes, throw into cold water, drain, wipe, and keep cool. They may be rubbed with melted butter and fried or broiled, or dipped in egg and crumbs and fried or broiled. Serve with a cream sauce or with a sauce of melted butter, lemon-juice, and minced parsley.

CHICKEN HASH

Use cold cooked chicken and proceed according to directions previously given. Cold turkey or tongue makes delicious hash. A shredded green pepper will usually improve it. Any hash may be served on toast with a poached egg on each slice.

FRIED HAM

Freshen a slice of ham a few moments in boiling water. Drain, wipe, and fry slowly. Eggs may be served with it. See Bacon and Eggs.

FRIZZLED HAM

Prepare as above. When the ham is half done, sprinkle with flour and fry brown. When brown, add a tablespoonful of made mustard to the gravy, and boiling water enough to cover the ham. Simmer five minutes and serve on a hot platter.

HAM AND POACHED EGGS

Prepare as directed above. Poach the eggs separately and serve on the slices of ham.

BROILED HAM

Freshen in cold water, drain, wipe, and broil. May be breaded and broiled on a buttered gridiron.

HAM BALLS

One cupful of cooked ham, finely chopped, one cupful of bread crumbs, two cupfuls of cooked potatoes, mashed fine, a heaping tablespoonful of butter, two eggs, and a dash of cayenne. Melt the butter and beat all together until very light. Shape into small flat cakes, dip in egg and crumbs, and fry brown. May be prepared beforehand.

HAM TOAST

Half a cupful of cold cooked ham, finely minced, half a teaspoonful of anchovy paste, a bit of cayenne and pounded mace. Add half a cupful of milk and an egg, well beaten. Stir till thick, take from the fire, and spread thinly on dry buttered toast. A poached egg may be placed on each slice.

HAM RÉCHAUFFÉ

Butter individual custard cups, fill three fourths full of minced ham reheated in a cream sauce, break an egg into each cup, sprinkle with crumbs, dot with butter, and bake till the egg is set. Tongue, chicken, turkey, or other meats may be used in this same way.

HAM AND EGGS À L'AURORE

Mince cooked ham and reheat in a cream sauce, to which the shredded whites of hard-boiled eggs have been added. Spread on buttered toast and sprinkle with the sifted yolks of the eggs, rubbed through a sieve.

KIDNEY BACON ROLLS

Season a cupful of bread crumbs with grated onion, salt and pepper, and minced parsley. Moisten with egg well beaten. Spread the crumb mixture over thin slices of bacon and wrap each slice of bacon around a small kidney. Fasten with toothpicks or skewers. Put in a baking-pan and bake in a hot oven until the bacon is crisp. Remove the skewers and serve on a hot plate, garnished with parsley.

FRIED KIDNEYS

Cut in halves, skin, sprinkle with salt and red pepper, and fry one minute in a spider, with no additional fat. Serve with dry toast.

KIDNEYS EN BROCHETTE

Cut the kidneys into small squares after parboiling and skinning. String on small steel skewers with small squares of bacon alternating. Broil or fry or cook in the oven, dredging with flour or not, as preferred. If the bacon is not very fat, soak the kidneys in olive oil a few moments before stringing. Serve on the skewers.

CRUMBED KIDNEYS

Parboil, drain, wipe, and split the kidneys, keeping them open with skewers. Season with pepper and salt, brush with oil, roll in crumbs, and broil, fry, or cook in a very hot oven. Make a sauce of melted butter, lemon-juice, and minced parsley, and pour over them if desired.

DEVILLED KIDNEYS

Parboil, drain, wipe, and slice the kidneys. Make a marinade of three tablespoonfuls of olive-oil, one of vinegar,—tarragon vinegar or lemon-juice may be used,—a teaspoonful of mustard, salt, and red pepper. Dip the sliced kidneys in this dressing and broil. Minced parsley is a pleasant addition to the marinade. After dipping in the dressing, they may be rolled in crumbs and fried. Serve plain, or with a sauce of melted butter, lemon-juice, and minced parsley, or with the remaining marinade heated and poured over the kidneys.

KIDNEY AND BACON

Parboil and slice mutton or lamb kidneys. Fry brown in bacon fat and serve on dry toast with the bacon.

STEWED BEEF KIDNEY

Parboil, drain, wipe, and cut into dice. Cook five minutes in boiling water, drain, add a small onion, grated, a pinch of sage, and a cup of water. Bring to the boil once more, add a pinch of salt, and two hard-boiled eggs, cut fine. Thicken with one tablespoonful of cornstarch, rubbed smooth in a little cold water. Serve on toast.

KIDNEYS À LA TERRAPIN

Parboil, drain, wipe, and cut into dice. Reheat in cream sauce, to which hard-boiled eggs, cut fine, and minced parsley are added. Serve on toast.

BROILED KIDNEYS—MAÎTRE D'HÔTEL

Use veal or lamb kidneys. Plunge for an instant into boiling water, skim out, and wipe dry. Split down the middle without cutting through, skin, and run a skewer through each to keep flat. Broil as usual. When brown, remove the skewers, lay on a hot platter, pour over melted butter, add a squeeze of lemon-juice, and sprinkle with chopped parsley. Kidneys and liver must be cooked very quickly, as long cooking makes them tough.

MINCED LAMB WITH POACHED EGGS

Chop cold roast lamb very fine. Season with salt, pepper, and a bit of mint. Reheat in the gravy, or in water, adding a little butter, or in a cream sauce. Spread thinly on thin slices of dry buttered toast, slip a poached egg on each slice, and serve at once, sprinkled with pepper and minced parsley.

BROILED LAMB'S LIVER

Cut the liver in thin slices, cover with olive oil, and soak half an hour. Drain, season with salt and pepper, dip in crumbs, and broil. Finish as for Broiled Kidneys.

CALF'S LIVER AND BACON

Cook the bacon first, skim out, and put the slices of liver, dredged with flour and seasoned with salt, into the hot fat. Cook very quickly.

LIVER À LA CRÊME

Parboil calf's liver, drain, wipe, and cut into dice or chop coarsely. Reheat in a cream sauce, seasoning with salt and pepper. Minced parsley, lemon-juice, or finely cut capers may be added to the sauce. Serve on toast. Cold cooked liver may be used in this way.

LIVER HASH

Equal parts of cold cooked liver and cold potatoes, cut fine. Reheat in a frying-pan, adding butter and boiling water as necessary. Almost any cold cooked meat may be used in this way.

BAKED HASH

Butter a shallow baking-dish, pile in the hash loosely, smooth the top, dot with butter, and bake until brown and crisp. Turn out on a platter or serve in the dish, a fresh napkin or a paper frill being arranged around the dish.

LIVER BOULETTES

Chop cold cooked liver fine. Reheat in a very thick cream sauce, well seasoned. Cool, shape into small flat cakes, dip in egg and crumbs, and fry brown.

LIVER AND BACON BALLS

Cold cooked liver cut fine and half as much cooked bacon, chopped. Shape into small flat cakes, using a raw egg to bind if necessary. Dip in egg and crumbs and fry brown.

MEAT AND RICE BALLS

One cupful of cold cooked rice, one cupful of finely chopped cooked meat,—any kind, or several kinds,—a pinch of salt, a dash of pepper, two tablespoonfuls of butter, half a cupful of milk, and one egg. Put the milk on to boil, add the rice, meat, and seasoning. When it boils, add the egg, well beaten, and stir one minute. Take from the fire, cool, form into small flat cakes, dip in egg and crumbs, and fry brown. May be prepared the day before using.

FRIED SALT PORK

Cut in thin slices, freshen in cold water gradually brought to the boil. Drain, wipe, trim off the rind, roll in flour, and fry. When brown, put on a hot platter and make a cream sauce, using the fat in the pan. Fried salt pork with cream sauce poured over it is a venerable New England dish of some three centuries' standing.

PHILADELPHIA SCRAPPLE

Use the head, heart, and feet of fresh pork. Boil until the flesh slips from the bone. Cool, take out the bones and gristle, and chop the meat fine. Set aside the water in which the meat was cooked, and when cold take the cake of fat from the surface. Bring the liquor to the boil once more, add the chopped meat, and when at a galloping boil, sprinkle in, slowly, enough corn-meal to make a thick mush. Cook slowly for an hour or more. Pour into a pan wet with cold water and let stand in a cold place over night. Turn out on a platter, cut in half-inch slices, and fry.

SAUSAGE

Prick the skins with a needle or fork to prevent bursting. Cover with boiling water, parboil five minutes, drain, wipe, and fry as usual. The sausage meat is made into small flat cakes, dredged with flour and fried. Bread crumbs may be used in making the sausage cakes if desired. If the cakes do not hold together readily, add a little beaten egg.

BAKED SAUSAGE

Prick the sausages and lay each one on a strip of buttered bread its own length and width. Arrange in a baking-pan and bake in a very hot oven till the sausages are brown and the bread crisp.

SAUSAGES BAKED IN POTATOES

Prick medium-sized sausages and brown quickly in a spider. Take out and keep warm. Core large potatoes, draw the sausages through the cores, and bake. A pleasant surprise for the person peeling the potato.

BROILED SWEETBREADS

Parboil, in slightly acidulated water, for five minutes, then throw into cold water. Remove pipes and fibres and let cool—the colder the better. Split, rub with melted butter, season with pepper and salt, and broil or fry. They may also be dipped in egg and crumbs and fried or broiled. Serve on a hot platter. A sauce of melted butter, lemon-juice, and minced parsley is a pleasing accompaniment.

FRIED TRIPE

Tripe as it comes from the market is already prepared. Wash thoroughly, boil until tender, drain, and cool. Cut into strips, season with salt and pepper, dip in egg and crumbs, and fry in butter or drippings until brown. It may be prepared for frying the day before and kept in a cool place. Breaded tripe may also be broiled on a buttered gridiron.

FRICASSEED TRIPE

Cut a pound of tripe in narrow strips, add a cupful of water, a piece of butter the size of an egg, and a tablespoonful of flour, rubbed smooth in a little cold water. Season with salt and simmer thirty minutes. Serve very hot, on toast if desired.

TRIPE À LA LYONNAISE

One pound of cooked tripe cut into inch squares, two tablespoonfuls of butter, one tablespoonful of chopped onion, one tablespoonful of vinegar, salt and pepper to taste. Put the butter and onion in a frying-pan. When the onion turns yellow, add the tripe and seasoning, boil up once more, and serve immediately, on toast.

TRIPE À LA POULETTE

Fry a chopped onion in three tablespoonfuls of butter. When brown, add a pound of tripe, cut into dice, season with salt and paprika, and fry until the mixture is partially dry. Add a heaping tablespoonful of flour, and when the butter has absorbed it, add slowly two cupfuls of stock or milk and a slight grating of nutmeg. Simmer till the tripe is tender. Beat together one tablespoonful of melted butter and one tablespoonful of lemon-juice, stir into the well-beaten yolks of two eggs, take the tripe from the fire, mix thoroughly, and serve at once.

MINCED VEAL AND EGGS

Chop cold cooked veal very fine. Add hard-boiled eggs cut fine, one to each two cupfuls of meat. Reheat in hot water, adding melted butter, or in a cream sauce. A bit of green pepper, parsley, grated onion, pimento, or capers finely cut may be used for flavoring. Other meats may be prepared in the same way.

SUBSTITUTES FOR MEAT

Certain things are well suited to replace meat at the breakfast table. It is a good idea to bar out the potato, unless in hash, for the simple reason that the humble vegetable appears at dinner about three hundred and sixty-five days in the year, and even a good thing may be worked to death. Americans have been accused, not altogether unjustly, of being "potato mad." Potato left-overs can be used at luncheon, if not in hash for breakfast.

FRIED EGGPLANT

Slice the eggplant in slices one third of an inch thick, pare, put into a deep dish, and cover with cold water well salted. Soak one hour. Drain, wipe, dip in egg and crumbs, and fry brown.

BROILED MUSHROOMS

Choose large, firm mushrooms. Remove the stems, peel, wash, and wipe dry. Rub with melted butter and broil. Serve with a sauce made of melted butter, lemon-juice, and minced parsley.

FRIED MUSHROOMS

Prepare as above, dip in egg and crumbs, and fry in deep fat. Or sauté in butter in the frying-pan. Breaded mushrooms may be broiled if dipped in melted butter or oil before broiling.

BAKED MUSHROOMS

Prepare as above. Place in a shallow earthen baking-dish, hollow side up, sprinkle with salt and pepper, and place a small piece of butter on each. Baste with melted butter and a few drops of lemon-juice. Serve very hot, on buttered toast.

GRILLED MUSHROOMS

Cut off the stalks, peel, and score lightly the under side of large, firm, fresh mushrooms. Sprinkle with pepper and salt and soak a few moments in oil. Drain and broil. Serve with lemon quarters and garnish with parsley.

FRENCH TOAST

Make a batter of two eggs, well beaten, a cupful of milk, a tablespoonful of melted butter, and spice or grated lemon- or orange-peel to flavor. Dip the trimmed slices of bread in this batter and fry brown in butter.

CORN OYSTERS

Two cupfuls of green corn, grated, half a cupful of milk, one cupful of sifted flour, two eggs, a teaspoonful of salt and one tablespoonful each of butter and lard. Beat the yolks of the eggs, add the milk, then the flour and salt. Beat to a smooth batter, add the corn, then beat again, adding the well beaten whites of the eggs last. Put the lard and butter into a frying-pan, and when very hot put in the batter by small spoonfuls. Brown on one side, then turn. If the batter is too thick, add a little more milk. The thinner the batter, the more delicate and tender the oysters will be. Canned corn may be used, if it is chopped very fine, but it is not so good. By scoring deeply with a sharp knife each row of kernels on an ear of corn, the pulp may be pressed out with a knife. The corn may be cut from the cob and chopped, but the better way is to press out the pulp.

Regardless of the allurements of wood and field, it is always safest to buy mushrooms at a reliable market. So many people are now making a business of raising them that they are continually getting cheaper. The silver spoon test is absolutely worthless. In fact, the only sure test is the risky one: "Eat it, and if you live it's a mushroom—if you die it's a toadstool." However, when buying mushrooms of a reliable dealer, one takes practically no risk at all, and, even at the highest price, a box of mushrooms is much cheaper than a really nice funeral.

EGGS

Various rules have been given for testing the freshness of eggs, but there is only one which is reliable, and it is, perhaps, the most simple of all. It is merely this: open the egg and look at the contents in a strong light. It is better to hold it near the eyes and at the same time take a deep breath inward.

Strictly fresh eggs come from the country sometimes with the date of their appearance stamped indelibly in purple on the egg. This is done by giving the hens chopped calendars with their meals. Care should be taken, however, to furnish this year's calendar. Nobody wants an egg with a last-year's date on it and the error is likely to disarrange the digestion of the hen. Eggs flavored with onions or tomatoes are secured by turning the hens into a neighbor's vegetable garden. A certain florist feeds his unsold roses to his hens and sells rose-flavored eggs to his customers at a fancy price. The hint is well worth remembering. Violet-flavored eggs might be had, doubtless, in the same way.

At a formal breakfast, all precautions should be taken to insure the freshness of the eggs. A conscientious hostess would be very much mortified if she served chicken out of its proper course.

POACHED EGGS

Use a skillet, or muffin-rings placed in a pan of water, not too deep. The water should barely cover the eggs. Bring the water to the boiling point, drop in the eggs carefully, one at a time, and remove from the fire immediately. Cover the pan and let stand until cooked. A teaspoonful of lemon-juice or vinegar in the water will keep the whites firm and preserve the shape of the eggs. Poached eggs are usually served on thin slices of buttered toast. Take up with a skimmer and let drain thoroughly before placing on the toast. Sprinkle with salt and pepper. As every other writer who has given directions for poaching eggs has said that "the beauty of a poached egg is for the yolk to be seen blushing through the veiled white," the author of this book will make no allusion to it.

SCRAMBLED EGGS

Put two heaping tablespoonfuls of butter into a frying-pan. When it sizzles, break into it quickly six fresh eggs and mix thoroughly with a silver spoon for two minutes without stopping. Season with salt and pepper and a slight grating of nutmeg if desired. Scrambled eggs should be thick and creamy.

SCRAMBLED EGGS—II

Beat the eggs thoroughly, add one teaspoonful of cold water or milk for each egg and beat again. Cook as above.

SCRAMBLED EGGS WITH ASPARAGUS TIPS

Have one cupful of cold cooked asparagus tips ready. In boiling asparagus its color will keep better if the smallest possible pinch of baking soda be added to the water. It should be cooked quickly in an uncovered saucepan. Prepare the eggs as for Scrambled Eggs—II, and when they begin to thicken, put in the asparagus tips and stir until the eggs are done. One half cupful of the asparagus tips to each three eggs is about the right proportion, but more may be added if desired. In making scrambles, allow one egg for each person and one extra for each three persons.

SCRAMBLED EGGS WITH DRIED BEEF

One cupful of minced dried beef, which has been soaked in boiling water for five minutes. Put it into melted butter, stir till the butter sizzles, then pour over six or seven-well-beaten eggs. Stir till the eggs are smooth and creamy. Serve at once. Any scramble may be served on toast if desired.

FRIED EGGS

Three tablespoonfuls of butter in the frying-pan. When it sizzles, slip in the broken eggs carefully, one at a time. Tip the pan and baste with the melted butter while cooking. If wanted crisp on both sides, turn the eggs over when the under side is done. Wet in cold water the saucer on which an egg is broken and the egg will not stick to it, but will slip easily into the pan. Olive oil may be used instead of butter, but the pan must be covered during the cooking, as the oil spatters.

FRIED EGGS AU BEURRE NOIR

Fry eggs as above, using butter or oil. When done, skim out, add more butter or oil to that in the pan, season with salt, pepper, vinegar, or lemon-juice, and let brown. When the butter is brown pour it over the fried eggs and serve.

EGGS À LA CRÊME

Make a cream sauce, using one tablespoonful of butter, two of flour, two cupfuls of milk, and pepper and salt to season. When the sauce is thick and creamy, add hard-boiled eggs coarsely chopped, and serve at once on toast. Sprinkle with chopped parsley.

EGGS À LA TRIPE

Fry two sliced onions in butter, but do not brown. Stir in one cupful of milk or cream and enough flour to thicken, rubbed smooth in a little of the cream or milk. Season with salt, white pepper, and a bit of grated nutmeg. Stir till thick, then add eight hard-boiled eggs, sliced crosswise. Heat thoroughly and serve.

EGGS AU MIROIR

Butter a stone platter that will stand the heat of the oven. Break into it carefully enough fresh eggs to cover it, taking care not to break the yolks. Place in the oven till the eggs are set. Sprinkle with salt and pepper and minced parsley and serve at once.

EGGS WITH CREAMED CELERY

Make the cream sauce and put into it enough boiled celery, coarsely cut, to serve as a vegetable. Spread on buttered toast and lay a poached egg on each slice. The tough, unsightly portions of celery stalks may be used in this way.

CHICKEN LIVER SCRAMBLE

Use one cupful of chopped cooked chicken livers and six or seven well-beaten eggs. Prepare like other scrambles.

CHEESE SCRAMBLE

One half cupful of grated American cheese and six well-beaten eggs. Mix the cheese with the eggs before cooking.

EGGS À LA PAYSANNE

Put one half cupful of cream into a baking-dish, break into it six fresh eggs, and place in the oven till the eggs are set. Sprinkle with salt and pepper, minced parsley, and sweet green pepper.

EGGS À L'AURORE

Make the cream sauce and add to it the shredded whites of six or eight hard-boiled eggs. Spread on buttered toast and rub the yolks through a sieve, sprinkling each slice of toast with the powdered yolk. Sometimes called "Eggs à la Goldenrod."

OYSTER SCRAMBLE

One cupful of oysters, cut fine. Pour boiling water over, drain on a fine sieve, and add six or seven well-beaten eggs. Prepare as other scrambles.

MUSHROOM SCRAMBLE

One cupful of cooked mushrooms, cut fine, six or eight well-beaten eggs. Serve on toast.

LOBSTER SCRAMBLE

One cupful of cold cooked lobster, six or eight well-beaten eggs. Mix before putting into the hot butter.

TOMATO SCRAMBLE

One cupful of stewed and strained tomato, or of fresh tomato peeled and rubbed through a sieve, six or eight well-beaten eggs. Mix before putting into the hot butter.

GREEN PEA SCRAMBLE

One cupful of cold cooked green peas, six or seven well-beaten eggs. Mix before beginning to cook.

HAM SCRAMBLE

One cupful of cold boiled ham, minced, mixed with eight well-beaten eggs. A little grated onion is an improvement.

BACON SCRAMBLE

Fry one cupful of shredded bacon until partially cooked, drain off part of the fat, add six or seven well-beaten eggs, and finish cooking, stirring constantly. A little grated onion may be added with the eggs.

CRAB SCRAMBLE

One cupful of cooked shredded crab-meat, six or seven well-beaten eggs. Shredded green peppers may be added at pleasure. The canned crab-meat is nearly as good as the fresh.

SHRIMP SCRAMBLE

One cupful of finely cut cooked shrimps, six or seven well-beaten eggs. Green peppers may be added. Canned shrimps may be used.

KIDNEY SCRAMBLE

One cupful of cold cooked kidneys, cut fine, six or seven well-beaten eggs. Prepare like other scrambles.

SAUSAGE SCRAMBLE

One cupful of cooked sausage-meat, finely minced, mixed with six or seven well-beaten eggs before cooking. Or, use uncooked sausage-meat and prepare like Bacon Scramble.

SARDINE SCRAMBLE

Add the juice of half a lemon to one cupful of finely cut sardines. Use the oil from the can instead of butter. Beat six or seven eggs thoroughly and mix with the sardines before cooking.

TONGUE SCRAMBLE

One cupful finely minced cooked tongue, six or eight well-beaten eggs. Season with grated onion, shredded green pepper, or minced parsley.

EGGS WITH FINE HERBS

Use a heaping tablespoonful of minced parsley, chives, and tarragon to eight well-beaten eggs, mixing before putting into the hot butter.

MEXICAN EGGS

Split three sweet green peppers, lengthwise, and take out the seeds. Fry two minutes in very hot butter. Fry six very thin slices of ham and place on slices of toast, lay the peppers over the ham, and put a fried or a poached egg on each slice.

SPANISH EGGS

Cook together one cupful of stewed and strained tomato, one bean of garlic, finely minced, one chopped onion, and two sweet green peppers, seeded and chopped. Cook gently till reduced one half. Spread on thin slices of toast and lay a fried or poached egg on each slice.

CREAMED CHICKEN AND POACHED EGGS

Make a cream sauce, add one cupful of minced cooked chicken, spread on toast, and lay a poached egg on each slice.

BOILED EGGS—I

Put the eggs into a saucepan of cold water and bring to the boil. Boil one minute and serve at once.

BOILED EGGS—II

Have a saucepan of water at a galloping boil. Drop in the eggs carefully, cover, and let stand till the eggs are cool enough to handle. They will be perfectly cooked and much more easily managed than if the shells were piping hot.

EGGS IN CRUSTS

Cut stale bread into slices an inch thick. Scoop out the centres of each slice and remove the crust. Rub with butter, drop an egg into each cavity, and put in a hot oven till the eggs are set.

EGGS IN RAMEKINS

Butter ramekins or custard cups. Drop an egg into each cup and place in a hot oven till the egg is set. This method of cooking eggs may be endlessly varied by filling the cups half full of minced meat, fish, seasoned crumbs, creamed vegetables, or anything else which combines well with eggs. Anything used in a scramble or an omelet may be placed in the bottom of the ramekin. If too dry, moisten with cream, milk, or water. The egg may be sprinkled with crumbs and dotted with butter. Grated cheese and minced parsley may be added at pleasure. A "left-over" which is otherwise hopeless may often be used advantageously in a ramekin with an egg. The small individual dishes are pleasing, when served on a fresh doily. Lacking the individual dishes, or for variety, a stoneware platter, or a baking-dish may be half filled with the mixture and the eggs broken on top.

BAKED EGGS WITH CHEESE

Make toast and hollow the slices slightly in the centre. Mix grated cheese to a paste with milk and spread over the toast. Arrange on a stoneware platter or in a baking-dish, break an egg over each slice, sprinkle with more cheese, and place in a hot oven till the eggs are set.

BAKED EGGS WITH HAM

Make the cream sauce and add to it one cupful of cold cooked ham, finely minced. Butter custard cups, break an egg into each, and stand in a pan of hot water in the oven till the eggs are firm. Spread the minced ham on a platter or on slices of toast, and turn the eggs on to it. Sprinkle with salt, pepper, and minced parsley.

CODDLED EGGS

Allow four tablespoonfuls of milk for each egg. Beat together thoroughly, cook in a double boiler till creamy, and serve on toast.

EGGS AND MUSHROOMS

(*May Irwin's Recipe*)

One pound of fresh mushrooms cleaned well in several waters, and wiped dry. Put into a saucepan with two ounces of butter, half a teaspoonful of salt, and a dash of white pepper. Set over the fire till thoroughly hot, then turn into a shallow baking-dish, and break over them six eggs. Sprinkle with stale bread crumbs, dot with butter, dust with salt and pepper, and bake in a hot oven till the eggs are set. Serve on buttered toast.

EGGS IN AMBUSH

Scoop out the crumb from stale rolls, first cutting an even slice off the top. Toast or fry the shells thus made, or rub freely with butter and set into a piping hot oven until crisp and brown. Drop a fresh egg into each shell, add a little minced parsley or a teaspoonful of cream, if desired, or any preferred seasoning of minced fish, or meat, or vegetable. (See Eggs in Ramekins.) Bake in a hot oven till the eggs set, put on the covers, and serve. A pleasant surprise for the person who expects to find only a roll.

EGGS À LA MAÎTRE D'HÔTEL

Make a sauce of half a cupful of melted butter, the juice of half a lemon, and a teaspoonful of minced parsley. Cut hard-boiled eggs in slices lengthwise, arrange on buttered toast, and pour the sauce over the eggs, or, pour over poached eggs on toast just before serving.

POACHED EGGS ON ANCHOVY TOAST

Work a teaspoonful of anchovy paste, or more, if desired, into half a cupful of butter. Spread on thin slices of crisp toast and lay a poached egg on each slice.

EGGS SUR LE PLAT

Beat the whites of eggs to a stiff froth, spread on a buttered platter, and make hollows in the froth with a spoon. In these hollows drop carefully the unbroken yolks. Sprinkle with salt and pepper and place in a hot oven until the eggs are set.

BIRDS' NESTS

Use recipe for Eggs sur le Plat. Arrange in ramekins or on slices of toast.

EGGS BAKED IN TOMATOES

Cut off a slice from the top (blossom end), of a small, ripe, well-shaped tomato. With a silver spoon scoop out the pulp carefully, sprinkle the inside with salt and drain for a few moments, upside down. Put a tablespoonful of seasoned bread crumbs in the bottom of the tomato, break a fresh egg into it, sprinkle with salt and pepper, and place in a hot oven until the egg is set. Prepare one tomato for each person.

SWISS EGGS

Rub a stoneware platter thickly with butter, cover it with very thin slices of fresh Gruyère cheese, break fresh eggs upon the cheese, sprinkle with grated nutmeg, pepper, and salt, pour half a cupful of cream over the eggs, sprinkle with the cheese, grated, and bake about a quarter of an hour in a hot oven. Serve on the same platter on which the eggs were baked.

CHICKEN SCRAMBLE

Use one cupful of cold cooked chicken, shredded or chopped, to seven well-beaten eggs, and prepare like other scrambles. A bit of green pepper or of chopped pimento is an agreeable addition.

EGGS À LA BONNE FEMME

Fry two sliced onions brown in butter, then add a tablespoonful of vinegar. Butter a platter, spread the fried onions over it, break upon it six fresh eggs, sprinkle with crumbs, dot with butter, and bake in a hot oven until the eggs are set.

EGGS À LA BOURGEOISE

Cut slices of bread half an inch thick and trim off the crust, lay on a buttered platter, and sprinkle with grated cheese. Beat eggs enough to cover the bread, season with salt and pepper and grated nutmeg, pour over the bread and bake in a moderate oven until the eggs are set.

EGGS À LA ST. CATHERINE

Select smooth, shapely potatoes and bake until soft. Cut in halves lengthwise and scoop out a part of the pulp. Break an egg into each half, sprinkle with salt and pepper, add a teaspoonful of cream to each egg and bake in a moderate oven until the eggs are set. In the meantime, beat the white of an egg to a stiff froth, and work gradually into it the potato pulp which has been scooped out. Heap roughly over the baked eggs and keep in the oven till well puffed and brown. A little grated cheese or minced parsley may be sprinkled over the top.

EGGS IN PEPPERS

Cut a thin slice from the stem end of a green pepper and take out the seeds. Cut a slice from the smaller end, so that the pepper may stand straight, and put on a slice of buttered toast. Make a small hollow in the toast under the pepper and break an egg into each one. Bake until the eggs are set.

EGGS POACHED IN MILK

Butter a frying-pan, add a pint of milk, and bring the milk to a boil. Slip in fresh eggs, one at a time, and poach as usual. Skim out, season with salt and pepper, and put each egg on a slice of buttered toast. Pour the milk over and serve immediately.

EGGS À LA WASHINGTON

Lay a slice of fresh fried tomato on each slice of buttered toast. On each slice of tomato arrange some shredded sweet pepper, fried. Lay a poached egg on each slice, and sprinkle with parsley and sweet pepper minced together.

PIMENTO SCRAMBLE

Use the scarlet pimentos which come in cans. Chop rather coarsely and use half a cupful to each four eggs. Prepare like other scrambles.

EGGS À LA ESPAGNOLE

Make a cream sauce and add to it half a cupful of shredded pimentos. Spread over buttered toast and put a poached egg on each slice.

CODFISH SCRAMBLE

Use one cupful of shredded salt cod which has been freshened, and seven well-beaten eggs. Salt Mackerel, Finnan Haddie, Smoked Salmon, or other salt fish may be used. Clams, Caviare, Herring, Sturgeon, and many other left-overs are also acceptable.

STEAMED EGGS

Break fresh eggs into buttered custard cups and steam until set.

BAKED EGGS ON RASHERS OF BACON

Have ready some thin slices of bacon fried until transparent, but not crisp. Lay two strips of bacon on each slice of toast, arrange in a baking-pan, break an egg over each slice of toast, and bake until the egg is set.

SCRAMBLED EGGS IN CUPS

Prepare stale rolls as for Eggs in Ambush, but bake the buttered rolls until crisp and brown. Fill with scrambled eggs and serve immediately.

RICE SCRAMBLE

Use a cupful of cold cooked rice and eight well-beaten eggs and proceed as for other scrambles. A little milk or water may be necessary.

SURPRISE EGGS

Boil fresh eggs four minutes, skim out, plunge into cold water for an instant, then remove the shells. Dip each egg into egg and crumbs, then fry in deep fat.

JAPANESE EGGS

Spread hot boiled rice on a platter, season with melted butter, lemon-juice, and minced parsley. Poach six eggs and arrange them on the rice.

RUMBLED EGGS

Beat three fresh eggs with two tablespoonfuls of butter, and add a teaspoonful of milk. Stir over a moderate fire until it puffs up, then serve at once on buttered toast.

EGGS À LA WALDORF

Beat six eggs with half a cupful of cream, half a teaspoonful of salt, and a sprinkle of pepper. Cut two large mushrooms into dice and fry one minute in two tablespoonfuls of butter. Pour the egg mixture over the mushrooms and stir rapidly until it begins to thicken, then take from the fire and beat until smooth and creamy. Serve at once on buttered toast.

WHIPPED EGGS

Beat six eggs separately, the whites to a stiff froth. Mix thoroughly, season with salt and pepper, and pour into two quarts of salted water at a galloping boil. Stir one minute, then drain through a fine sieve. Serve on buttered toast and garnish with crisp rashers of bacon.

ESCALLOPED EGGS

Make the cream sauce. Have ready eight hard-boiled eggs and some dried bread crumbs. Butter ramekins, put in a layer of crumbs, then sliced eggs, then butter in tiny dots, then sauce, and so on, until the dish is full, having crumbs and butter on top. A little grated cheese may be sprinkled over the top. If too dry, moisten with a little milk or cream. Bake until brown.

POACHED EGGS WITH CREAMED SALMON

Make a cream sauce and reheat in it either canned salmon, or a cupful of salt or smoked salmon. Spread on buttered toast and lay a poached egg on each slice. Sprinkle with minced parsley and garnish with lemon quarters.

EGGS À LA MARTIN

Boil six eggs four minutes, plunge into cold water, then remove the shells. Arrange in a baking-dish, or in ramekins, cover with cream sauce, sprinkle with bread crumbs and a little grated cheese, dot with butter, and bake until brown.

OMELETS

"To make an omelet, you must first break eggs."—French Proverb.

So many different methods for making omelets are given, in works of recognized authority, that it seems as if any one who had an egg and an omelet pan could hardly go amiss. Yet failures are frequent, as every omelet-maker knows.

French writers say positively that no liquid of any sort must be added to an omelet—that it contains eggs and eggs alone, beaten just enough to break the yolks. American authorities add milk or water, or beat the eggs separately, the whites to a stiff froth. One of them makes a clear distinction between an omelet and a puffy omelet; the puffy omelet, of course, being made by folding in the stiffly beaten whites before cooking. Some say milk makes it tough, and others say water makes it stringy. Suffice it to say, however, that a perfect omelet is a matter of experience and a deft hand. All writers agree that small omelets are more easily made than large ones, and it is better to do it twice or even three times than to have too many eggs in one omelet. Below are given the various methods, from which the would-be omelet-maker may choose. All of them have the stamp of good authority.

OMELET—I

Beat six eggs well, yolks and whites together. Put two tablespoonfuls of butter into a frying-pan. When it is hot, pour in the beaten eggs, which have been seasoned with salt and pepper. With a fork, draw the cooked egg from the outside of the pan to the centre. As soon as it is all thick, lift half of the omelet on to a plate, and turn the other half over it. It should be turned while the centre is still soft, and the fire should not be too hot.

OMELET—II

Break the eggs into a bowl, add as many tablespoonfuls of cold water as there are eggs. Beat the eggs well, then season with salt and pepper, and pour into a thin, smooth frying-pan which contains a tablespoonful of melted butter. With a thin knife lift the cooked portion of the egg and allow the uncooked portion to run down into the butter, meanwhile gently rocking the pan back and forth. When creamy, begin at the side of the pan nearest the handle and roll the omelet, using a little butter if needed.

OMELET—III

Prepare as above, using milk instead of water.

OMELET—IV

Separate the whites and yolks of the eggs. Beat the yolks till thick and lemon colored and the whites until they stand alone. Fold together carefully, seasoning with salt and pepper, and adding a tablespoonful of cold water for each egg. Have two tablespoonfuls of butter in the frying-pan. When it is hot, pour in the egg mixture and let stand until the egg is set around the edge and a knife plunged into the centre comes out nearly clean. Then set the pan into the oven till the omelet puffs. Score slightly across the middle with a sharp knife, fold, and serve at once on a hot platter.

OMELET AUX FINES HERBES

Prepare Omelet I, and mix a tablespoonful of chopped parsley and chives with the eggs before cooking.

PEA OMELET

Prepare Omelet I. As soon as the eggs are in the frying-pan, add a cupful of cooked and drained peas, arranging carefully in the outermost half so that the other portion will fold over it. Finish as usual.

OMELET WITH ASPARAGUS TIPS

Have ready one cupful of cooked and drained asparagus tips. Prepare according to directions given for Pea Omelet.

MUSHROOM OMELET

Use fresh mushrooms, if possible. Fry, and drain on brown paper. When the eggs are in the frying-pan, spread the mushrooms on the outermost half of the omelet, so that the other portion will fold over it. Finish as usual.

OMELET WITH TOMATO SAUCE

Spread the outermost half of an omelet with tomato sauce, fold, and finish as usual.

OMELET AU FROMAGE

Prepare Omelet I, adding half a cupful of grated Parmesan cheese, or dried and grated American cheese, to the egg mixture.

HAM OMELET

Have ready one cupful of cooked ham, very finely minced. Spread on half of the omelet and fold the other part over it.

OYSTER OMELET

One cupful of cooked oysters, minced or not, as preferred. Lay on half of the omelet and fold.

CLAM OMELET

See Oyster Omelet.

SHRIMP OMELET

One cupful of cooked and shredded shrimps. See Oyster Omelet

CRAB OMELET

One cupful of minced cooked crab meat. See Oyster Omelet.

LOBSTER OMELET

One cupful of cooked and shredded lobster. See Oyster Omelet.

TOMATO OMELET

One half cupful of stewed and strained tomatoes, or of fresh tomatoes peeled and rubbed through a sieve. Spread on the outermost half of the omelet, sprinkle with salt and pepper, and fold.

DRIED BEEF OMELET

One cupful of dried beef, shredded or minced. Cook five minutes in boiling water, drain in a cloth, spread on the outermost half of the omelet, and fold.

KIDNEY OMELET

Cut the kidneys into inch pieces, fry, drain, and finish as for Mushroom Omelet.

CHICKEN LIVER OMELET

One cupful of cooked chicken livers, cut in small pieces. See Oyster Omelet.

SAUSAGE OMELET

Spread the outer portion of an omelet with cooked sausage meat and fold as usual.

SARDINE OMELET

Rub to a paste with melted butter and lemon-juice enough sardines to make half a cupful. Spread thinly on the outer half of an omelet, and fold.

CHEESE OMELET II

Spread one cupful of grated cheese, Swiss, American, or Parmesan, on the outer portion of an omelet when the eggs are first put in the pan. Cook and fold as usual.

BLAZING OMELET

Make a plain omelet. Pour over it rum, kirsch, or brandy, ignite, and send to the table blazing. Serve as soon as the fire has gone out.

BACON OMELET

Cook a plain omelet in bacon fat instead of in butter and garnish with crisp rashers of bacon.

BACON OMELET II

Fry one cupful of minced bacon until crisp, drain off the fat, spread the bacon on half the omelet, and fold.

BREAD OMELET

Soak half a cupful of bread crumbs in half a cupful of milk and mix with the eggs before cooking.

OMELET À LA CRÊME

Make the cream sauce. Mix half a cupful of it with the omelet before cooking. Spread the rest of it on the outermost half of the omelet, finish, and fold as usual.

JELLY OMELET

Spread half of an omelet thinly with jelly—crabapple, currant, gooseberry, or quince, and fold.

SPANISH OMELET

Cook until thick one half can of tomatoes, one grated onion, one very finely minced bean of garlic, and one minced green pepper. Season with salt and paprika, spread on half the omelet, and fold.

TONGUE OMELET

Have ready a cupful of cold cooked tongue, minced or shredded. Spread on half the omelet, and fold.

CHICKEN OMELET

One cupful of cold cooked chicken, shredded or minced. Spread on half of the omelet, and fold.

CAULIFLOWER OMELET

One cupful of cold cooked cauliflower, with its sauce. Cut fine, spread on half the omelet, and fold.

ANCHOVY OMELET

Add a teaspoonful of anchovy paste to half a cupful of melted butter. Mix thoroughly, spread on half the omelet, and fold.

POTATO OMELET

One cupful of cooked potatoes, creamed or fried, cut in dice. Spread on half the omelet, sprinkle with salt, pepper, and minced parsley, and fold.

Almost any left-over can be advantageously used in an omelet. Fish, especially salt fish, meats, and vegetables, in quantities of half a cupful or more, preserved and fresh fruits, cereals—everything but soups, salads, and puddings. Roughly speaking, any omelet mixture can be added to the eggs before cooking, but as a general rule, it is better to spread it on half of the omelet and fold the other half over it, as otherwise the omelet is more likely to be heavy.

Sweet omelets are delicious. A teaspoonful of powdered sugar should be added to the eggs before cooking, and the fruit, jam, jelly, or preserves should be very thinly spread, as flavor is desired, not a dessert. Fresh fruits are cut fine and sprinkled with powdered sugar, spread on half the omelet, and the other half folded over. In the case of juicy fruits, such as oranges, the juice of the fruit is carefully saved and poured over the folded omelet just before serving.

Among the fresh fruits suitable for omelets are Apricots, Bananas, Blackberries, Cherries, Gooseberries, Grapefruit, Plums, Huckleberries,

Oranges, Pineapples, Peaches, Raspberries, and Strawberries—all crushed very fine and sweetened; the juice, if any, being poured over the omelet.

Among the stewed and preserved fruits are Apples, Apricots, Cherries, Currants, Figs, Gooseberries, Peaches, Pears, Plums, Quinces, Rhubarb, and the various fruit jams. Rum or brandy poured over the omelet and set on fire just before serving is a pleasant addition to many of the fruit omelets, Fig especially.

QUICK BREADS

People who can eat hot breads for breakfast are always sorry for those who cannot. Quite often the internal dissension ascribed to the hot bread is due to something else, or to an undesirable combination of food elements in one and the same meal. Besides, hot bread is so good that it is sometimes eaten too quickly. This hint is of medical origin and is worth consideration. Almost any hot bread will be found harmless when baked a second time.

BAKING POWDER BISCUIT

Four cupfuls of sifted flour, shortening the size of an egg,—equal parts of butter and lard preferred,—two heaping teaspoonfuls of baking powder, and a pinch of salt. Mix thoroughly, rubbing with the finger-tips till the flour is granular, like corn-meal. Add cold sweet milk to make a dough as soft as can be handled, roll out an inch thick, cut into rounds with a biscuit cutter, and bake in a hot oven. The dough must be handled as little as possible after putting in the milk.

QUICK BISCUIT

Two cupfuls of buttermilk, or of sour milk, a teaspoonful of baking soda, a tablespoonful of melted butter or lard, and flour to make a soft dough. Handle as little as possible, roll out, cut into circles with a biscuit cutter, and bake in a quick oven.

BUTTERMILK BISCUIT

Sift four cupfuls of flour, add a tablespoonful of melted lard, a pinch of salt, a teaspoonful of soda, and enough buttermilk to make a soft dough. Roll thin, handling as little as possible, cut into rounds, and bake in a quick oven.

EGG BISCUIT

Sift three cupfuls of flour, add a teaspoonful of salt, a tablespoonful of sugar, two eggs well beaten, a tablespoonful of melted lard, and a cupful of sweet milk to which has been added half a teaspoonful each of soda and cream of tartar. Work to a smooth dough, roll out half an inch thick, cut into circles with a biscuit cutter, and bake on buttered pans.

SOUR MILK BISCUIT

Four cupfuls of flour, one teaspoonful of soda, one teaspoonful of salt, one tablespoonful of butter or lard, and two cupfuls of sour milk. Or, leave out the butter and use sour cream. Mix the salt and soda with the flour and sift it. Rub in the shortening, mix with the milk, roll the dough half an inch thick, and cut into rounds with a biscuit cutter. Bake from twelve to fifteen minutes in a quick oven.

NEW YORK BISCUIT

Two eggs well beaten, one cupful of milk, one tablespoonful of melted lard, a pinch of salt, two teaspoonfuls of baking powder and four cupfuls of sifted flour. Roll out, cut into circles, and bake in a hot oven.

SOUTHERN BATTER BREAD

Half a cupful of cold boiled rice, two eggs beaten separately, two cupfuls of corn-meal, one tablespoonful of lard or butter, melted, a teaspoonful of salt, and two cupfuls of milk. Beat together till thoroughly mixed and bake quickly in buttered muffin-rings or in shallow baking-tins.

SPOON BREAD

Pour one cupful of boiling water over one cupful of white corn-meal. Add a pinch of salt, one cupful of cold boiled rice, three eggs, well beaten, two teaspoonfuls of baking powder, and a cupful and a half of milk. Mix thoroughly and pour two inches deep into a buttered earthen baking-dish and bake till done. It should be like a baked custard and is served from the dish with a spoon. Cereals other than rice may be used, especially cerealine.

KENTUCKY BATTER BREAD

Two cupfuls of corn-meal, three eggs well beaten, one teaspoonful of salt, and one tablespoonful of melted butter. Mix with enough milk to make a thin batter. Pour into shallow buttered tins and bake about forty-five minutes in a quick oven.

SOFT BATTER BREAD

Two cupfuls of sweet milk, two cupfuls of buttermilk, one cupful of white corn-meal, half a teaspoonful of soda, one teaspoonful of salt, three eggs, and one tablespoonful of melted butter. Boil the milk and add the meal slowly, making a mush, then add the salt and butter, and cool. Add the eggs and a tablespoonful of milk in which the soda has been dissolved. Bake in a buttered pan in a moderate oven.

COLONIAL BREAKFAST BREAD

One cupful of flour, half a teaspoonful of salt, two cupfuls of rich milk, and seven eggs, well beaten. Bake in a buttered cake-tin and serve quickly.

ENGLISH BUNS

Rub half a cupful of butter into two cupfuls of flour, mix with a teaspoonful of salt and two of baking powder. Add three tablespoonfuls of sugar and half a cupful of cleaned currants. Mix well, add two eggs, well beaten, and enough milk to make into a dough. Roll out, cut into rounds with a biscuit cutter, and bake in a slow oven. The buns should be an inch thick when put into the oven.

SOUTHERN CORN PONE

Two cupfuls of yellow corn-meal, one cupful of flour, two cupfuls of milk, two teaspoonfuls of baking powder, one tablespoonful each of lard and butter, melted, and two well-beaten eggs. Mix thoroughly, spread thinly on a buttered baking-pan, and bake in a moderate oven.

SOUTHERN CORN PONE—II

Four cupfuls of corn-meal, one teaspoonful of salt, one tablespoonful of melted lard, and enough cold water to make a soft dough. Mould into thin oblong cakes and bake quickly in a well-buttered pan.

SOUTHERN CORN PONE—III

One and three quarter cupfuls of white corn-meal, half a teaspoonful each of salt and soda, two tablespoonfuls of melted butter, one egg, well beaten, and one cupful of buttermilk. Bake in a buttered pan for half an hour.

CORN MUFFINS

Sift together three quarters of a cupful of corn-meal and the same of flour, half a teaspoonful each of salt and soda, and a tablespoonful of sugar. Mix with one egg, well beaten, and one cupful of thick sour milk. Bake from twenty to thirty minutes in well-buttered muffin-tins.

CORN MUFFINS

Make as Oatmeal Gems and bake in muffin-tins.

CORN MUFFINS—II

Mix one cupful of corn-meal with one cupful of boiling water, spread with butter, and let stand over night. In the morning, mix with one tablespoonful of sugar, two eggs, well beaten, three quarters of a cupful of sour milk, and one cupful of flour, sifted in with half a teaspoonful each of salt and soda. Bake half an hour in buttered muffin-rings.

CORN BREAD

Two heaping cupfuls of corn-meal, one cupful of flour, three eggs beaten separately, one tablespoonful of melted lard, two of sugar, two and a half cupfuls of milk, one teaspoonful of salt, and two of baking powder. Sift the dry materials into the milk, eggs, and shortening. Beat thoroughly, and bake half an hour in a buttered tin.

JOHNNY CAKE

One cupful of sweet milk, one cupful of buttermilk, one teaspoonful of salt, one of soda, and one tablespoonful of melted butter. Add enough corn-meal to roll into a sheet half an inch thick. Lay on a buttered baking-pan and bake till brown and crisp, basting occasionally with melted butter meanwhile. Break instead of cutting, and serve hot.

CORN DODGERS

Pour two cupfuls of boiling water over two cupfuls of corn-meal. Add a pinch of salt and drop by spoonfuls in a well-buttered shallow pan. Dot with butter and bake till crisp and brown, or bake on a griddle.

NEW ENGLAND CORN DODGERS

Two cupfuls of white corn-meal, two pinches of salt, and a teaspoonful of sugar sifted together. Dampen with boiling water and thin with cold milk to a batter which will keep its shape on a griddle. Butter the griddle and drop the batter on by spoonfuls. Put dots of butter on each dodger, and when crisp and brown on one side turn and brown on the other. Keep hot in the oven a few minutes before serving.

CORN DODGERS—III

Mix a teaspoonful of salt with two cupfuls of corn-meal. Pour over it enough boiling water to moisten and let stand ten minutes. Add three eggs, beaten separately, one cupful of milk, and a teaspoonful of baking powder. Thin with more milk if necessary and bake on a buttered griddle. Ham or bacon fat may be used in place of butter.

SOUTHERN HOECAKES

Add a teaspoonful of salt and a heaping teaspoonful of baking powder to one cupful and a third of corn-meal. Beat the yolks of two eggs until light, add a cupful of milk and beat hard for a few moments, then add the whites of the eggs beaten to a stiff froth. Put a tablespoonful of lard into a spider and drop in the batter by spoonfuls, turning when done on one side. Serve very hot.

CORN BREAD—II

One cupful of corn-meal, a teaspoonful each of salt and baking powder, a tablespoonful of butter or lard, melted, three eggs and a cupful and a half of milk. Mix the salt with the meal, beat the eggs, mix with the milk and pour over the meal, then sift in the baking powder, beat hard, and add the melted butter last. Pour into a baking-pan and bake in a hot oven.

CORN MUFFINS—III

One cupful of corn-meal, two cupfuls of buttermilk, a pinch of salt, one teaspoonful of soda, one egg, and a tablespoonful of melted lard. Beat the eggs, add the soda to the milk and lard, then mix with the meal. Bake in hot buttered muffin-rings filled half full.

CORN AND RICE MUFFINS

Two cupfuls of buttermilk, one cupful of white corn-meal, one teaspoonful of soda, a pinch of salt, one egg, half a cupful of cream, and half a cupful of boiled rice. Mash the rice, add the salt, egg, and cream, then the buttermilk mixed with the soda, then the meal. Bake in buttered muffin-pans in a quick oven.

BREAKFAST CORN BREAD

Two cupfuls of corn-meal, two cupfuls of sifted flour, one tablespoonful of sugar, one tablespoonful of lard or butter, one teaspoonful of salt, three teaspoonfuls of baking powder, two cupfuls of milk, and three eggs well beaten. Sift the dry ingredients and rub in the cold butter. Beat the eggs separately, the yolks with the milk, then the dry ingredients, and add the whites of the eggs last. Bake about half an hour in buttered shallow pans.

APPLE JOHNNY CAKE

Mix two cupfuls of corn-meal with half a cupful of sugar, a pinch of salt, and a teaspoonful of cream of tartar. Dissolve half a teaspoonful of soda in a cupful and a half of milk, stir in, and add three peeled and cored apples sliced very thin. Bake in a buttered shallow tin thirty-five minutes in a moderate oven.

CORN MUFFINS—IV

Beat two eggs very light, add one tablespoonful of melted butter, three tablespoonfuls of corn-meal, one teaspoonful of brown sugar, one heaping tablespoonful of flour, half a teaspoonful of baking powder and one cupful of milk. Mix thoroughly, pour into buttered muffin-tins, and bake in a quick oven.

CORN DODGERS—IV

Two cupfuls of corn-meal, one cupful of sour milk or buttermilk, one pinch of salt, one teaspoonful of soda, one egg well beaten. Bake on a hot griddle.

CORN MUFFINS—V

One cupful of yellow corn-meal, one cupful of flour, one heaping tablespoonful of sugar, one heaping teaspoonful of baking powder, one egg, well beaten, one cupful and a half of sweet milk, and a pinch of salt. Beat hard and bake in well buttered muffin-pans.

CORN PUFFS

Sift together one and two thirds cupfuls of flour, one cupful of meal, and two level teaspoonfuls of baking powder. Rub two tablespoonfuls of butter to a cream with three tablespoonfuls of sugar, add three well-beaten eggs and two cupfuls of milk. Combine mixtures, beat thoroughly, pour into well-buttered muffin-tins and bake.

FRUIT CORN MUFFINS

Two cupfuls of yellow corn-meal, one cupful of flour, two tablespoonfuls of sugar, a pinch of salt, two teaspoonfuls of baking powder, one tablespoonful of melted butter, two eggs, well beaten, one and one half cupfuls of milk, and one cupful of fruit. Dates, figs, prunes, or other fruits may be used. Stones should be removed and the fruit cut fine. Bake in well-buttered muffin-pans for about twenty minutes.

CORN AND HOMINY MUFFINS

Mash one cupful of cold boiled hominy with one cupful of corn-meal. Add a pinch of salt, a tablespoonful of sugar, a teaspoonful of baking powder, a tablespoonful of melted butter, one egg, well beaten, and one cupful of milk. Beat hard for five minutes, pour into buttered gem-pans, and bake fifteen or twenty minutes in a hot oven.

SOFT CORN BREAD

One cupful of corn-meal, one cupful of sour milk, a pinch of soda, one cupful of sweet milk, a tablespoonful of melted butter, a pinch of salt, and two well-beaten eggs. Mix thoroughly and bake in a deep baking-dish, well buttered.

FLORIDA CORN BREAD

One cupful of buttermilk, one cupful of sweet milk, one half teaspoonful of soda, two eggs, one cupful of corn-meal, and one teaspoonful of salt. Mix the buttermilk, sweet milk, and soda together, and when the soda is thoroughly dissolved, pour the milk over the beaten eggs. Add the corn-meal and beat thoroughly. Spread lard over the bottom and sides of the baking-tin, place in the oven until very hot, then pour in the batter and bake in a quick oven until a delicate brown.

CHARLESTON BREAKFAST CAKE

Beat together one cupful of sugar and one tablespoonful of melted butter. Add two eggs, beaten very light, a pinch of salt, a grating of nutmeg, and one cupful of milk. Sift in two cupfuls of flour and three level teaspoonfuls of baking powder. Bake in hot buttered muffin-tins or in a shallow baking-pan.

DATE GEMS

One cupful of dates, seeded and chopped fine, two cupfuls of milk, two tablespoonfuls of melted butter, one heaping teaspoonful of baking powder, three cupfuls of flour, and one egg well beaten. Mix the egg and milk, sift the dry ingredients together, add the chopped dates, and combine mixtures. Beat hard and bake in well-buttered gem-irons for about twenty minutes. Figs or prunes may be used instead of dates.

GRAHAM BISCUIT

Three cupfuls of Graham flour, one cupful of white flour, three cupfuls of milk, two tablespoonfuls of lard, one heaping tablespoonful of sugar, a pinch of salt and two heaping teaspoonfuls of baking powder. Mix and bake like Baking Powder Biscuits.

GRAHAM PUFFS

Two cupfuls of Graham flour, four cupfuls of boiling milk, and a teaspoonful of salt. The dough should be as soft as it can be handled. Roll an inch thick, cut into circles, arrange on a buttered pan and bake in the hottest kind of an oven. If the oven is right, they will be very light.

GRAHAM MUFFINS

Prepare like Rye Muffins, using Graham flour or meal instead of rye meal. A teaspoonful of caraway seed is sometimes added to Rye Muffins.

GRAHAM DROP CAKES

Sift together a cupful and a half of Graham meal, half a teaspoonful each of salt and soda, and a quarter of a cupful of brown sugar. Add enough sour milk to make a stiff batter. Drop by spoonfuls on a buttered baking-tin and bake a quarter of an hour in a quick oven.

GRAHAM MUFFINS—II

Four cupfuls of Graham flour, one tablespoonful of brown sugar, one teaspoonful of salt, two heaping teaspoonfuls of baking powder, one egg, well beaten, and two cupfuls of milk. Sift the dry ingredients together, add the beaten egg and milk, mix thoroughly, fill well-buttered muffin-tins two thirds full and bake in a hot oven about twenty minutes.

HOMINY MUFFINS

Two cupfuls of cold fine hominy, three eggs, three cupfuls of sour milk, half a cupful of melted butter, two tablespoonfuls of sugar, one teaspoonful of baking soda dissolved in hot water, and flour to make a good batter—probably about a cupful and a half. Add the milk to the hominy, then the salt, sugar, butter, and eggs, then the soda, and the flour last. Bake in a quick oven.

HOMINY DROP CAKES

Two cupfuls of cold boiled hominy, one tablespoonful of cold water, two eggs, well beaten, a pinch of salt, and a teaspoonful of baking powder sifted into enough flour to make a good batter. Drop by spoonfuls on a buttered baking-sheet and bake brown in a quick oven.

MUFFINS—I

Sift together four cupfuls of flour, a teaspoonful of salt, and two heaping teaspoonfuls of baking powder. Add a tablespoonful of sugar. Stir in two cupfuls of milk, four eggs well beaten, and three tablespoonfuls of melted butter. Bake twenty-five or thirty minutes in muffin-tins. Half of this recipe is sufficient for a small family.

MUFFINS—II

Two cupfuls of flour, two eggs, one cupful of milk, one teaspoonful of sugar, one heaping teaspoonful of baking powder, a pinch of salt, and two tablespoonfuls of melted butter. Sift the dry ingredients together, beat the eggs till very light, mix with the milk and melted butter. Sift the dry mixture gradually into the milk and eggs, stirring constantly. Bake twenty-five minutes in muffin-tins.

CREAM MUFFINS

Four cupfuls of flour, four cupfuls of rich milk, six eggs, beaten separately, two tablespoonfuls of shortening, melted—equal parts of butter and lard. Bake in buttered muffin-rings half full of the batter and serve immediately.

BUTTERMILK MUFFINS

Four cupfuls of buttermilk, or of curdled milk, two eggs, a teaspoonful of soda dissolved in a little hot water, a teaspoonful of salt, and enough sifted flour to make a good batter. Mix thoroughly, adding the soda last. Bake in a quick oven.

MUFFINS—III

Sift together two cupfuls of flour, two tablespoonfuls of baking powder, a pinch of salt, and a tablespoonful of sugar. Add one tablespoonful of melted butter or lard, one cupful of milk, and one egg well beaten. Mix thoroughly and bake quickly in muffin-rings.

MUFFINS—IV

Make like Muffins V, using a quarter cupful each of sugar and melted butter, and two or three eggs, well beaten.

BLUEBERRY MUFFINS

Use any muffin mixture, lessening slightly the quantity of milk. Add a cupful of blueberries and bake quickly.

MUFFINS—V

Four cupfuls of flour, three eggs, beaten separately, the whites very stiff, three cupfuls of milk, and a pinch of salt. Beat hard until thoroughly mixed and bake in a quick oven.

MUFFINS—VI

Six cupfuls of flour, two eggs well beaten separately, two rounded teaspoonfuls of baking powder, four cupfuls of milk, one teaspoonful of salt. Sift the dry materials, mix with the eggs and milk, beat hard, and bake in muffin-tins in a quick oven.

CEREALINE MUFFINS

Three fourths of a cupful of flour, a pinch of salt, one egg, well beaten, one cupful of cerealine, and one cupful of milk. Bake in buttered muffin-pans.

BATTER MUFFINS

Three cupfuls of sour milk and one teaspoonful of soda beaten together. Beat the yolks of three eggs and add to the milk, then stir in a pinch of salt and flour enough to make a moderately stiff batter. Beat the whites of the eggs to a stiff froth and fold in the last thing. Bake in buttered muffin-tins.

SOUTHERN MUFFINS

Two eggs, two cupfuls of milk, two cupfuls of flour, a pinch of salt, and a teaspoonful of melted butter. Beat the eggs separately, then add the milk and butter to the yolks, then the flour, then the stiffly beaten whites. Bake in hot buttered muffin-tins.

MUFFINS—VII

Two cupfuls of flour, two teaspoonfuls of baking powder, one teaspoonful of salt, two tablespoonfuls of melted butter, two tablespoonfuls of sugar, one cupful of milk and one egg, well beaten. Bake in buttered muffin-tins.

MUFFINS—VIII

Four cupfuls of flour, two and one half cupfuls of milk, three eggs, beaten separately, two tablespoonfuls of butter, one teaspoonful of salt, one tablespoonful of sugar, and three teaspoonfuls of baking powder. Sift the dry ingredients together, add the melted butter and the beaten yolks to the milk, combine the two mixtures, and add the well-beaten whites of the eggs last. Fill buttered muffin-rings two thirds full and bake in a hot oven about twenty minutes. Serve immediately.

SOUR MILK MUFFINS

Three cupfuls of sour milk, three cupfuls of flour, two eggs, well beaten, one teaspoonful each of soda, cream tartar, and salt. Sift the dry ingredients together, add the milk, then the eggs, and bake in buttered muffin-tins in a hot oven.

WHITE MUFFINS

One tablespoonful of soft butter, two tablespoonfuls of sugar, rubbed to a cream. Add two eggs, well beaten, a pinch of salt, a cupful of milk, and two cupfuls of flour sifted with two rounded teaspoonfuls of baking powder. Beat thoroughly and bake in buttered muffin-tins in a moderate oven.

ENTIRE WHEAT MUFFINS

Sift thoroughly, with three cupfuls of entire wheat flour, two tablespoonfuls of baking powder, a pinch of salt, and a tablespoonful of sugar. Add one and one half cupfuls of sweet milk in which the well-beaten yolk of an egg has been stirred, and two tablespoonfuls of melted butter. Add the white of the egg, beaten to a stiff froth, mix thoroughly, and bake about twenty minutes in hot buttered muffin-pans in a moderate oven.

HONEY MUFFINS

Sift together three cupfuls of flour, three heaping teaspoonfuls of baking powder, and a pinch of salt. Add two tablespoonfuls of melted butter, three eggs well beaten, one cupful of strained honey, and one cupful of milk. Bake in well-buttered muffin-tins.

GEORGIA MUFFINS

One cupful of milk, one egg, well beaten, two cupfuls of flour, a pinch of salt, and a teaspoonful of baking powder. Mix thoroughly, and bake in buttered gem-irons made piping hot before the batter is put in.

BLUEBERRY MUFFINS—II

One cupful of sugar, two eggs, one cupful of milk, two teaspoonfuls of baking powder, butter the size of an egg, melted, and two cupfuls of flour sifted with the baking powder. Add two cupfuls of blueberries, stir thoroughly, and bake in buttered muffin-tins in a quick oven.

SWEET MUFFINS

One half cupful of butter and one half cupful of sugar rubbed to a cream. Add two eggs, well beaten, and mix thoroughly. Add one cupful of sweet milk and stir and mix thoroughly. Sift three and three fourths cupfuls of flour and three rounded teaspoonfuls of baking powder into the muffin mixture, beat again, pour into hot buttered gem-pans, and bake about half an hour.

PERFECTION MUFFINS

Mix together three cupfuls of flour, one cupful of corn-meal, two teaspoonfuls of baking powder, one tablespoonful of sugar, and one teaspoonful of salt. Work in one heaping tablespoonful of butter or lard, add three well-beaten eggs and two cupfuls of milk. Beat quickly into a firm batter. Bake in well-buttered muffin-tins.

NEW HAMPSHIRE MUFFINS

Beat together three eggs and one cupful of milk. Add a pinch of salt and one teaspoonful of powdered sugar. Sift together two cupfuls of flour and one heaping teaspoonful of baking powder. Combine mixtures, beat well, and bake in hot buttered gem-irons. The cups should be about half full of the batter and the oven only moderately hot.

OATMEAL GEMS

Pour one cupful of boiling water over one cupful of steam-cooked oatmeal and let it stand over night. Mix one cupful of flour, two teaspoonfuls of baking powder, and a half a teaspoonful of salt. Sift, mix with the soaked oatmeal, and add enough flour to make a batter that will drop easily from the spoon. Bake in buttered muffin-pans.

POPOVERS

One cupful of flour, measured after sifting, one egg, unbeaten, one cupful of milk, and a pinch of salt. Butter a gem-pan and put it into a hot oven. Mix all the ingredients together, stirring hard with a wooden spoon. When the pan is hissing hot, pour in the batter, filling each compartment half or two thirds full. Bake in a very hot oven till well puffed and golden brown, cover with a paper and finish baking. This quantity makes a dozen popovers.

POPOVERS—II

Two eggs, well beaten, one cup of flour, one cupful of milk, one teaspoonful of salt. Prepare as above and bake in buttered custard cups.

FRUIT POPOVERS

Make the batter for Popovers I. Drop a piece of banana, a few blueberries, or a bit of preserved fruit or jam, or a steamed fig into each small cup of batter, which will rise in the cup and almost cover the fruit. These may be served with a simple syrup in place of pancakes or waffles.

PUFFS

Boil two cupfuls of milk with half a cupful of butter. Stir in one cupful and a half of sifted flour and let cool. Beat five eggs separately and add. Fill buttered custard cups half full of the batter and bake in a quick oven. Serve on a hot plate and sprinkle with sugar if desired.

RICE MUFFINS

One cupful of cold boiled rice, two cupfuls of flour, two eggs, beaten separately, two tablespoonfuls of lard or butter, a teaspoonful of salt, and milk enough to make a thin batter. Beat hard and bake in a quick oven.

RICE MUFFINS—II

One cupful of milk, one and one half cupfuls of flour, half a cupful of cold boiled rice, two level teaspoonfuls of baking powder, a pinch of salt, a teaspoonful of sugar, a heaping teaspoonful of butter, and one egg well beaten. Mix the dry ingredients, then melt the butter and rub it into the rice, add the egg, then the milk. Combine the two mixtures, beat well, and bake twenty-five minutes in buttered muffin-tins in a moderate oven.

RYE MUFFINS

Sift together one cupful each of rye meal and white flour, add two teaspoonfuls of baking powder, a pinch of salt, and a tablespoonful of sugar. Mix with one egg, well beaten, and one cupful of milk. Bake in buttered muffin-rings.

RYE CRISPS

One cupful of rye meal and one half cupful of white flour. Sift into a bowl with one teaspoonful of baking powder and mix thoroughly with one third of a cupful of finely minced beef suet. Add half a teaspoonful of salt, and enough milk to make a soft dough that may be easily handled with a spoon. Have well-buttered muffin-tins piping hot. Fill them two-thirds full and bake quickly in a very hot oven. They should be done in from twelve to fifteen minutes.

SALLY LUNN

Four cupfuls of sifted flour, four eggs, beaten separately, one cupful of milk, one cupful of melted butter and lard, equal parts, one teaspoonful of salt, two heaping teaspoonfuls of baking powder. Mix, adding the whites the last thing. Bake in muffin-rings.

SCONES

Spread a rich biscuit or muffin dough in a well-buttered pan, mark deeply into squares, brush with the yolk of an egg, and sprinkle with sugar.

SNOW BALLS

Make a batter of one cupful of cream—the top of milk will do nicely—two tablespoonfuls of sugar, the yolks of four eggs, a heaping teaspoonful of baking powder, and flour enough to mix. Add the whites of the eggs last, beaten to a stiff froth. Fill buttered cups two thirds full, and bake in a hot oven.

SCOTCH SCONES

Four cupfuls of sifted flour, one cupful of buttermilk, one tablespoonful of butter, one tablespoonful of sugar, one half teaspoonful of baking soda, and one half teaspoonful of salt. Rub the butter into the flour, add the sugar and salt, stir the soda into the buttermilk, and mix with the flour. Roll into a thin sheet, cut into triangles, and bake about thirty-five minutes on a floured tin. Just before they are done, rub a cloth dipped in milk over the tops and put back into the oven to glaze.

Note.—Sour milk may be made from fresh by keeping the milk some hours in a warm place, or, more quickly, by adding a little lemon-juice or vinegar to the amount of milk required.

RAISED BREAKFAST BREADS

Although many recipes included in this section may seem, at first glance, to be unsuitable for breakfast on account of the length of time taken for rising, there are ways in which the time can be considerably shortened.

A competent authority says that any mixture for rolls or muffins can be made ready for its second rising at night, and kept over night in any place where the dough will not freeze, or where the temperature is not so high as to cause too rapid rising and consequent souring of the dough.

Moreover, rolls or muffins may be baked in the afternoon until done thoroughly, but not brown, wrapped in a cloth, and put away in a cool place. In the morning, they need only to be rubbed with melted butter and set into a hot oven for a very few moments. They will come out crisp and flaky, and free from all objections on the score of indigestibility. Bread twice baked is always much more digestible than fresh bread.

Brioche, the most delicious of all hot breads, needs to stand in the refrigerator over night, and the second process is a quick one when the paste is once made. The paste will keep a week or more in a very cold place, and be the better for it. It is a French dough, for which many complicated recipes are given, but the following will be found satisfactory, and not difficult after one or two trials.

BRIOCHE PASTE

One cake of compressed yeast, a pinch of salt, one and one fourth cupfuls of butter, four cupfuls of flour, one tablespoonful of sugar, two tablespoonfuls of warm water, and seven eggs. Dissolve the yeast in the water, adding a little more water if necessary, and rubbing the yeast cake with a spoon until thoroughly dissolved. Stir in enough sifted flour to make a stiff dough, rolling and patting with the hands until thoroughly mixed. Drop this ball of paste into a kettle of warm water and let stand in a moderate temperature until it has a little more than doubled in bulk. (Some recipes for Brioche say that the ball of paste should be light enough to float.) Put the remainder of the four cupfuls of flour into a mixing bowl, add the sugar, salt, and butter, softened but not melted, and four of the eggs, unbeaten. With the hand mix carefully to a paste, beat smooth, and add the rest of the eggs, unbeaten, one at a time. Take the ball of paste, when light, out of the warm water with a skimmer, and, still using the hand, incorporate it carefully with the egg mixture, folding the two together as lightly as possible. Let rise, in a moderate temperature, until double in bulk. Then turn the paste on a floured board and pat and fold with the hands until smooth in texture and inclined to stay in shape. Let rise once more until very light, then put into the refrigerator and let stand over night.

BRIOCHE ROLLS

Roll a large lump of Brioche dough into a thin sheet on a floured board or pastry slab, working lightly and quickly, spread with softened butter, and fold so that the paste will be in three layers. Cut in strips an inch wide and twist, working from the ends, and arrange in circles on a baking-sheet, the ends of the strips pointing inward. The rolls should be very close together in the pan. Beat the yolk of an egg, dilute it with as much milk, and brush the rolls with the mixture. Let them rise a few minutes, then bake about half an hour in a moderate oven. A little sugar and water may be spread over the tops if desired.

BRIOCHE BUNS

Shape the chilled paste into small balls, and put a bit of citron or a few raisins on the top of each one. Let rise a few moments and bake half an hour in a moderate oven.

BRIOCHE BREAKFAST CAKE

Butter a round cake-tin which has a tube in the centre, fill it half full of chilled Brioche paste, and let rise till the pan is two thirds full. Bake in a moderate oven and turn out. It should be torn apart with the fingers—not cut.

BATH BUNS

Dissolve a cake of yeast in two cupfuls of warm water. Add enough flour to make a moderately stiff sponge, let rise about two hours. Cream together one half cupful each of butter and sugar, add one cupful of lukewarm milk, a pinch of salt, and two eggs, well beaten. Mix with the sponge, let rise an hour longer, then knead, shape into buns, arrange close together in a baking-pan, and let rise till very light. Bake in a moderate oven.

*"Bath Bunny, Currant Bunny, sang a comic song,Bath Bunny, Currant Bunny, sang it loud and long;When his friends had told him that he gave them all a pain,Bath Bunny, Currant Bunny, sang it twice again."*Louis Wain.

ENGLISH BATH BUNS

Dissolve half a cake of compressed yeast in one cupful of milk, and add two cupfuls of flour, or enough to make a sponge. Let rise until light, then add two thirds of a cupful of melted butter and four eggs, well beaten. Knead and let rise again for about an hour. Make into balls the size of a small apple and press into each one some currants and bits of candied peel. Let rise ten or fifteen minutes in a warm place, sprinkle with sugar, and bake.

HOT CROSS BUNS

Rub one half cupful of butter into eight cupfuls of sifted flour, then add half a cake of compressed yeast dissolved in three cupfuls of scalded milk. Let rise two hours. Work into the sponge one cupful of sugar, one cupful of cleaned currants, and half a nutmeg grated. Knead, shape into buns, arrange in pans, score deeply with a cross, brush with butter, and let rise fifteen minutes. Bake forty-five minutes in a brisk oven. This is the genuine English recipe, and the buns are good at any time, but the cross is made only on Good Friday, or for Easter.

RISEN MUSH MUFFINS

One cupful of hominy, cerealine, corn-meal mush, oatmeal, rice, or other left-over cooked cereal, one teaspoonful of butter, one tablespoonful of sugar, one pinch of salt, one fourth of a cake of yeast (compressed) dissolved in one cupful of scalded milk, and two cupfuls of sifted flour. Mix thoroughly and let rise over night. In the morning, beat well and fill well-buttered muffin-pans half full. Let rise until double in bulk, then bake half an hour.

FINGER ROLLS

Mix one cupful of scalded milk with one tablespoonful of butter. When cool, add a teaspoonful of sugar, a pinch of salt, and one half cake of yeast dissolved in half a cupful of warm water. Add enough flour to make a soft dough—about three cupfuls. Mix thoroughly, knead for fifteen minutes, and set to rise in a warm place for three or four hours. When light, knead again, shape into balls, and roll into cylinders on a floured board, pointing the ends. Arrange in a shallow pan, and let rise until double in size—about an hour—glaze with beaten egg, and bake fifteen minutes in a hot oven.

SOUTHERN ROLLS

Six cupfuls of flour, two eggs, one cake of compressed yeast, one cupful of milk, two tablespoonfuls of lard, melted, and a teaspoonful of salt. Mix as other sponges, let rise five hours, knead, shape into rolls, let rise two hours longer, and bake about twenty minutes.

FRENCH ROLLS

Eight cupfuls of flour, four eggs, four teaspoonfuls of sugar, one tablespoonful of butter, one cake of compressed yeast dissolved in two cupfuls of milk. Mix like other sponges, let rise until light, knead, shape, let rise the second time, and bake in a moderate oven.

KENTUCKY ROLLS

Four cupfuls of flour, one tablespoonful of sugar, one teaspoonful of salt, two eggs, half a cupful of lard, and half a cake of compressed yeast. Mix the lard, sugar, and flour, then stir in the other ingredients, the yeast being dissolved in a little water, and add enough milk or warm water to make a thin batter. Let rise in a warm place, then add enough flour to make a stiff dough, and let rise again. When light, knead, shape, and put to rise for a third time. Bake in a quick oven.

ALABAMA ROLLS

Rub two hot baked potatoes through a colander. Stir in one cupful of melted butter, two eggs well beaten, half a cake of compressed yeast, dissolved, and mixed with one cupful of sifted flour. Work with the hand into a smooth sponge, and let rise three hours. Then work into the sponge two cupfuls of sifted flour and let rise five hours longer. Knead, make into roll shape, set to rise two hours more, and bake.

CORN ROLLS

To four cupfuls of well-salted hot corn-meal mush add one cupful of mixed butter and lard and half a cupful of sugar. When cool, add one cake of compressed yeast dissolved in a little warm water, and set to rise in a warm place. When light, work in enough sifted flour to make a stiff dough, knead thoroughly, and let rise again. Late at night, knead again and set in a cool place over night. In the morning, roll and cut out like biscuit. Spread half of each circle with softened butter and roll the other half over it. Let rise a few moments and bake. If the weather is very warm, add a teaspoonful of soda, dissolved in a little warm water, to the sponge.

PARKER HOUSE ROLLS

Dissolve one cake of compressed yeast in one cupful of lukewarm water, and add enough flour to make a thin batter. Put this sponge in a warm place to rise. Add one tablespoonful of lard, one tablespoonful of butter, two tablespoonfuls of sugar, and one teaspoonful of salt to two cupfuls of milk, and bring to the boil. Take from the fire and let cool. When the sponge is light stir in the milk, and add enough sifted flour to make a dough, usually about eight cupfuls, though the thickening qualities of various brands of flour vary greatly. Knead for fifteen or twenty minutes, then set to rise until very light. Shape, place in a baking-pan, let rise once more, and when light bake in a quick oven.

WHOLE WHEAT ROLLS

One teaspoonful of salt, one teaspoonful of sugar, one tablespoonful of butter, one cake of compressed yeast, one cupful of scalded milk, and three cupfuls of whole wheat flour. Add the salt, sugar, and butter to the scalded milk. Dissolve the yeast in two tablespoonfuls of warm water and add to the milk when it has cooled. Add half of the flour and beat hard for ten minutes, then work in the rest of the flour. Set it to rise for two hours. Roll out into a sheet an inch thick and cut into small rolls. Place close together in a well-buttered baking-pan, and let rise from fifteen to thirty minutes. Bake fifteen or twenty minutes in a quick oven. Brush with an egg-white beaten with a little milk if a glossy surface is desired. This should be done about ten minutes before taking out of the oven.

SWEDISH ROLLS

Use any plain roll mixture. When shaping for the last rising, roll the dough very thin, spread with softened butter, sprinkle with sugar and cinnamon, and add a few cleaned currants, bits of citron, and stoned raisins. Roll the dough like jelly cake, cut in half-inch slices from the ends, arrange flat in a well-buttered pan, let rise until double in bulk, and bake as usual.

PARIS ROLLS

Four cupfuls of milk, one half cake of compressed yeast, six cupfuls of flour, and the yolks of two eggs, well beaten. Mix thoroughly and set the sponge to rise. When it is very light, work into it two tablespoonfuls of melted butter, one whole egg, well beaten, one teaspoonful of salt, and half a teaspoonful of baking soda dissolved in hot water, one tablespoonful of white sugar, and enough sifted flour to make a soft dough. Let rise five hours. Roll out, shape into balls, score each one deeply crosswise with a sharp knife, and arrange close together in a well-buttered baking-pan. Let rise for an hour or more and bake about half an hour. This recipe makes a large number of rolls. They may be taken from the oven when beginning to turn brown and wrapped in a cloth. Five minutes in a hot oven, if brushed first with melted butter, will render them crisp, flaky, and very digestible.

RUSK

Two cupfuls of flour, two cupfuls of sugar, one cupful of melted lard, half a cake of compressed yeast, dissolved in a little warm water, and three cupfuls of lukewarm water. Make into a batter, let rise all day in a warm place. At night work into the sponge six cupfuls of sifted flour and two eggs, well beaten. Let rise over night in a moderately cool place. In the morning, shape the dough into rolls, let rise a few minutes in a warm place, and bake. The dough should be soft. These rolls may be sprinkled with sugar and spice.

GEORGIA RUSK

One cupful of milk, scalded and cooled, one tablespoonful of sugar, one teaspoonful of salt, one quarter of a cake of compressed yeast, dissolved in the milk, and two cupfuls of sifted flour. Set the sponge, and, when light, work into it half a cupful of melted butter, half a cupful of sugar, and one well-beaten egg. When very light, shape into small pointed rolls and let rise again. Brush with milk and egg and sprinkle with sugar just before baking.

SOUTHERN SALLY LUNN

Four cupfuls of flour, three eggs, one teaspoonful of butter, one cake of compressed yeast, and two cupfuls of milk. Beat the yolks of the eggs until very light. Stir in the butter, flour, and milk, the yeast being dissolved in the milk. Beat the whites to a stiff froth and add last. Set to rise, and when light bake in well-buttered muffin-tins.

SOUTHERN SALLY LUNN—II

Four cupfuls of flour, one teaspoonful of salt, two cupfuls of milk, one half cupful of sugar, and one cake of compressed yeast, dissolved in the milk. Make a batter and let rise in a warm place about three hours. Then work into it gradually five eggs, beaten separately, and one half cupful of melted butter. Add flour enough to make a stiff batter, fill buttered muffin-tins two thirds full, let rise, and bake.

SOUTHERN SALLY LUNN—III

Three cupfuls of flour, three eggs, one cake of compressed yeast dissolved in two cupfuls of milk, one half cupful of melted butter, and one tablespoonful of sugar. Beat well together into a stiff batter and let rise five or six hours. Then add a little warm water in which half a teaspoonful of baking soda has been dissolved, and pour the batter into a well-buttered cake-pan having a tube in the centre. Bake about three quarters of an hour and serve hot. It should be torn apart, not cut.

ZWIEBACK

One cake of compressed yeast dissolved in one cupful of scalded milk, a pinch of salt, and enough sifted flour to make a soft dough. Let rise until very light, then stir in one fourth of a cupful of melted butter, one fourth of a cupful of sugar, and one unbeaten egg. Mix thoroughly, and sift in enough more flour to make a smooth, elastic dough. Shape into a loaf and let rise until very light. A Russian-iron bread-pan holding one loaf is best for Zwieback. Let it rise once more until very light, then bake in a quick oven. Glaze with sugar dissolved in milk just before taking from the oven. When the loaf is cold, cut in half-inch slices and place in an open oven until golden-brown, dry, and crisp.

PANCAKES

The edible varieties of pancakes are readily distinguished from the poisonous growths. The harmless ones are healthful and nutritious and grow in private kitchens. The dark, soggy, leaden varieties are usually to be found in restaurants, but have been known to flourish in private kitchens also.

Batter for pancakes should be thoroughly beaten. A soapstone griddle is best, but an iron one will do, and many a savory pancake has come from a humble frying-pan. A pancake turner is essential, and no pancake should be turned more than once, as twice turning makes a soggy pancake from the most promising batter. In the following recipes, where exact proportions are given, they are not arbitrary as regards flour. The thickening properties of various brands of flour vary so much that no exact rule can be given. A perfect pancake batter will be smooth, light in texture, seem somewhat elastic to the touch of the mixing spoon, and will keep its shape on a griddle. Batter enough for one pancake should be dipped from the bowl with a cup or large spoon, as adding uncooked batter to that on the griddle even an instant after it has begun to cook will work disaster to the pancake—and the hapless mortal who eats it.

Maple syrup is the syrup *par excellence* for pancakes and waffles, but alas, it is difficult to procure. Much of it is made from corn cobs and molasses, sealed in tin cans bearing gaudy labels, and, sailing under false colors, is sold to the trusting consumer at a high price.

Even the bricks of maple sugar are not wholly trustworthy, though, as a rule, a better quality of syrup can be obtained by making it at home from the bricks. The ordinary adulterants cannot so readily be added to a crystallized as to a liquid product, though promising maple bricks are often made of brown sugar flavored with a little maple syrup.

Other syrups can be made easily and may possibly give welcome variety even to those fortunates who can secure the real maple syrup. Maraschino, noyeau, kirsch, and other cordials, orange-flower water, grated orange- and lemon-peel, and the fruit juices left from canned and preserved fruits, can all be used to advantage in flavoring a simple syrup made of sugar and water boiled till it hairs from the spoon. Always add flavoring to syrup just before taking it from the fire, and do not allow it to boil.

SOUTHERN BUCKWHEAT CAKES

Four cupfuls of buckwheat flour, sifted, one half cake of compressed yeast dissolved in a little lukewarm water, one teaspoonful of salt, and one tablespoonful of molasses. Mix with enough warm water to make a thin batter and set to rise over night. If the batter is sour in the morning add a bit of baking soda.

QUICK BUCKWHEAT CAKES

Three cupfuls of buckwheat flour and one cupful of white flour, one cupful each of milk and water, three heaping teaspoonfuls of baking powder, one teaspoonful of salt, and one tablespoonful of molasses. Sift the dry ingredients together, mix, and fry as usual.

KENTUCKY BUCKWHEAT CAKES

One cupful of flour, two cupfuls of buckwheat flour, one teaspoonful of salt, one cake of compressed yeast dissolved in lukewarm water, and one tablespoonful of molasses. Beat well together and let stand over night. Fry on a soapstone griddle greased with suet, salt pork, or bacon. A bit of suet or salt pork tied in a bit of cloth was the old-fashioned method of greasing a griddle for buckwheat cakes.

BUCKWHEAT CAKES WITH SOUR MILK

Take two cupfuls of thick sour milk, add a teaspoonful of salt, and enough buckwheat flour to make a thin batter. Let stand over night. In the morning add a teaspoonful of soda dissolved in two tablespoonfuls of lukewarm water and beat thoroughly. Fry at once.

CRUMB BUCKWHEAT CAKES

Two cupfuls of buckwheat flour, two and one half cupfuls of warm water, one cupful of dried bread crumbs, one cupful of milk, one tablespoonful of salt and half a cake of compressed yeast. Dissolve the yeast in the water and mix with the buckwheat flour. Add the salt, beat until well mixed, then cover and let stand over night in a warm place. Put the dried crumbs into the milk and let soak over night in a cool place. In the morning, mash the soaked crumbs and toss with a fork until light and dry, then mix with the risen buckwheat batter and fry as usual.

BLUEBERRY PANCAKES

Stir one cupful of blueberries into the batter for strawberry pancakes and fry as other pancakes.

CORN-MEAL PANCAKES

One cupful of corn-meal, one cupful of flour, four cupfuls of milk, one tablespoonful of melted butter, two tablespoonfuls of sugar, one teaspoonful of salt, and three eggs. Add the melted butter to the corn-meal, boil the milk and pour it, scalding hot, over the corn-meal. Sift the dry ingredients together, and after the meal and milk have cooled stir the dry mixture into it. Add the well-beaten eggs last, beat hard, and bake like other griddle cakes.

CORN-MEAL PANCAKES—II

Two cupfuls of corn-meal, one cupful of flour, one tablespoonful of sugar, one teaspoonful of salt, one teaspoonful of soda, one tablespoonful of melted butter, three eggs, and sour milk to thin the batter. Scald the meal with enough boiling water to mix it, then add the sugar and melted butter. Sift the flour and salt together and add to the meal. Add the eggs, beaten separately, the whites to a stiff froth, and the soda dissolved in a teaspoonful of warm water. Thin the batter with enough sour milk to make it of the right consistency and bake like other pancakes.

CORN-MEAL FLAPJACKS

Two cupfuls of corn-meal, one cupful of buttermilk, half a teaspoonful of salt, half a teaspoonful of soda, half a cupful of boiling water, and one egg, well beaten. Mix the salt with the meal, pour over the boiling water, mix thoroughly and let cool. Add the buttermilk, in which the soda is dissolved, and the eggs, well beaten. If too thin add a very little sifted flour. Fry in butter or in equal parts of butter and lard.

CRUMB PANCAKES

Two cupfuls of bread crumbs soaked in milk until very soft. Add a pinch of salt, one cupful each of sweet milk and buttermilk, one teaspoonful of soda and one egg beaten separately, the white to a stiff froth. Beat hard and add enough sifted flour to make a good batter—probably about a heaping tablespoonful. Fry in butter on a griddle.

GREEN CORN GRIDDLE CAKES

One cupful of milk, one cupful of grated green corn, a pinch of salt, half a teaspoonful of baking powder, one egg, beaten separately, and enough sifted flour to make a thin batter. Butter the cakes while hot and serve at once.

DANISH PANCAKES

One cupful of flour, three eggs beaten separately, one pinch each of salt and soda dissolved in a teaspoonful of vinegar, and enough milk to make a thin batter.

FLANNEL CAKES

Beat two eggs thoroughly. Add one teaspoonful of salt, one tablespoonful of sugar, three cupfuls of milk, and enough flour, sifted in with one teaspoonful of cream tartar and half a teaspoonful of soda, to make a thin batter. Bake on a greased griddle, butter, and serve very hot.

FRENCH PANCAKES

One and one half cupfuls of flour, one and one half cupfuls of milk, one teaspoonful each of salt and melted butter, two teaspoonfuls of brandy, and four eggs. Beat the yolks of the eggs till light-colored and creamy, add the other ingredients gradually and fold in the stiffly beaten whites last. Fry in a very hot frying-pan, using equal parts of lard and butter to fry in. Bake in small cakes, and after taking up spread very thinly with marmalade, honey, or jam, and roll up like a jelly roll. Sift powdered sugar over the rolls and serve at once, without butter or syrup.

FEATHER PANCAKES

Scald two cupfuls of milk, dissolve in it one half cake of compressed yeast, and add a teaspoonful of salt. Sift in enough flour to make a thin, smooth batter, and set to rise over night. In the morning add to it one cupful of thick sour milk, one tablespoonful of melted butter, two eggs, beaten separately, one teaspoonful of soda sifted in with enough flour to make a smooth, thin batter. Let stand twenty or thirty minutes, then bake as usual.

FRUIT PANCAKES

Add apple sauce, berries, chopped dates, figs or prunes, orange marmalade, chopped preserved quinces, or any desired fresh fruit or preserves to any good pancake batter, in the proportion of one heaping tablespoonful of fruit to each cupful of batter. The grated pineapple which comes in cans is particularly satisfactory and needs no further preparation. The fruit juice, sweetened, should be used instead of syrup wherever possible.

GRAHAM GRIDDLE CAKES

One cupful of wheat flour and one cupful of Graham flour, sifted with one teaspoonful of salt and one tablespoonful of sugar. Beat two eggs separately, the whites to a stiff froth. Add two cupfuls of thick sour milk in which a teaspoonful of soda has been dissolved, mix with the eggs, and stir the flour into the liquid. When the batter is well mixed, add a heaping tablespoonful of butter, melted, beat hard, and fry like other griddle cakes.

HOMINY GRIDDLE CAKES

Soak two cupfuls of fine hominy all night and cook it in a double boiler all day or until soft. When wanted for griddle cakes add two cupfuls of white corn-meal, sifted, three tablespoonfuls of butter, melted, a pinch of salt, three eggs, well beaten, and four cupfuls of milk, or less if necessary, to make a thin batter.

MARYLAND GRIDDLE CAKES

Three cupfuls of flour, three cupfuls of milk, one teaspoonful of salt, two teaspoonfuls of baking powder, and three eggs. Beat the eggs thoroughly, stir into the milk, sift the dry materials together, beat hard, and fry at once.

POTATO PANCAKES

Peel eight or ten good-sized potatoes and drop into cold water to prevent discoloration. Grate rapidly on a coarse grater. To the pulp add four eggs, well beaten, two teaspoonfuls of salt, and half a cupful of flour sifted with half a teaspoonful of baking powder. Mix lightly but thoroughly, and bake on a hot griddle. Serve with butter, but without syrup. Germans add a little grated onion to potato pancakes.

RAISED PANCAKES

Four cupfuls of milk, one half cake of compressed yeast, three tablespoonfuls of melted butter, one teaspoonful of sugar, one teaspoonful of salt, half a teaspoonful of soda, two eggs, and enough flour for a batter. Scald the milk and cool it, then dissolve the yeast in it and add the salt and sugar. Add enough sifted flour to make a smooth, thin batter, cover, and let stand over night in a warm place. In the morning add the melted butter, the soda dissolved in a little warm water, and the eggs, beaten separately. Cover and let stand half an hour in a warm place. Bake like other griddle cakes and serve immediately.

RAISED PANCAKES—II

Mix one cupful of scalded and cooled milk, in which one quarter of a yeast cake has been dissolved, with one heaping tablespoonful of butter, melted, one teaspoonful of sugar, one pinch of salt, and one cupful of sifted flour. Let rise over night. In the morning add one egg beaten separately, the white to a stiff froth. Beat to a smooth, thin batter and fry as usual.

SOUTHERN RICE PANCAKES

Boil one cupful of well-washed rice as directed in the chapter on Cereals. Add to it one half cupful of cream, two tablespoonfuls of flour sifted with one tablespoonful of baking powder, and two eggs, beaten separately, the whites to a stiff froth. Use only enough butter to keep the cakes from sticking to the griddle and serve as soon as done.

RICE PANCAKES—II

Mix two cupfuls of boiled rice with two cupfuls of milk and let stand over night in a cool place. In the morning, add three cupfuls of sifted flour, one teaspoonful of salt, one tablespoonful of melted butter and one tablespoonful of sugar. Beat until thoroughly mixed, with two cupfuls of milk and a tablespoonful of baking powder, then add three eggs, beaten separately, folding in the stiffly beaten whites last. A cupful of cream may be used instead of the butter.

RICE PANCAKES—III

Dissolve a teaspoonful of soda in a tablespoonful of cold water, and stir it into two cupfuls of thick sour milk. Add two cupfuls of sifted flour, a pinch of salt, two eggs, beaten separately, and one cupful of cold boiled rice. Fry brown on a well-greased griddle.

STRAWBERRY PANCAKES

Six eggs, beaten separately, two cupfuls of milk, two cupfuls of sifted flour, and one teaspoonful of salt. Mix the flour and salt, then add the milk and stir in the well-beaten yolks. Beat hard until the mixture is very light. Then fold in the whites, beaten to a stiff froth. Bake on a well-greased griddle and serve two to each person, with butter and crushed and sweetened strawberries between. Sprinkle with powdered sugar. Half this recipe is sufficient for a small family.

SOUR MILK PANCAKES

Two cupfuls of sour milk, two and one half cupfuls of sifted flour, one teaspoonful of soda, one tablespoonful of warm water, one teaspoonful of salt, one teaspoonful of sugar, two tablespoonfuls of melted butter, and two eggs. Beat the yolks of the eggs till light-colored and creamy, add the sour milk, salt, and sugar, and beat till thoroughly mixed. Add the flour gradually, beating constantly, then the soda dissolved in warm water, then the melted butter, then the stiffly beaten whites of the eggs. Fold together carefully and bake at once.

SOUR MILK PANCAKES—II

To four cupfuls of sour milk add enough flour to make a batter that will pour, sifted in gradually and thoroughly mixed. Add two eggs, well beaten, one tablespoonful of melted butter, one teaspoonful of salt, and a teaspoonful of soda dissolved in a little warm water. Bake on a very hot griddle, well greased.

WHEAT PANCAKES

Three cupfuls of flour, two cupfuls of milk, two teaspoonfuls of baking powder, one tablespoonful of melted butter, three eggs, and one teaspoonful of salt. Sift the dry ingredients together. Beat the yolks of the eggs till light-colored and creamy and stir into the milk. Mix with the flour, then add the melted butter and beat to a smooth batter. Add a little more milk if the batter seems too thick. Add the whites of the eggs, beaten to a stiff froth, fold in carefully, and bake as usual.

WHEAT PANCAKES—II

Three cupfuls of milk, two cupfuls of sifted flour, three eggs, one pinch of salt, and two heaping teaspoonfuls of baking powder. Beat the yolks of the eggs till light-colored and creamy, and mix thoroughly with the milk. Put the flour in a bowl and pour on a part of the milk, making a thick batter. Beat this thick batter hard until very smooth, dissolve the baking powder in the rest of the milk and add it, beating thoroughly, and add the stiffly beaten whites of the eggs last. This batter may be used for waffles. The thinner it is the more delicate the cakes will be.

COFFEE CAKES, DOUGHNUTS, AND WAFFLES

BABA À LA PARISIENNE

Prepare the yeast as for French Coffee Cake. Beat four tablespoonfuls of sugar to a cream with one cupful of butter and the grated yellow rind of a lemon. Add seven unbeaten eggs, one at a time, incorporating each egg thoroughly into the mixture before the next is added. Make a sponge of the yeast, one cupful of milk, scalded and cooled, and one cupful of sifted flour. Let it rise until very light—about half an hour—and mix with the hand into the egg mixture, adding two more cupfuls of sifted flour. Butter a tube-pan, put in the dough, sprinkle with chopped almonds, sugar, and spice, let it rise two hours, and bake very slowly.

GERMAN COFFEE BREAD

Scald and cool to lukewarm one cupful of milk. Add one heaping tablespoonful of butter and two heaping tablespoonfuls of sugar, one quarter of a yeast cake dissolved in one tablespoonful of warm water, a pinch of salt, and enough sifted flour to make a soft dough. Let it rise over night. In the morning, roll out and spread in a flat buttered tin. Rub with softened butter, sprinkle with sugar and cinnamon, and bake about half an hour in a moderate oven. Cut into squares and serve hot.

GERMAN COFFEE CAKE

One tablespoonful of butter, one cupful of sugar, one egg, one cupful of milk, one and one half cupfuls of flour, one heaping teaspoonful of baking powder, the juice and grated rind of half a lemon. Mix thoroughly, spread the dough in a shallow buttered baking-pan, sprinkle with chopped nuts, sugar, cinnamon, and dots of butter. Bake until brown and crisp, cut in squares, and serve piping hot.

AUSTRIAN COFFEE CAKE

Four cupfuls of flour, one teaspoonful of salt, two teaspoonfuls of baking powder, five eggs, well beaten, with two tablespoonfuls of sugar, two cupfuls of milk, and one tablespoonful of softened butter. Mix thoroughly, spread in a buttered baking-pan, dot with butter, sprinkle with sugar and cinnamon, and bake in a quick oven. Serve hot.

HUNGARIAN ROYAL COFFEE CAKE

Six cupfuls of flour, two cupfuls of butter, four cupfuls of milk, three eggs, three quarters of a pound of cleaned and seeded raisins, one half cupful of sugar, three cakes of compressed yeast, half a cupful of shredded citron, and eight pulverized cardamon seeds. Mix the sugar, butter, flour, and milk thoroughly, the yeast having been dissolved in the milk, previously scalded and cooled. Dredge the fruit with flour and add last. Let rise four hours, or more, if necessary. When ready for baking, rub with softened butter, sprinkle with cinnamon, granulated sugar, and chopped almonds. Bake in a tube-pan or in a ring on a large baking-sheet.

FRENCH COFFEE CAKE

Dissolve a cake of compressed yeast in two tablespoonfuls of tepid water. Add a pinch of salt and a tablespoonful of sugar. Cream a cupful of butter with three fourths of a cupful of powdered sugar, and add, gradually, the unbeaten yolks of six eggs, one at a time, and the grated yellow rind of a lemon. Sift two cupfuls of flour into a bowl and make into a thin batter with the dissolved yeast and one cupful of scalded and cooled milk. Add the egg mixture, and beat with the hand till the dough leaves the sides of the bowl. Add a handful of sultanas, half a cupful each of blanched and shredded almonds and shredded citron, and, lastly, the stiffly beaten whites of the eggs. Put into a tube-pan which has been well buttered, and set in a warm place to rise. Bake very slowly. When fully risen and beginning to brown, rub with softened butter, and sprinkle with sugar and spice.

VIENNA COFFEE CAKE

Dissolve a cake of compressed yeast in one cupful of scalded and cooled milk, add a pinch of salt and one tablespoonful of brown sugar. Sift one cupful of flour into a bowl, add the milk and yeast, beat to a smooth, light batter, free from lumps, and set away in a warm place till very light. Cream three quarters of a cupful each of butter and powdered sugar, add four whole eggs, unbeaten, three unbeaten yolks, and two cupfuls of sifted flour, working with the hand, and adding egg and flour alternately. Incorporate gradually into the risen batter, working thoroughly with the hand. Dredge half a cupful of blanched and shredded almonds, a tablespoonful of shredded citron, and half a cupful of cleaned and seeded raisins thoroughly with flour, and work into the dough with the hand. Put into a buttered tube-pan or mould and let rise in a warm place for three or four hours, then bake an hour in a moderate oven. When beginning to brown, rub with softened butter, sprinkle with granulated sugar and spice, and set back into the oven until done. All risen coffee cakes will keep well if wrapped closely in a cloth, and may be served cold, or reheated in a brisk oven for a few minutes just before serving.

BERLIN COFFEE CAKE

Make a sponge with two cupfuls of milk, scalded and cooled, a cake of compressed yeast dissolved in the milk, a pinch of salt, and one cupful of sifted flour. Let rise two hours in a warm place, then add one half cupful of melted butter, one cupful of cleaned and seeded raisins, one fourth cupful of finely shredded citron, one cupful of sugar, and three eggs, well beaten. Add enough sifted flour to make a stiff dough, knead thoroughly, roll into a long thin strip, cut in three strips, lengthwise, braid, and twist into a ring. Arrange in a circle on a well-buttered baking-sheet and let rise till very light, then bake half an hour. It will be more delicate if the strips are rubbed with softened butter before braiding and will come apart more easily. Before taking from the oven glaze with sugar and milk, or rub with butter and sprinkle with sugar and spice.

QUICK COFFEE CAKE

Cream one fourth of a cupful of butter with one cupful of sugar, add one egg, well beaten, one half cupful of milk, a pinch of salt, and one and one half cupfuls of flour sifted, with a heaping teaspoonful of baking powder. Spread in a pan, sprinkle with seeded and cleaned raisins or currants, a little shredded citron, dot with butter, and sift over sugar and spice, cinnamon preferred. Serve hot, cut in small squares.

CRULLERS

Three eggs, a pinch of salt, two cupfuls of flour, three tablespoonfuls of milk, six tablespoonfuls of melted butter, and six tablespoonfuls of sugar. Roll out half an inch thick, cut out with a small cake cutter which has a hole in the centre, and fry in very hot lard. Drain on brown paper and sprinkle with powdered sugar.

PLAIN DOUGHNUTS

Sift two teaspoonfuls of baking powder with four cupfuls of flour. Dissolve half a cupful of sugar in one cupful of milk. Add to the milk one teaspoonful of salt, half a nutmeg, grated, and two well-beaten eggs. Combine with the dry mixture, roll out, cut in rings, and fry in deep fat. Drain on brown paper.

DOUGHNUTS—II

Half a cupful of butter, one cupful of sugar, three cupfuls of flour, one egg, and one and one half cupfuls of milk, and a slight grating of nutmeg. Make into a soft dough, roll out, cut into shapes, and fry in hot fat. Sprinkle with powdered sugar.

RAISED DOUGHNUTS

One cupful of butter, one cupful of sugar, one teaspoonful of powdered cinnamon, and two eggs, well beaten. Work this mixture into two cupfuls of bread dough or roll mixture made ready for its second rising, and let rise an hour or more. When light, roll out, cut into circles or squares, let rise until very light, and fry in smoking-hot fat. Let drain on brown paper and sprinkle with granulated sugar.

LIGHT DOUGHNUTS

Three quarters of a cupful of granulated sugar, two eggs, beaten separately, one cupful of milk, three tablespoonfuls of melted butter, three cupfuls of flour, three heaping teaspoonfuls of baking powder, and half a teaspoonful of grated nutmeg. Fold in the stiffly beaten whites of the eggs last, then work in enough more sifted flour to make a soft dough, probably about two cupfuls. Roll very thin, cut out, fry in smoking-hot fat, and drain on brown paper. This recipe makes about five dozen doughnuts, and half of it will be sufficient for an ordinary family unless they are especially fond of doughnuts.

RAISED FRUIT DOUGHNUTS

Cream together one heaping tablespoonful of butter and one fourth cupful of sugar. Dissolve one half a cake of compressed yeast in one cupful of milk that has been scalded and cooled. Add half a teaspoonful of salt to the milk and yeast, combine mixtures, and work in two cupfuls of flour. Let rise until double in bulk. Mix together one half cupful of sugar, a pinch of cinnamon, a grating of nutmeg, and a pinch of allspice, one half cupful of cleaned currants, cleaned and seeded raisins, and shredded citron, mixed, and a scant two cupfuls of sifted flour. Lastly, add one egg, well beaten, knead thoroughly, and let rise until very light. Cut or tear off pieces of dough the size of an egg, drop into smoking-hot fat, and fry like other doughnuts. Drain on brown paper and sprinkle with granulated sugar.

BLUE GRASS WAFFLES

Two cupfuls of thick sour cream, two cupfuls of flour, three eggs, well beaten, and half a teaspoonful of soda sifted with the flour. Mix quickly, folding in the stiffly beaten whites of the eggs last, and bake until golden brown and crisp on hissing-hot, well-greased waffle-irons.

CREAM WAFFLES

Sift together one cupful of flour, three tablespoonfuls of corn starch, and a pinch of salt. Mix one egg, well beaten, one scant teaspoonful of soda, and two cupfuls of sour milk together and gradually combine mixtures, beating hard meanwhile. Bake in hot, well-greased waffle-irons and butter the waffles before serving.

FEATHER WAFFLES

Four cupfuls of milk, three eggs, beaten separately. Add the milk to the yolks and a pinch of salt, then add one and one half tablespoonfuls of rich cream or melted butter and sifted flour enough to make the batter a little stiffer than pancake batter. Add the whites of the eggs last, beaten to a stiff froth, and stir in quickly two teaspoonfuls of baking powder.

GEORGIA WAFFLES

Two cupfuls of flour, a pinch of salt, two cupfuls of buttermilk, one cupful of melted lard, one scant teaspoonful of soda, and one egg. Sift the flour and salt together and beat into a smooth batter with the buttermilk. Add the well-beaten egg, then the hot lard, beat thoroughly, add the dry soda, beat hard for a minute or two, and bake in hissing-hot waffle-irons.

HOMINY WAFFLES

One cupful of cold cooked hominy, one egg, well beaten, one tablespoonful of melted butter, one pinch of salt, two cupfuls of milk, and two cupfuls of flour sifted with one teaspoonful of baking powder. Mix thoroughly and bake in very hot waffle-irons, well buttered.

RAISED HOMINY WAFFLES

To one cupful of cold cooked hominy add two cupfuls of scalded milk in which one half a yeast cake has been dissolved, one tablespoonful of butter, melted, a pinch of salt, one tablespoonful of sugar, and two cupfuls of flour. Mix thoroughly and set to rise over night. In the morning add two eggs, beaten separately, folding in the stiffly beaten whites last. Bake in very hot, well-greased irons.

INDIAN WAFFLES

One cupful each of flour and corn-meal, two cupfuls of thick sour milk, one cupful of sour cream, half a teaspoonful of salt, one teaspoonful of soda, two tablespoonfuls of sugar, and two eggs, beaten separately, the stiffly beaten whites being folded in last. Bake in a very hot, well-greased waffle-iron and serve very hot.

KENTUCKY WAFFLES

Make a smooth paste of two cupfuls of sifted flour and two cupfuls of milk, add one half cupful of softened butter, not melted, then the well-beaten yolks of three eggs, then the stiffly beaten whites, and, just before baking, one heaping teaspoonful of baking powder. Beat very hard for five minutes and bake in a hissing-hot iron.

MARYLAND WAFFLES

Beat four eggs separately, the whites to a stiff froth. To the beaten yolks add a pinch of salt, two cupfuls of milk, and enough sifted flour to make a stiff batter. Beat hard until perfectly smooth and free from lumps. Thin the batter by adding gradually the beaten whites of the eggs, and a little more milk in which a level teaspoonful of baking powder has been dissolved. Add lastly one tablespoonful of melted butter or lard. Have the waffle-irons very hot and well greased, and butter each waffle as soon as done. Crisp light waffles are delicious when served with cream and sifted maple-sugar.

PLAIN WAFFLES

Two cupfuls of sifted flour, two cupfuls of milk, one tablespoonful of melted butter, one tablespoonful of melted lard, two teaspoonfuls of baking powder sifted with the flour, two eggs well beaten, and half a teaspoonful of salt. Beat thoroughly and have the irons hot before mixing.

RICE WAFFLES

One cupful of cold boiled rice beaten light with one cupful of milk. Add one tablespoonful of melted butter, half a teaspoonful of soda dissolved in a little of the milk, two eggs well beaten, and enough flour, sifted in with one teaspoonful of cream tartar, to make a thin batter. Beat thoroughly and bake in well-greased waffle-irons. Cream tartar and spices are practically certain to be pure when bought of a druggist instead of a grocer. (Not knocking the groceryman.)

RICE AND CORN-MEAL WAFFLES

One cupful of cold boiled rice, one half cupful each of wheat flour and corn-meal, one tablespoonful of melted butter, one half teaspoonful of soda dissolved in hot water, one teaspoonful of salt, two eggs, beaten separately, and enough milk to make a thin batter. The waffle-irons must be very thoroughly greased and the baking must be done with great care, as these waffles are likely to burn.

SWEDISH WAFFLES

Two cupfuls of cream, whipped stiff, one half cupful of sugar, one egg beaten with one fourth cupful of cold water, one half cupful of melted butter, and enough flour, sifted, to make a thin batter. Fold the whipped cream in carefully just before baking, and sprinkle with sugar when done.

TENNESSEE WAFFLES

Two cupfuls of sifted flour, half a teaspoonful of salt, one tablespoonful of melted butter or lard, one egg, beaten separately, and milk enough to make a thin batter. Bake until brown in a well-greased waffle-iron.

VIRGINIA WAFFLES

Three eggs, well beaten, two cupfuls of milk, one half cupful of melted butter, two teaspoonfuls of baking powder, a pinch of salt, and enough flour to make a thin batter. Bake in hissing-hot waffle-irons.

BREAKFAST BEVERAGES

The breakfast beverage *par excellence* is coffee, at least in American households, but, rather than have coffee poorly made, it is better to have no coffee at all. The French method of coffee making has practically superseded the old-fashioned boiled coffee. Cheap coffee, carefully made in the proper kind of a pot, has a better flavor than the more expensive brands can possibly have when improperly made.

The best coffee-pot on the market, which publishing ethics forbid us to mention by name, is made of nickel, comes in five or six different sizes, has a close fitting cover, a wooden handle, and has inside a finely woven wire strainer, which does away entirely with the questionable, and often unclean, cloth strainer. A cloth, no matter how carefully kept, will eventually become saturated with the grounds, and add the flavor of reheated coffee to the fresh brew in the pot.

The nickel coffee-pots having the wire strainer inside are easily kept clean with boiling water alone, and about once a month may be boiled out with a weak solution of baking soda.

Various blends of coffee have their champions, and the blended package coffees are, in the main, very good. It is better to buy in small quantities, a pound or two at a time, have the coffee pulverized very finely at the grocery, and keep a watchful eye on the man while he does it, lest he add alien elements to the coffee. Pulverized coffee keeps perfectly in ordinary Mason jars, tightly sealed, if bought in small quantities, as suggested.

The ideal coffee blend is two thirds Mandeheling Java and one third Arabian Mocha, but very little genuine Mocha ever reaches this country, though trusting consumers often pay high prices for what the man says is sure-enough Mocha.

Pure Java is easier to get, and South American, Mexican, Cuban, and Porto Rican coffees are beginning to deserve consideration.

Presuming that we have the pot and a good quality of coffee, finely pulverized, we will proceed to brew the nectar of the gods. The water must be fresh and captured while on its first boil. Scald the coffee-pot, and put into it one heaping tablespoonful of pulverized coffee for each person and another for the poor, neglected pot. If the coffee is desired extra strong, put in another tablespoonful, or even two. Pour in one cupful of boiling water for each tablespoonful of coffee, keeping the pot over steam, but never over the fire itself. Occasionally the grounds may be lifted from the bottom of the strainer with a spoon in order to hasten the process a bit. The strength of Samson may be given the brew by pouring out a cupful or two of the coffee after it is made, and compelling it to go over the ground(s) again.

Put the desired amount of sugar in each cup, and add a liberal quantity of cream. Fill three fourths full with coffee and weaken slightly with freshly boiling water. Coffee poured into cream and afterward weakened with boiling water is an entirely different beverage from that which results when the process is reversed. Anybody knowing why, please write.

Never, never, never under any circumstances use the same coffee twice, or add fresh coffee to the remnant in the pot, if by chance there should ever be any left. Trim over last year's hat, if you must, and buy no books for a year except this one, but do have the daily coffee *right*.

Our deep feeling on this subject is caused by our own cherished reputation for coffee making, which extends as much as three blocks in every direction of the compass.

BOILED COFFEE

One cupful of ground coffee, mixed with a raw, unbeaten egg, and part of the shell. Add half a cupful of cold water, and put it into the coffee-pot. Pour over four cupfuls of boiling water, and as it rises and begins to boil, stir it with a silver spoon. Let boil hard for ten or fifteen minutes, then take from the fire. Pour out one cupful of the coffee, then put it back, and set the pot on the back of the stove for five minutes to settle.

CAFÉ GLACÉ

A welcome variant in summer, even for people who do not like cold coffee. Fill iced-tea glasses three fourths full of inch cubes of ice, add a lump or two of sugar, and pour in the coffee, boiling hot. Do not stir, but add the cream immediately. For some strange reason, it is better than if the hot coffee is poured over the ice, sugar, and cream. Anybody knowing why, please write.

CHOCOLATE

Make exactly like cocoa, using milk instead of water. A few drops of vanilla added to chocolate pleasantly accentuates its flavor.

COCOA

Directions are given on the package the cocoa comes in. If not, buy another kind.

TEA

Cheap tea contains sawdust, dried and powdered hay, grass-seed, and departed but unlamented insects. Moral—buy good tea, or go without. Have the kettle boiling, and take the water at the first boil. Scald out the tea-pot, which must never be of metal, and put into it one teaspoonful of tea for each person, and one for the pot, or more, if curly hair for the drinker is desired. Pour one cupful of boiling water for each person and another for the pot upon the tea, and pour off the tea inside of three minutes. After that the boiling water busies itself in taking tannic acid out of the tea grounds. Tannic acid hardens albumen into a leathery substance of which the most courageous stomach is rightfully suspicious, and also puckers the mucous membrane of the stomach into smocking. Persistent drinking of boiled tea is quite likely to relieve the stomach altogether of its valued and hard-worked mucous membrane.

SIMPLE SALADS

A salad with mayonnaise dressing is an ideal *pièce de résistance* for luncheon. It furnishes the necessary carbon in a light and easily assimilated form, and, if well made, is always palatable.

Strictly speaking, there are but two salad dressings, French and mayonnaise. The boiled dressing, with all its variations, is, technically, a sauce. A true salad dressing is made almost entirely of oil.

To make French dressing, put into a bowl or soup plate a pinch of salt, a dash of red pepper, and three tablespoonfuls of olive-oil. Stir with a silver spoon until thoroughly mixed, then add one tablespoonful of tarragon vinegar, and stir until thick. French dressing must not be made until it is to be used, as it very quickly wilts a vegetable salad. Four or five tablespoonfuls of oil may be used to one of vinegar or lemon-juice if desired, and French dressing may also be seasoned with tabasco sauce, Worcestershire, dry mustard, celery salt, or any preferred condiment.

To make mayonnaise, put into an earthen bowl the yolk of a fresh egg and a pinch of salt, a dash of red pepper and half a teaspoonful of dry mustard. Place the bowl on ice or in ice water. Pour one cupful of olive-oil into a small pitcher from which it will drop easily. When the egg and seasoning are thoroughly mixed, begin to add the oil, using a silver teaspoon, and rubbing rather than stirring. Add the oil until a clear spot is formed upon the egg, then mix until smooth. Only a few drops can be added at first, but the quantity may be gradually increased. The clear spot upon the egg is an infallible test of the right quantity of oil. If too much oil is added, the dressing will curdle. A few drops of lemon-juice and long beating will usually make it right again. If this fails, set the bowl directly on the ice in the refrigerator, and let stand half an hour. If it is still curdled, begin again with the yolk of another egg and add the curdled mayonnaise by degrees to the new dressing.

When the mayonnaise is so thick that it is difficult to stir it, add the juice of half a lemon, or more if desired. If wanted still thinner, add a little cream at serving-time, but a stiff, creamy-yellow mayonnaise is a culinary triumph.

With a little experience, mayonnaise is very quickly made. It need not take more than ten or fifteen minutes to make enough abundantly to serve six people. Packed in jelly glasses, and covered with wax paper, or the cover of a jelly glass, mayonnaise will keep a week or more in a cool place.

A quick mayonnaise can be made by putting into a bowl half a teaspoonful of salt, a dash of red pepper, half a teaspoonful of dry mustard, the yolk of an egg, four tablespoonfuls of olive-oil, one tablespoonful of lemon-juice or tarragon vinegar, and beating all together with the egg beater. If it fails to thicken, it is because the egg is not strictly fresh, but even if it does not thicken, it is palatable. A small jar of mayonnaise dressing, kept upon the ice, is an ever present help in time of trouble.

All vegetables used for salads must be in prime condition. Lettuce must be crisp, and only the perfect leaves used. Ragged edges may be trimmed off with the scissors. The head lettuce is best for all salads, but the leaf lettuce may be used if the other is not obtainable. It is sometimes shredded into ribbons with a sharp knife or scissors, but lettuce should be torn rather than cut, as cutting breaks and bruises the fibres.

Salads with mayonnaise dressing are too rich to serve at dinner, and hence are relegated to luncheons, Sunday-night suppers, and hot-weather dinners, where no other meat is served.

The variety of salads is inexhaustible, and new combinations are invented every day, many of them elaborate and very difficult to make. The following salads, however, will be found simple, convenient, and in every way satisfactory.

CHICKEN SALAD

Mix cold, cooked, shredded chicken with half the quantity of finely cut celery, mix with mayonnaise dressing, and serve on a bit of lettuce. Garnish with parsley and slices of hard-boiled egg. Canned chicken may be used, but it is not as good.

CHICKEN AND MUSHROOM SALAD

Equal parts of chicken and cooked mushrooms. Mayonnaise.

MOCK CHICKEN SALAD

Cold roast pork, shredded with the fingers and mixed with half as much finely cut celery. Mayonnaise.

CHICKEN AND SWEETBREAD SALAD

Cold, cooked, shredded chicken, and half the quantity of cooked sweetbreads cut fine. Mayonnaise.

CHICKEN AND NUT SALAD

Add a few pecans or English walnuts, cut coarsely, to chicken salad.

ALMOND SALAD

Stone and chop six olives. Add half a cupful of blanched and shredded almonds, and half a cupful of tender celery cut fine. Serve on lettuce leaves, with mayonnaise.

ASPARAGUS SALAD

Boil, drain, and cool the asparagus. Serve on lettuce leaves with French dressing, and garnish with slices of hard-boiled egg.

APPLE AND CRESS SALAD

Cut sour apples into dice. Mix with watercress, carefully picked over, and French dressing.

APRICOT SALAD

Chill the fruit, pare, stone, cut in halves, arrange on lettuce leaves, and pour over French dressing made with lemon-juice.

ASPARAGUS AND SALMON SALAD

Flake cold, boiled salmon, mix with cooked asparagus tips, and add a little finely cut celery. Mayonnaise.

BEAN SALAD

Lima beans boiled, drained, and cooled, chopped onion and minced parsley. Mayonnaise.

BORDEAUX SALAD

Celery and olives, coarsely cut. Mayonnaise.

BANANA SALAD

Chill the fruit, peel, slice thin, pour over French dressing made with lemon-juice, and serve at once on lettuce leaves.

BANANA AND CHERRY SALAD

Prepare as above, mixing the bananas with a few maraschino cherries, cut into quarters.

BANANA AND PIMENTO SALAD

Prepare as above, using shredded scarlet pimentos instead of the cherries.

BANANA AND CELERY SALAD

Six bananas, half a cupful of nuts cut fine, and two stalks of celery cut fine. Peel the bananas carefully, cut the fruit into dice, mix with the nuts and celery, addmayonnaise, fill the banana skins, chill, and serve on lettuce leaves.

BIRD'S-NEST SALAD

Take the yolks of hard-boiled eggs and rub to a paste with an equal quantity of Neufchatel cheese. Season with salt and paprika, and make into egg-shaped balls. Make a mound of the shredded whites and lay the egg-balls upon it, flecking them with black pepper. Surround the dish with the heart-leaves of head lettuce, and servemayonnaise dressing in a dish apart.

CELERY SALAD

Crisp, tender celery cut fine, mixed with a little chopped onion and mayonnaise. Serve on lettuce.

CAULIFLOWER SALAD

Boil a large cauliflower in salted water until tender. Drain, cool, separate the flowerets, sprinkle with chopped onion and parsley, and set on ice. When thoroughly chilled, mix with mayonnaise, and serve on lettuce leaves.

BOHEMIAN SALAD

Mix fried oysters or fried scallops, cold, with half the quantity of finely cut celery. Serve very cold on lettuce leaves with mayonnaise.

CRAB SALAD

Use the meat of boiled crabs flaked into pieces of uniform size. The canned crab meat is very good. Add half the quantity of finely cut celery, mix with mayonnaise, and serve on lettuce leaves.

CRESS SALAD

Watercress and nasturtium leaves. French dressing. Garnish with nasturtium blossoms.

CALF'S-BRAIN SALAD

Parboil the brains in acidulated water, blanch, cool, and remove all veins and membranes. Break in pieces and proceed as for Crab Salad.

CUCUMBER SALAD

Peel, slice, and chill the cucumbers. Drain, mix with chopped onion, or small bits of the large white onions. French dressing.

CUCUMBER AND RADISH SALAD

Prepare as above, and add a few radishes, sliced but not peeled. The onion may be omitted.

COTTAGE CHEESE SALAD

Make soft cottage cheese into balls the size of a bird's egg. Arrange carefully with cucumber dice and a little chopped onion. French dressing.

CREAM CHEESE SALAD

Prepare cheese as above, coloring the balls with spinach juice or green color paste. Sprinkle with chopped parsley, arrange on lettuce leaves, and pour over French dressing.

CUCUMBER JELLY

Cut peeled tomatoes and cucumbers into dice, saving the juice. Season with grated onion, pepper, and salt. Mix with hot water, in which gelatine has been dissolved, let cool, break up and serve in tomato shells with mayonnaise. When gelatine is used in salads, half a package to each two cupfuls of salad material is about the right proportion.

CHERRY SALAD

Maraschino or ox-heart cherries stuffed with hazel nuts. Serve very cold on lettuce leaves with mayonnaise.

CELERY AND NUT SALAD

Celery and pecans, or English walnuts, coarsely cut. Mayonnaise.

CAULIFLOWER AND BEET SALAD

Cooked cauliflower flowerets and dice of cold, boiled beets. Serve on lettuce with mayonnaise.

CHEESE AND TOMATO SALAD

Slices of tomato with small bits of Edam cheese. Serve on lettuce leaves with French dressing.

CELERY JELLY SALAD

Put into a saucepan two cupfuls of strained tomatoes, a tablespoonful of grated onion, a bay leaf, and a pinch of celery seed. Bring to a boil, set aside for fifteen minutes, add half a package of gelatine that has been soaked in half a cupful of cold water, half a teaspoonful of salt, and the juice of half a lemon. Stand over boiling water until the gelatine is all dissolved. Strain, stir in a quantity of finely cut celery, set on ice, stir until it begins to thicken, mould in small cups, and chill. At serving-time, turn out on a bed of lettuce leaves and mask with mayonnaise.

CHESTNUT SALAD

Shell and blanch the nuts, boil until tender, drain, and peel. Add an equal quantity of finely cut celery and some bits of pimento. Mayonnaise.

CHICKEN ASPIC SALAD

Use strong, clear chicken stock or the chicken juice which comes in cans, and half a package of gelatine to each pint. When the jelly begins to thicken, stir in lightly broken English walnuts, mould, chill, turn out on plates covered with lettuce leaves, and mask with mayonnaise.

TOMATO ASPIC SALAD

Use the juice and strained pulp of fresh or canned tomatoes. Season highly with salt, pepper, grated onion, and vinegar. Use half a package of gelatine to each two cupfuls of juice and pulp, mould in small cups, chill, turn out on lettuce leaves, and mask with mayonnaise.

BELLEVUE SALAD

Make the tomato aspic according to directions given above. When it begins to stiffen, stir in lightly flaked shrimps and cucumber dice, mould, chill, turn out on individual serving dishes, surround with the tender heart-leaves of head lettuce, and mask with mayonnaise dressing.

CHICKEN SALAD EN BELLEVUE

Make the tomato aspic and mould in a border mould. At serving-time turn out upon a platter, fill the centre with chicken salad and surround with tomato aspic. Garnish with the heart-leaves of head lettuce.

CUCUMBER ASPIC SALAD

Chop cucumbers fine, or grate on a coarse grater. Season with onion and celery, or a little celery seed. Add salt, pepper, and vinegar to taste, and save every drop of the juice. Tint with green color paste if desired. Use one package of gelatine to each quart of the pulp, and proceed according to directions given for other aspic salads. Turn into a border mould and chill on ice. At serving-time cover the platter with lettuce leaves, turn the border out of the mould and fill the centre with a fish salad.

CELERY AND RADISH SALAD

Prepare the celery as usual, but do not peel the radishes. Slice them thin and leave the little red line around each slice. Chill thoroughly, mix with mayonnaise, and serve on lettuce leaves. Garnish with whole radishes.

CABBAGE SALAD

Select a small, heavy, shapely head of white cabbage. Cut a slice off the top and scoop out the interior carefully, leaving a thin shell. Shred the inner portion with an equal quantity of crisp celery, mix with mayonnaise and serve in the cabbage. A few nut meats may be added. Sometimes the cabbage bowl is filled with fried oysters, and the celery and cabbage salad served on lettuce leaves.

SALAD À L'ESPAGNOLE

Scald, skin, and cool large, smooth tomatoes, cut a slice off the blossom end and scoop out the pulp with a silver spoon. Drain the pulp, add an equal quantity of cucumber dice, cut small, and a little grated onion to season, mix with a French dressing and fill the tomato shell with the mixture. Put a spoonful of mayonnaise on top of each tomato and serve on individual plates covered with lettuce leaves.

GRAPE SALAD

Use large, white, California grapes, peel, seed, and cut in halves. Mix with sour orange slices, and any preferred nuts. Use French dressing made with lemon-juice, and serve on lettuce leaves.

GRAPE SALAD—II

Prepare as above, using apples in place of the oranges.

GRAPEFRUIT SALAD

Break the pulp of grapefruit into small bits and drain, reserving the juice. Arrange on lettuce leaves, sprinkle with cut English walnuts, and pour over a French dressing made of oil and the juice of the fruit.

ITALIAN SALAD

Six cold, cooked potatoes, cut in dice, six flaked sardines, three small cucumber pickles, chopped, and a stalk of celery cut fine. French dressing.

LETTUCE SALAD

Use the crisp heart-leaves of head lettuce, and dress with French dressing. Serve with cheese and toasted crackers.

ENDIVE SALAD

Use the crisp leaves of endive and prepare as above.

MARGUERITE SALAD

Make a bed of lettuce leaves on each individual dish. Slice hard-boiled eggs lengthwise, and remove the yolks whole. Put a yolk in the centre of each plate and arrange the white around it, cut in strips to resemble the petals of a Marguerite. French dressing.

MARQUISE SALAD

Tomatoes sliced and sprinkled with chopped onion, parsley and finely cut celery. Serve on lettuce leaves with French dressing.

NORMANDY SALAD

Three cucumbers and three hard-boiled eggs, cut in dice, a cupful of olive meat, and half a cupful of pecan or English walnut meat, broken, but not chopped.Mayonnaise. The egg may be omitted.

NUT AND SWEETBREAD SALAD

A can of shrimps, a pound and a half of sweetbreads, cooked and cut into dice, a can of French peas, a can of mushrooms, a cupful of English walnuts, half a cupful of blanched almonds, and a cupful of finely cut celery. Mix with mayonnaise and serve on lettuce leaves. Half, or even a third, of this quantity is sufficient for a small family.

ORANGE SALAD

Thin slices of very sour oranges, sprinkled with cut English walnuts. Serve on lettuce leaves with French dressing made with lemon-juice. Especially good with game.

PIMENTO SALAD

Shredded pimentos, sliced olives, finely cut celery, and a tablespoonful of chopped onion to each pint. Mayonnaise. This salad should be half celery, one fourth pimentos, and one fourth olives.

PIMENTO SALAD—II

Hard-boiled eggs cut into eighths. Half the quantity of shredded pimentos, and as much olive meat as pimentos. To each pint of the salad add one tablespoonful of the tiny pearl onions which come in bottles. Mix with mayonnaise, and serve on lettuce leaves.

PEPPER SALAD

Sliced tomatoes and cucumbers, shredded green peppers, chopped onion, and French dressing.

PARISIAN SALAD

Boil French peas in their own juice, drain, cool, and mix with cut walnut meats. Soak for an hour in French dressing, drain, put into lemon cups on lettuce leaves, and serve with a spoonful of mayonnaise on top.

PORTUGUESE SALAD
Celery, English walnuts, and shredded pimentos. Mayonnaise.

PEACH SALAD
Prepare according to directions given for Apricot Salad, and stuff the halves with maraschino cherries and chopped nuts.

RUSSIAN SALAD
Make tomato aspic in a border mould, turn out on a platter and fill the centre with celery mayonnaise.

PINEAPPLE SALAD
Pineapple, oranges, bananas, and strawberries, cut coarsely. French dressing made with lemon-juice. Serve in the pineapple shell, or in orange baskets, or banana skins.

SCALLOP SALAD
Parboil the scallops, drain, and cool. Cut coarsely, and mix with half the quantity of finely cut celery. Mayonnaise.

OYSTER SALAD
Prepare according to directions given above. Mushrooms may be added if desired.

STUFFED-TOMATO SALAD
Scald, drain, skin, and chill large, well-shaped, ripe tomatoes. Cut a slice off the blossom end, scoop out the pulp, drain, mix with an equal quantity of finely cut celery and a little minced onion. Mix with mayonnaise, fill the shells, put a spoonful of stiff mayonnaise on top, with a little sprig of parsley upright for a garnish, or an English walnut meat. Any salad which combines well with the flavor of tomato may be served in tomato shells, and as a cupful of salad will stuff several tomatoes, the problem of insignificant salad left-overs is often solved in this way.

SHRIMP SALAD
Use either canned or fresh shrimps. Break into small bits, mix with mayonnaise, and serve on lettuce leaves.

SUMMER SALAD
Slice peeled tomatoes, drain, and mix with sliced cucumbers and finely chopped onion. Mayonnaise.

SALMON SALAD
Use boiled, fresh salmon. Free from skin, fat, and bone, and flake. Mix with finely cut celery and a few capers. Mayonnaise.

SALMON SALAD—II
Prepare as above, using cucumber dice and a bit of chopped onion instead of the celery and capers. Mayonnaise.

SARDINE SALAD

Drain the sardines, sprinkle with lemon-juice, and alternate with hard-boiled egg quarters on a bed of lettuce leaves. French dressing.

SHAD ROE SALAD

Boil the roe, chill, slice, and add finely cut celery and boiled beet dice. Mayonnaise.

SHAD ROE SALAD—II

Prepare the roe as above and mix with sliced cucumbers. Season with chopped onion and mix with mayonnaise.

SWEETBREAD SALAD

Prepare according to directions given for Calf's-Brain Salad.

SALSIFY SALAD

Boil, drain, and cool, cut into dice and combine with an equal quantity of potatoes, lima beans, or cauliflower. French dressing.

SPINACH SALAD

Mould cooked and chopped spinach in small cups. Turn out on individual dishes, garnish with hard-boiled eggs and beet dice. French dressing.

STRING BEANS SALAD

String the beans, but do not cut them. Boil, drain, and cool. Serve on lettuce leaves with French dressing and garnish with nasturtium blossoms.

SHRIMP AND CUCUMBER SALAD

Cut the shrimps coarsely and sprinkle with French dressing. At serving-time, drain, mix with an equal quantity of crisp cucumber dice, and serve on lettuce leaves with mayonnaise.

VIENNA SALAD

Finely cut celery, apple dice, and shreds of green pepper. Mayonnaise.

WALDORF SALAD

Sour apples, peeled and sliced, English walnuts, and finely cut celery. Mayonnaise.

MUTTON SALAD

Cut cold roast or boiled mutton into dice, using none of the fat. Arrange on lettuce leaves, season with salt and pepper, add a few capers, and mix with mayonnaise dressing.

MUTTON AND ASPARAGUS SALAD

Prepare according to directions given above, using an equal quantity of cold, cooked asparagus instead of the capers.

MUTTON AND PEA SALAD

Prepare according to directions given above, using peas instead of asparagus.

CHESTNUT SALAD—II

Prepare according to directions given for Chestnut Salad—I. Mix with an equal quantity of sour apples cut into dice. Mayonnaise.

CRESS AND WALNUT SALAD

Wash and drain a bunch of watercress, pick off the tender sprigs and place in a salad bowl. Add half the quantity of broken English-walnuts which have been soaked in lemon-juice. Dress with a French dressing made of twice as much oil as vinegar and no seasoning except salt.

SHAD ROE SALAD—III

Cook the roe with a slice of onion in salted, acidulated water for twenty minutes. Drain, cool, cut into slices, and sprinkle with French dressing. Add cucumber dice and chopped olives. Mix with mayonnaise, garnish with peppers, and serve on lettuce leaves.

SALMON SALAD—III

Open a can of salmon, break into large pieces, remove the bones, skin, and fat, and lay on a plate. Slice two tomatoes and mince finely a few small cucumber pickles. Mix the tomatoes with the pickle and put around the salmon, with a little on top. Cover with a mayonnaise, to which chopped pickles and capers have been added, and garnish with lettuce and parsley.

ITALIAN SARDINE SALAD

Four sardines, three large potatoes, three eggs, seasoning, four anchovies, half a cupful of lima beans cooked, and plenty of oil and vinegar. Bake the potatoes, peel them, and set them aside to cool. Boil the eggs hard. Slice the potatoes into a bowl and add the beans. Skin and bone the sardines and anchovies, break into bits, and mix them with the vegetable. Put the yolks of two of the eggs into a bowl, add a pinch each of mustard and salt and enough oil to make a smooth cream. Add one third as much vinegar as oil. Pour this dressing over the vegetables and add the shredded whites of the eggs. Garnish with the whole egg cut in slices and a few stoned olives.

EGG AND CHEESE SALAD

Slice half a dozen hard-boiled eggs. Line a salad dish with lettuce leaves, cover with a layer of the eggs, and sprinkle thickly with grated cheese. Thin some mayonnaisewith a little cream and spread over the cheese. Add another layer of eggs and cheese and a sprinkling of chopped cucumber pickle. Put in the remainder of the eggs, cover with mayonnaise and sprinkle more cheese over all.

CELERY AND PINEAPPLE SALAD

Use equal parts of shredded pineapple and celery, cut fine. Sprinkle with lemon-juice, and chill. Add a few blanched and pounded almonds, mix with mayonnaise, and serve on lettuce leaves.

VEAL SALAD

One cupful of cold roast veal cut into dice. Add one cupful of cooked peas. Sprinkle with celery salt, chopped capers and pickles, and pour over a French dressing, seasoned with dry mustard and chopped mint. In making the French dressing for this salad, use ordinary cider vinegar instead of tarragon vinegar.

TOMATOES STUFFED WITH ASPARAGUS TIPS

Prepare tomato shells according to directions previously given. Cut cold, cooked asparagus tips in small bits, mix with mayonnaise, and fill the shells. Season with grated onion if desired.

TUTTI-FRUITTI SALAD

One half pound of figs, cut in small pieces, one quarter pound of stoned dates, four oranges cut into small slices, one cupful of canned strawberries, one cupful of canned pineapple, the juice of one lemon, three or four tablespoonfuls of sugar, and one cupful of sherry. While this is not strictly a salad, it is served on lettuce leaves in place of a salad. Half or a third of the quantity is sufficient for a small family.

SPAGHETTI SALAD

Shredded celery, boiled spaghetti broken into inch pieces, and bits of Spanish pimento. Mix with mayonnaise and serve on lettuce leaves.

SWEETBREAD AND CUCUMBER SALAD

Mix cooked sweetbreads, cut into dice, with half the amount of cucumbers cut the same size, and a little finely cut celery. Mix with mayonnaise and serve on lettuce leaves.

HAM AND CELERY SALAD

Cut cold, cooked ham into bits and mix with half as much celery cut fine. Mix with mayonnaise and serve on lettuce leaves. Garnish with hard-boiled eggs cut in slices.

EGG AND POTATO SALAD

Dress slices of cold, hard-boiled eggs and potatoes with French dressing, arrange on lettuce leaves, and garnish with stoned olives.

CHEESE AND PARSLEY SALAD

Moisten Neufchatel or cream cheese with cream, and shape in tiny balls. Roll in very finely minced parsley, and serve on lettuce leaves with French dressing.

CHERRY AND PINEAPPLE SALAD

Half of a banana, one orange, one cupful of shredded pineapple, one cupful of stoned cherries, one fourth cupful of blanched almonds, the juice of half a lemon, and one tablespoonful of powdered sugar. Use the cherry juice in a French dressing.

SHRIMP AND CELERY SALAD

Equal parts of shredded shrimps and finely cut celery. Mix
with mayonnaise and serve on lettuce leaves.

POTATO AND NUT SALAD

Three cold, boiled potatoes, three hard-boiled eggs, one half cupful of walnuts,
and a dozen olives. Cut the potatoes and eggs into dice, stone the olives, cut
fine, break up the nut meats and mix all together. Pour over a small quantity
of French dressing and let stand on ice. At serving-time, mix with a
little mayonnaise.

EGG AND CHICKEN SALAD

Chop cold roast chicken very fine. Mix the yolks of hard-boiled eggs with the
chicken, adding enough mayonnaise to make the mixture easily into balls. Cut
the whites of the eggs into rings, and serve the balls and the rings together on
lettuce leaves.

CABBAGE AND PEPPER SALAD

Shred finely a crisp, raw cabbage. Mix with half as much shredded green
pepper. Serve on lettuce leaves with mayonnaise.

CHEESE AND CELERY SALAD

Cut crisp, tender celery into small bits, sprinkle with grated Parmesan cheese
and serve on lettuce leaves with French dressing.

CELERY AND CAULIFLOWER SALAD

Equal parts of finely cut celery and cold, cooked cauliflower broken into bits.
Either French dressing or mayonnaise.

CAULIFLOWER AND CARROT SALAD

Cold, cooked cauliflower broken into bits, and one third the quantity of cooked
carrots cut into dice. Either French or mayonnaise dressing.

PEA AND WALNUT SALAD

Equal quantities of cold, cooked peas and English walnuts broken into small
bits. Sprinkle with French dressing, let stand half an hour and mix
with mayonnaise. Serve on lettuce leaves or in lemon cups.

RUSSIAN SALAD—II

Equal quantities of cooked potato dice, peas, carrots, lima beans, shredded
celery, sliced tomatoes, chopped onion, cucumber dice and anchovies broken
into small bits.French dressing, using more vinegar than usual.

GERMAN CAULIFLOWER SALAD

Use cold, cooked cauliflower separated into flowerets. Fry shredded bacon until
crisp, drain, and mix with the cauliflower. Make a French dressing, using the
bacon fat instead of oil, and cider vinegar instead of tarragon. Pour hot over the
salad and set away to cool.

SPANISH SALAD

Cut into dice three slices of stale bread. Add an equal quantity of cold, cooked potatoes, three tomatoes, sliced, and one onion chopped fine. Rub the salad bowl with the cut side of a clove of garlic, put in the salad, and pour over plenty of French dressing.

ONION SALAD

Peel two or three onions, soak in water two hours, chop, put into a salad bowl, add a tablespoonful of minced parsley and pour over French dressing. The large, white Spanish onions are best for this salad. One large onion is usually enough.

RUSSIAN SALAD—III

Cut crisp, tender celery into small bits, add one fourth the quantity of Russian caviare and the same quantity of anchovies as caviare. Add half as much tomato pulp as celery and mix with mayonnaise. Serve in tomato shells.

STRAWBERRY SALAD

Arrange tender, white lettuce leaves in cup shapes. Fill each cup with strawberries and put a tablespoonful of mayonnaise in each cup. Mayonnaise for this salad should have the mustard and tarragon vinegar omitted.

BANANA AND PEANUT SALAD

Slice bananas lengthwise, cover with finely ground peanuts, and serve on lettuce leaves with mayonnaise.

EGG AND ASPARAGUS SALAD

Cut boiled, fresh asparagus into bits. Mix with slices of hard-boiled egg and serve on lettuce leaves with a French dressing to which chopped pickles and capers have been added.

EGG AND CUCUMBER SALAD

Slice cucumbers and hard-boiled eggs. Alternate slices of each in a circle around a bed of watercress, and serve with French dressing.

TOMATO AND CHIVE SALAD

Peel and chill the tomatoes, and cut into halves. Sprinkle with finely chopped chives, and put a spoonful of mayonnaise on each half. Serve on lettuce.

GRAPEFRUIT AND CELERY SALAD

Mix grapefruit pulp with finely cut celery, using twice as much grapefruit as celery. Serve on lettuce leaves with mayonnaise.

CUCUMBER AND PIMOLA SALAD

Mix in equal parts, slicing both thin. Use French dressing and serve on lettuce.

EGG AND CELERY SALAD

Two heads of celery cut fine, two hard-boiled eggs, and half a cupful of English walnuts. Break the nuts into small pieces, slice the eggs and mix all together. Serve on lettuce with mayonnaise.

CABBAGE SALAD—II

Mix shredded, raw cabbage with mayonnaise, and sprinkle with celery seed.

CABBAGE SALAD—III

Cut off the small ends of green peppers, scoop out the seeds, and fill with cabbage salad prepared as above.

EGG-BALL SALAD

Separate the whites and yolks of hard-boiled eggs. Cut the whites into shreds with the scissors. Rub the yolks through a sieve and mix to a paste with mayonnaise, adding sardines, anchovies, salmon, or any preferred meat or fish which has been cooked and pounded fine. Shape the egg mixture into balls the size of marbles. Spread lettuce leaves with mayonnaise, sprinkle it with the shredded whites of the eggs, and drop the balls of yolk paste upon it.

STUFFED-EGG SALAD

Divide hard-boiled eggs in the middle, take out the yolks, cut a thin slice from the bottom of each to make them stand firm, and drop in a little mayonnaise. Mix the yolks to a paste with mayonnaise, using any preferred minced meat, fish, or vegetable for seasoning. Fill the shells, spread with mayonnaise, and sprinkle with chopped parsley.

CELERY AND APPLE SALAD

Mix equal parts of finely cut celery and shredded sour apple. Serve on lettuce leaves with mayonnaise.

TOMATO AND CELERY SALAD

Peel large, ripe tomatoes and cut into cubes. Drain in a colander until dry. Mix with half as much finely cut celery, and serve on lettuce leaves, with mayonnaise.

SHRIMP AND NUT SALAD

Break the shrimps into thirds. Use one half or one third the quantity of pecan or English walnut meats. Serve on lettuce with mayonnaise.

SMOKED HERRING SALAD

Skin and bone the herring and flake the meat. Use as much hard-boiled egg as herring, and twice as much potato dice as herring. Season with grated onion, and mix withFrench dressing.

HALIBUT SALAD

Steam halibut steaks until tender, arrange on a bed of lettuce and remove the skin and bone. Cover with a layer of shredded sweet pepper, hard-boiled eggs, and olives sliced thin. Serve with a French dressing which has been seasoned with grated onion.

HALIBUT SALAD—II

Prepare halibut steaks according to directions given above. Sprinkle with French dressing, cover with cucumbers sliced thin, and spread with mayonnaise.

HALIBUT SALAD—III

Prepare the fish according to directions given above, and flake it. Add half the quantity of finely cut celery. Serve on lettuce leaves with mayonnaise.

HALIBUT SALAD—IV

Prepare according to directions given for Halibut Salad—III, adding as much cucumber dice as celery.

SMELT SALAD

Boil the smelts, drain, cool, and flake the meat. Mix with cucumber dice, or finely cut celery, and serve on lettuce leaves with mayonnaise.

LOBSTER SALAD—I

Pick out the meat of a cold, boiled lobster, mix with mayonnaise, and serve on lettuce leaves.

LOBSTER SALAD—II

Prepare according to directions given for Lobster Salad—I, adding half the quantity of finely cut celery to the fish.

SHRIMP AND TOMATO SALAD

Break the shrimps into half-inch bits, and mix with twice the quantity of peeled, sliced, and drained tomatoes. Serve on lettuce leaves with mayonnaise. The tomatoes may be cut into quarters, instead of slicing.

CRAB AND CUCUMBER SALAD

Use equal quantities of crab meat, broken into inch pieces, and cucumber dice. Season with a little grated onion, and mix with mayonnaise.

TURKEY SALAD

Use cold roast turkey and prepare according to directions given for Chicken Salad.

EGG AND CABBAGE SALAD

Boil six eggs hard. When cold, cut in two lengthwise, and take out the yolks. Rub the yolks through a sieve, season with salt, pepper, and grated onion, and mix to a paste with mayonnaise. Mould into small balls and set aside. Shred the whites with the scissors, and add twice as much shredded cabbage. Mix with mayonnaise, arrange on a bed of lettuce leaves, and drop the egg balls on the salad.

EGG AND SARDINE SALAD

Boil three eggs hard. Cut in two lengthwise, and take out the yolks. Rub the yolks through a sieve with four sardines, season with salt and pepper, and add enough cream or oil to make a paste. Shape into balls. Shred the whites of the eggs with the scissors, and mix with twice the quantity of finely cut celery. Mix the celery and egg together with mayonnaise, arrange on lettuce leaves, and drop the balls of egg paste upon the salad.

TONGUE AND POTATO SALAD

Cut cold, cooked, pickled lamb's tongues into dice, mix with twice the quantity of cold, boiled potatoes cut into dice, and add a little hard-boiled egg, finely chopped. Pour over a French dressing to which a tablespoonful of chopped cucumber pickle has been added.

SHREDDED LETTUCE SALAD

Use the leaf lettuce and cut crosswise into narrow ribbons, using scissors or a very sharp knife. Serve with French dressing. Sliced hard-boiled eggs may be mixed with this salad.

GERMAN CABBAGE SALAD

Fry a cupful of finely cut bacon until crisp, and drain off the fat. Add the bacon to three times the quantity of shredded, raw cabbage. Make a salad dressing of the bacon fat and vinegar, seasoning to taste. Pour hot over the cabbage and set away to cool.

IRWIN SALAD

Six medium-sized tomatoes, peeled and quartered, two or three cucumbers cut in thin slices, one Spanish onion chopped fine, three green peppers, shredded, and two large sour apples cut into dice. Rub the salad bowl with the cut side of a clove of garlic and put in the salad. Make a dressing with six tablespoonfuls of oil, three of wine vinegar, half a teaspoonful of mustard, a teaspoonful each of Worcestershire sauce, brown sugar, and salt. Sprinkle liberally with red pepper and set the bowl on ice until thoroughly cold.

ONE HUNDRED SANDWICH FILLINGS

1. One half pound of Roquefort cheese, one fourth as much butter, and half a teaspoonful of paprika. Mix to a paste with sherry wine. Spread on wafers or toasted rye bread.

2. Remove all the seeds from a pepper, chop fine, and simmer ten minutes in a tablespoonful of butter. Add a dash of salt, and set aside to cool.

3. Chopped dates seasoned with grated lemon-peel and clove or cinnamon.

4. Corned beef cut in thin slices and spread with mustard.

5. Tongue cut in thin slices, spread with mustard.

6. Grated horseradish spread on buttered bread.

7. Swiss cheese cut in thin slices.

8. Dutch cheese made into a paste with cream.

9. Same as above with chopped nuts added.

10. The meat of a liver sausage seasoned with chopped onion and celery.

11. Prunes chopped with half the quantity of English walnut meats, seasoned with lemon-juice and powdered sugar.

12. Equal parts of chicken and cold ham, finely minced and seasoned with curry powder.

13. Drained and boned anchovies pounded to a paste with butter.

14. Thin slices of cucumber dipped in French dressing.

15. Minced tongue and hard-boiled eggs, seasoned with mustard.

16. Thin slices of roast veal covered with chopped pickles.

17. Sardines made to a paste with lemon-juice.

18. Shrimps picked fine, seasoned with lemon-juice.

19. Cold roast turkey cut into thin slices.

20. Minced hard-boiled eggs, one sardine to every three, seasoned with lemon-juice.

21. Thin slices of cold roast chicken.

22. Watercress chopped fine and seasoned with salt and pepper.

23. Same as twenty-two, mix with chopped, hard-boiled eggs.

24. Minced hard-boiled eggs mixed with grated cheese, seasoned with mustard.

25. Cold baked beans mashed to a paste and seasoned with mustard or chopped celery.

26. Thin slices of banana dressed with oil and lemon-juice.

27. Finely cut celery mixed with mayonnaise.

28. Dutch cheese mixed with chopped olives.

29. Large figs cut in halves.

30. Equal parts of minced ham and celery mixed with mayonnaise.

31. Ham mixed with chopped pickle and celery.

32. Petals or leaves of nasturtiums.

33. Equal parts of grated Swiss cheese and chopped English walnuts.

34. Olives chopped fine and mixed with mayonnaise.

35. Peanuts mashed to a paste with mayonnaise.

36. Caviare mixed with a little lemon-juice.

37. Cold roast beef cut in thin slices.

38. Minced hard-boiled eggs mixed with mayonnaise.

39. Lobster meat mixed with mayonnaise.

40. Canned salmon mixed with hard-boiled eggs chopped fine.

41. Strawberries mashed with powdered sugar and seasoned with a little lemon-juice.

42. Figs and nuts chopped fine.

43. Nuts and raisins chopped fine.

44. Cold roast chicken and cold, cooked oysters chopped fine.

45. Cold chicken and one fourth the quantity of blanched almonds chopped fine and mixed to a paste with cream.

46. Five heaping teaspoonfuls of powdered sugar, two of cocoa, and two of boiling water. Stir over the fire until smooth. Add a few drops of vanilla and cool.

47. Minced hard-boiled eggs, grated cheese, and made mustard, mixed to a paste with olive-oil.

48. Equal parts of cold roast beef, boiled tongue, ham, and cold roast turkey. Season with chopped pickle and mix with mayonnaise.

49. One cupful of cold roast chicken, three olives, one pickle, and a tablespoonful of capers. Mince fine and mix with mayonnaise.

50. Orange marmalade.

51. Cream cheese, lettuce leaves, and French dressing.

52. Lettuce leaves and mayonnaise.

53. Salmon, capers, chopped chives, and mayonnaise.

54. Cold, cooked veal chopped fine with hard-boiled eggs. Season with tomato catsup.

55. Hard-boiled eggs cut into slices, sprinkled with salt and pepper and chopped parsley.

56. Cold roast chicken and finely cut celery mixed with mayonnaise.

57. Lettuce leaves, pimentos, and mayonnaise.

58. Cottage cheese seasoned with mustard and chopped olives, mixed with mayonnaise.

59. Minced ham, olives, and parsley.

60. Cold corned-beef and green peppers, minced.

61. Cold roast lamb, minced, seasoned with minced olives and tomato catsup.

62. Raisins and candied lemon-peel chopped and made into a paste with lemon-juice.

63. Dates chopped fine, with half the quantity of English walnuts or pecans.

64. Chinese preserved ginger chopped fine.

65. Equal parts of grated cheese and English walnuts, chopped fine, and rubbed to a paste with cream.

66. Cold, cooked sweetbreads chopped fine.

67. Cold mutton chopped fine, and seasoned with mint sauce.

68. Hard-boiled eggs and watercress finely minced and mixed with mayonnaise.

69. Pickled lambs' tongues chopped very fine with capers.

70. Olives and pimentos finely chopped, lettuce leaves, and mayonnaise.

71. Dutch cheese and finely minced watercress.

72. Sour apples and celery, minced very fine, and mixed with mayonnaise.

73. Cucumber, grated onion, and mayonnaise.

74. Leaves of endive and French dressing.

75. Grated cheese, seasoned with salt, paprika, mustard, vinegar, and anchovy paste.

76. Same as seventy-five, with chopped olives or pickles added.

77. Cold, fried oysters chopped fine, lettuce leaves, and French dressing.

78. Equal parts of banana pulp and crushed red raspberries, mashed with sugar, and made into a paste with cream.

79. Grated cocoanut, chopped nuts, sugar, and lemon-juice.

80. Orange marmalade and English walnut meats.

81. Preserved ginger and candied orange-peel chopped fine.

82. Maraschino cherries and nut meats chopped fine.

83. Cottage cheese and jam or marmalade.

84. Cream cheese and bar le duc mixed to a paste.

85. Hard-boiled eggs, chopped fine, and seasoned with anchovy paste.

86. Chopped figs and chopped peanuts, seasoned with lemon-juice.

87. Chopped English walnuts mixed with quince-jelly.

88. Cabbage, finely chopped, and mixed with salad dressing.

89. Thinly sliced bananas spread with mayonnaise.

90. The tender tops of celery, minced fine, and mixed with mayonnaise.

91. Figs and raisins chopped together.

92. Boiled ham, sardines, and pickles, minced, seasoned with mustard, catsup, and vinegar.

93. Cottage cheese, lettuce leaves, and French dressing.

94. Cold, cooked chicken and mushrooms mixed with mayonnaise.

95. Cottage cheese and minced hard-boiled eggs, mixed with mayonnaise.

96. Cold roast beef, chopped fine, seasoned with tomato catsup, celery salt, Worcestershire, and grated onion.

97. Raisins chopped fine and worked to a paste with sherry.

98. Cream cheese and shredded green peppers.

99. Equal parts of tongue and chicken, minced fine, and mixed with mayonnaise.

100. Cold, boiled shad roe and cucumbers, finely minced, and mixed with French dressing or mayonnaise.

101. People who are not satisfied with the above fillings are at liberty to invent their own.

LUNCHEON BEVERAGES

Inasmuch as coffee usually appears both at breakfast and dinner, it is well to bar it out absolutely from the luncheon table. Too much coffee drinking is injurious, as the makers of imitation coffees assure us daily through the medium of expensive advertisements. Though nothing else is quite as good as coffee, yet there are many other beverages which will prove acceptable at luncheon.

MILK

Serve from an earthen pitcher, either hot or cold as preferred.

BUTTERMILK

Buttermilk is always served ice cold. On a hot day a glass of buttermilk, and a cracker or a bit of salted toast will often prove a sufficient luncheon.

TEA

Use the best tea. The cheap tea is dear at any price. Scald out the tea-pot, which should never be of metal, and put into it a teaspoonful of tea for each person and one for the pot. Add as many cupfuls of hot water as there are teaspoonfuls of tea. Cover and let steep for a moment, but never allow it to boil. The water for tea must be freshly boiled and taken at the first vigorous boil. When tea is boiled, tannin is extracted from the grounds, and tannin, even in the most minute quantities, has a very injurious effect upon the lining of the stomach.

VIENNA CHOCOLATE

Three heaping tablespoonfuls of grated chocolate mixed to a paste with cold water. Pour it into a double boiler with four cupfuls of milk boiling hot. Add sugar to taste, and let cook five minutes. Beat the whites of two eggs to a stiff froth and put into the chocolate pot. Put a teaspoonful of vanilla into the chocolate after taking from the fire, and pour the hot chocolate very slowly upon the eggs, stirring constantly with a silver spoon or the wooden stick which comes for the purpose. It makes a delicious, frothy chocolate. The cocoa which comes in packages may be used instead of grated chocolate.

COCOA

Directions are given on the package the cocoa comes in. If not, buy another kind next time.

LEMONADE

Select perfect lemons and roll until soft. Extract the juice, using a glass lemon squeezer, and rejecting the seeds and pulp. Rub cut loaf sugar over the peel of the lemon to extract the oil, and add to the lemon-juice. Fill a glass pitcher one third full of broken ice, pour the lemon-juice upon the ice, and add granulated sugar and water to taste.

ICED TEA

Make tea according to directions given above, using two or three extra teaspoonfuls of tea. Fill a glass pitcher half full of broken ice, and pour the tea, scalding hot, upon the ice, being careful that the stream strikes the ice, and not the pitcher. Serve with cut loaf sugar, and slices of lemon.

PINEAPPLE CUP

Put into a bowl the juice of three lemons, two oranges, sliced and seeded, one grated pineapple, and one cupful of sugar. Let stand an hour to extract the juice, then strain through a fruit press. Add to the juice as much cold water as desired, and two slices of pineapple, shredded. Pour into glasses half full of cracked ice.

RASPBERRY CUP

Mash and strain two cupfuls of currants stripped from the stems. Mash also an equal quantity of raspberries. Mix the juices, sweeten to taste, and serve in glasses with cracked ice and cold water.

PINEAPPLE LEMONADE

One cupful of sugar, one cupful of canned pineapple, one cupful of water and the juice of two lemons. Boil the sugar and water until it threads. Put the pineapple through the fruit press and add to the syrup with the juice of the lemons. When ready to serve, add water and sugar to taste. Serve ice cold.

GRAPE JUICE

Stem ripe Concord grapes. Do not wash unless necessary. Cover with cold water and put into a saucepan over a slow fire. Boil until the grapes are in pieces, then strain through coarse cheese-cloth and sweeten to taste. Serve in glasses with plenty of cracked ice.

BLACKBERRY SHRUB

For every cupful of fruit juice take one half cupful of cider vinegar and two cupfuls of sugar. Put the fruit, sugar, and vinegar over the fire, stir until the sugar dissolves, and boil until a thick syrup. Skim if necessary, strain, and bottle. When served, allow one fourth cupful of syrup to half or three fourths of a cupful of ice water.

RASPBERRY SHRUB

Use ripe red raspberries, and prepare according to directions given for Blackberry Shrub.

RASPBERRY DASH

Fill the tumbler half full of cracked ice. Add one tablespoonful of sweetened raspberry juice and one tablespoonful of cream. Fill the glass with soda water.

MINT SANGAREE

Crush two or three sprays of mint with a lump of sugar. Put into a glass half full of cracked ice. Add four tablespoonfuls of grape juice and fill the glass to the brim with charged water. Shake thoroughly and strain into another glass.

SELTZER LEMONADE

Squeeze the juice of a lemon into a tall glass, add two inches of shaved ice, two heaping teaspoonfuls of sugar and fill the glass with seltzer or Apollinaris.

TEMPERANCE PUNCH

Upon a tablespoonful of good tea pour two quarts of boiling water. In the meantime have ready the juice and peelings of three lemons and one orange in a pitcher. When the tea has steeped for five minutes, strain through a fine strainer into the pitcher. Add a cupful of sugar and cool slowly. At serving-time put into glasses with plenty of ice.

EATING AND DINING

There is an old saying to the effect that "all may eat, but ladies and gentlemen dine." The difference lies more in the preparation and manner of serving than in the food itself, and whether her evening meal is a banquet or a repast of the lunch-counter sort rests wholly with the housewife.

We pause long enough to pay our disrespects to that barbarous institution known in America as the Sunday Dinner. On six days in the week, the average business man eats a light luncheon or none at all. On the seventh day, at an unaccustomed hour, he eats a heavy meal, goes to sleep shortly afterward, and wonders why Monday is a "blue day."

Our uncivilized Sundays are responsible for our Monday morning headaches and for the gloom which, in many a household, does not wear off until Tuesday morning. If Sunday were a day of fasting instead of a day of feasting, Monday might be radiant occasionally instead of riotous or revolutionary.

We make Sunday a hard day for the women of the household, especially the servants, and the imperial liver appertaining to the Head of the Establishment balks sometimes at the strain. The American Sunday Dinner is one cause of the American Servant Problem—and everybody knows what that is.

In more than one household, a twelve or one o'clock breakfast has proved both hygienic and satisfactory. Coffee and rolls are served to those who want them at eight or nine o'clock, if they come into the dining-room. At noon the family sits down to a simple breakfast—fruit, broiled chicken, creamed potatoes, hot bread and coffee, for example. The maid has few dishes to wash, is not too tired to enjoy her afternoon off, and gets away two or three hours earlier than her less fortunate sisters. Also she remains where she is hired—which has its advantages. Only a light lunch is needed in the evening which the mistress may serve, leaving the dishes to be washed in the morning.

Owing to the aforesaid American Servant Problem an increasing number of women do their own housework—not from choice, but from stern necessity. This book is intended for the woman in a small house or apartment, who is her own cook, who earnestly desires to do her duty by her family, yet be something more than a wearied and soul-sickened drudge; who has to look after her dimes and nickels, if not her pennies, and who wants more than the weekly "afternoon off" accorded to the stronger women who undertake domestic tasks.

Simplicity—and, as a general rule, economy—has been the standard by which each recipe has been judged. All are within the capabilities of the most inexperienced cook, who is willing to follow directions, and, in the case of such variable materials as flour and eggs, trust, now and then, to her own judgment.

THIRTY-FIVE CANAPÉS

I

Cover thin circles of fried or toasted bread with chopped hard-boiled eggs, lay a curled anchovy in the centre of each piece and serve either hot or cold, garnishing with minced parsley or capers.

II

Cut thin slices of bread into fancy shapes, toast, spread with butter, and lay a curled anchovy in the centre around half a pimola. Fill the spaces with the minced whites and sifted yolks of hard-boiled eggs and border with minced capers or parsley.

III

Serve pitted olives on rounds of fried bread with an anchovy curled around each olive. Fill the space to the edge with chopped olives or rings of hard-boiled eggs. Garnish with cress.

IV

Fry small rounds of bread in clarified butter, sprinkle with grated cheese, season with salt and cayenne, and put in the oven until the cheese is melted. Fillets of anchovies may be laid on these canapés and they may be served hot or cold, garnishing with minced parsley.

V

Pound anchovies to a smooth paste with butter and season with cayenne and lemon-juice. Spread on strips of toast or bread and lay strips of anchovy on each piece. Fill the spaces between with hard-boiled eggs chopped separately.

VI

Chop watercress and pickles with the yolks of hard-boiled eggs and rub to a smooth paste with butter. Spread on strips of fried or toasted bread and lay an anchovy on each one.

VII

Slice large tomatoes, cut circles of bread to fit, and toast or fry the bread. Lay a slice of tomato on each piece, put a pimola in the centre, curl an anchovy around it and border with stiff Mayonnaise, using the pastry bag and tube. Serve ice cold.

VIII

Beat together two eggs, a tablespoonful of melted butter, a teaspoonful of anchovy sauce, and salt and cayenne to season. Add three tablespoonfuls of grated cheese and one tablespoonful of flour wet with cream. Spread thickly upon small slices of toast and bake until brown.

IX

Chop two hard-boiled eggs fine, mix to a smooth paste with melted butter, season with anchovy essence, and serve on small circles or squares of buttered toast.

X

Spread strips of toast with caviare rubbed to a smooth paste with butter, sprinkle with chopped watercress, and serve cold.

XI

Heat caviare with enough cream to moisten, spread on rounds of fried or toasted bread, and sprinkle with hard-boiled egg-yolks rubbed through a fine sieve. Garnish with cress.

XII

Spread thin rounds of toasted rye-bread with caviare, seasoned with lemon-juice. Lay a slice of hard-boiled egg on each one and serve with a garnish of parsley.

XIII

Spread thin squares of toast with caviare seasoned with lemon-juice, sprinkle with minced parsley, and border with chopped hard-boiled eggs. Garnish with lemon and parsley.

XIV

Chop fine, olives, pimentos, and cucumber pickles. Season caviare with lemon-juice and spread upon circles of fried or toasted bread. Cover with a thin layer of the chopped mixture.

XV

Spread butter upon thin round slices of rye-bread or Boston brown-bread and lay a thin slice of cucumber, which has been dipped in French dressing, on each piece. Remove the yolk from slices of hard-boiled egg, lay the ring of white on the cucumber, and fill the centre with caviare.

XVI

Season caviare with lemon-juice and spread upon rounds of toasted bread. Lay an oyster on each piece and serve on a plate with a garnish of cress and lemon.

XVII

Mix caviare to a cream with lemon-juice and spread on buttered toast cut into squares or diamonds. Garnish with hard-boiled eggs, chopped finely, and sprinkle with minced onion. Skinned and boned anchovies may be used instead of caviare.

XVIII

Heat a can of caviare with a little melted butter, season with lemon-juice and cayenne, and serve on small squares of hot buttered toast.

XIX

Fry small rounds of bread in butter, drain and cool. Chop watercress very fine, rub it to a paste with butter and spread on the toast. Sprinkle with salt and paprika, cover with caviare seasoned with lemon-juice, and serve with a garnish of cress.

XX

Spread thick rounds of fresh bread with butter and anchovy paste, cover with crab-meat, sprinkle with minced green pepper, press firmly, and serve with a garnish of cress.

XXI

Rub to a smooth paste the yolks of hard-boiled eggs and an equal quantity of skinned and boned sardines, seasoning with lemon-juice. Spread on narrow strips of buttered toast and serve either hot or cold.

XXII

Drain and skin boned sardines. Sauté in butter, season with salt, cayenne, and lemon-juice, and serve hot on small strips of buttered toast.

XXIII

Drain, skin, bone, and mash sardines. Rub to a smooth paste, moistening with melted butter and lemon-juice. Spread on small circles of bread, lay a ring of hard-boiled egg-white in the centre, fill the space with minced olives and surround with the sifted yolk. Serve with cress or parsley.

XXIV

Toast small slices of rye-bread and spread with sardines, pounded to a paste and rubbed smooth with butter. Arrange alternate rows of chopped hard-boiled egg yolks and whites, garnish with parsley and serve.

XXV

Rub boned and skinned sardines to a paste with butter and the yolks of hard-boiled eggs, seasoning with chopped pickle and parsley, lemon-juice, and mustard. Spread the paste on rounds or strips of fried bread, lay a skinned and boned sardine on each piece, heat thoroughly and serve.

XXVI

Spread rounds of fried bread with anchovy paste and cover with Mayonnaise to which has been added chopped capers, olives, and onion. Garnish with cress and serve cold.

XXVII

Fry small rounds of bread, spread with anchovy paste, lay a slice of tomato on each and serve ice cold, garnishing with cress or parsley.

XXVIII

Sprinkle rounds of fried bread with grated cheese, heat until the cheese melts, and serve very hot.

XXIX

Spread rounds of fried bread with caviare seasoned with lemon-juice, lay a slice of hard-boiled egg on each one, and sprinkle with chopped cress.

XXX

Rub chopped ham to a smooth paste, moistening with cream, milk, or melted butter. Spread on small rounds of fried bread, sprinkle with grated Parmesan cheese and cayenne, and brown in a hot oven.

XXXI

Spread small strips of bread with butter and sprinkle with salt and paprika. Cover with grated cheese, bake until the cheese softens, and serve immediately.

XXXII

Butter small rounds of toast, cover with thin slices of Swiss cheese or sprinkle with grated Swiss cheese, brown in the oven, and serve hot.

XXXIII

Spread grated cheese on small rounds of bread seasoned with salt and cayenne, and bake until the cheese is melted. The bread may be spread with French mustard before the cheese is put on.

XXXIV

Rub two chicken livers to a smooth paste with butter, seasoning with salt and paprika, spread on rounds of fried bread, and serve hot.

XXXV

Mix equal quantities of minced cooked chicken, ham, or tongue with a little very thick Cream Sauce. Season with curry-powder and lemon-juice. Spread on small rounds of toast and serve hot, or make sandwiches of toast with the mixture between.

ONE HUNDRED SIMPLE SOUPS

BEEF SOUPS
BARLEY SOUP
Cook one cupful of barley slowly until soft. Drain, and add to beef stock made according to any preferred method. Serve very hot.
BLACK BEAN SOUP
Soak two cupfuls of black beans in cold water over night. In the morning, drain, and cover with fresh boiling water. Boil until tender, add four cupfuls of beef stock, and two cupfuls of boiling water. Rub through a fine sieve, return to the fire, and bring to the boil. Season with salt, pepper, and a wineglassful of sherry. Cut into slices one lemon, and two hard-boiled eggs. Put into a tureen, pour the hot soup over, and serve.
BOSTON SUMMER SOUP
Cook together one cupful of peas and one cupful of tomatoes. Rub through a sieve, and add to four cupfuls of beef stock. Thicken with two tablespoonfuls of cornstarch rubbed smooth in a little cold stock. Simmer fifteen minutes, add two tablespoonfuls of butter and three tablespoonfuls of cooked peas. Season with salt and pepper, reheat and serve.
CREOLE SOUP
Half a can of tomatoes, three tablespoonfuls of rice, one half can of okra, and a red pepper, added to two quarts of beef stock. Simmer until the rice is cooked. Blend together two tablespoonfuls of flour, mix with a little cold stock, pour into the soup, and stir until it thickens. Season with salt and serve at once.
ENGLISH SPINACH SOUP
Cook half a peck of spinach, rub through a fine sieve, add six cupfuls of strong beef stock, season with salt, pepper, sugar, and mace, thicken with butter and flour, bring to the boil, and serve immediately.
ENGLISH TOMATO SOUP
Add one can of tomatoes to four cupfuls of beef stock, and simmer together for an hour, with a small onion cut fine. Rub through a sieve, reheat, season with salt, pepper, and sugar, and thicken with a tablespoonful of butter, rubbed smooth with a tablespoonful of flour, boiled in the soup, while stirring. When thick, add three tablespoonfuls of cold boiled rice, reheat, and serve with croutons.
ITALIAN ONION SOUP WITH CHEESE

Slice four large onions very thin, fry brown in butter, and add to four cupfuls of beef stock. Put into an earthen pot and arrange slices of toast on top, liberally sprinkled with grated Parmesan cheese. Serve from the dish with one slice of toast for each person.

JULIENNE SOUP

Cut into thin, match-like strips carrots, turnips, and celery, having half a cupful of each. Cover with boiling water, season with salt and pepper, and cook until soft. Add to two quarts of boiling beef stock.

SOUP OF MIXED VEGETABLES

One cupful each of chopped onion, carrot, celery, and tomatoes; one-half cupful each of chopped turnip, parsnip, and cabbage. Fry the onions and carrot in a little butter, then add four cupfuls of boiling water and four cupfuls of beef stock. Simmer until the vegetables are tender. Season with salt, pepper, sugar, and minced parsley.

NOODLE AND TOMATO SOUP

Add a five-cent can of tomato paste to three pints of boiling beef stock. Season to taste, and cook in it noodles made according to directions given elsewhere. Serve hot with grated Parmesan cheese.

QUICK BEEF SOUP

Cook together in two quarts of water for half an hour, half an onion, three stalks of celery, and a sliced carrot. Season with salt, pepper, and mace. Strain, and add to the water two tablespoonfuls of extract of beef. Stir until dissolved, reheat and serve.

RICE AND CURRY SOUP

Melt in a saucepan two tablespoonfuls of butter, add a chopped onion, and a tablespoonful of chopped raw ham. Fry for three minutes. Add one tablespoonful of curry powder and two tablespoonfuls of flour. Mix thoroughly, add three quarts of beef stock, boil for one hour, skim, and press through a fine strainer into another saucepan. Add a pint of rice which has been cooked in stock, reheat, skim, and serve.

SPANISH ONION SOUP

Chop fine five onions and fry brown in butter, adding a teaspoonful of sugar. When brown, pour over eight cupfuls of hot beef stock. Add a bay leaf, half a dozen pepper-corns, and a tablespoonful of minced parsley. Simmer fifteen minutes, strain, and serve with dice of fried or toasted bread.

VEAL SOUP

Put a knuckle of veal into three quarts of cold water, with a teaspoonful of salt, and a tablespoonful of uncooked rice. Simmer gently for four hours, take from the fire, and strain through a colander. Beat the yolk of one egg with a cupful of milk, add a teaspoonful of butter, and strain the hot soup upon it, stirring constantly. Pour into the tureen and serve immediately.

WREXHAM SOUP

One pound of lean beef chopped fine. Peel and slice one large carrot, one large turnip, six small onions, a stalk of celery, and two cupfuls of tomatoes. Tie up in a muslin cloth a small bunch of parsley, six cloves, six pepper-corns, and a sprig of thyme. Put all these ingredients into a bean-pot, with a tablespoonful of salt, a teaspoonful of sugar and a pinch of pepper. Cover with five pints of cold water, and bake very slowly for five hours. Take out the bag of spices, and serve the soup with croutons.

BISQUES AND PURÉES

BISQUE OF CLAMS

Reheat four cupfuls of veal stock, and thicken with two tablespoonfuls of butter, blended with two tablespoonfuls of flour, and rubbed smooth in the stock, while boiling. Add a small can of minced clams with their liquor, or twenty-five clams, chopped very fine. Season to taste, add two cupfuls of boiling cream, and serve immediately.

CRAB AND TOMATO BISQUE

Blend together two tablespoonfuls each of butter and flour. Add one quart of cold milk, and cook slowly until it thickens, stirring constantly. Add one cupful of cooked crab meat, two cupfuls of stewed and strained tomatoes, a pinch of soda, and salt and pepper to season. Boil up once and serve.

PURÉE OF ASPARAGUS

Cut the tops from two bunches of asparagus, and set aside. Boil the stalks in salted water until tender, and rub through a sieve. Add the pulp to three pints of boiling beef stock, and season with salt, pepper, and butter. Simmer fifteen or twenty minutes. Stir in three tablespoonfuls of cream, strain the soup, add the cooked asparagus tips, and serve. This soup may be thickened if desired.

PURÉE OF GREEN PEAS

Boil four cupfuls of green peas in salted water with an onion, a small bunch of parsley, and two sprigs of mint. Rub through a colander and reheat. Add a cupful of veal stock, season with salt, pepper, and sugar, and thicken with one tablespoonful of butter blended with one tablespoonful of flour, and rubbed smooth in the soup, while boiling. Serve with croutons.

PURÉE OF KIDNEY BEANS

Soak over night two cupfuls of red kidney beans. Drain, and cook slowly until very soft in enough beef stock to cover. Rub through a coarse sieve. Add one-half cupful of salt pork, cut into dice and fried until brown and crisp, two onions, one carrot, and a tablespoonful of powdered sweet herbs. Add four cupfuls of beef stock, and simmer for an hour. Strain, add two tablespoonfuls of sherry or claret, reheat, and serve.

PURÉE OF PEAS AND RICE

Rub through a sieve one cupful of cooked peas, and one cupful of cold boiled rice. Mix with six cupfuls of boiling beef stock, thicken with butter and flour, according to directions previously given, and serve very hot.

PURÉE OF TOMATOES

Boil together for half an hour one can of tomatoes, and one large onion, chopped fine. Run through a sieve, return to the fire, and season with pepper, salt, and sugar. Blend together two tablespoonfuls of butter, and one tablespoonful of flour. Add two cupfuls of cold milk, and cook until smooth and thick, stirring constantly. Add the tomatoes and a pinch of soda. Reheat, add half a cupful of cracker crumbs, and serve immediately.

PURÉE OF TOMATOES AND MACARONI

Cook together for an hour, one can of tomatoes, a sprig of parsley, a teaspoonful of celery seed, a teaspoonful of sugar, a blade of mace, a bay-leaf, and a small onion chopped fine. Rub through a coarse sieve, add two cupfuls of beef stock, season with salt and pepper, and thicken with one tablespoonful each of butter and flour, rubbed together and boiled in soup, while stirring. When thickened add one cupful of cooked macaroni, cut into small bits.

CHICKEN SOUPS

CHICKEN BOUILLON

Cut up a chicken, cover with cold water, add a small onion sliced, a stalk of celery cut fine, and a small bunch of parsley. Simmer until the meat falls from the bones, strain through cheese-cloth, cool, skim, reheat, season with salt and pepper, and serve in cups.

CHICKEN SOUP

Select an old fowl and cut it in pieces. Put into the soup-kettle, with a sliced carrot, two onions, two cloves, and water to cover. Simmer for three or four hours, and strain. Reheat the liquor, add one cupful each of washed rice and meat of the chicken, a small turnip chopped, and a blade of mace. Simmer for three hours, rub through a sieve, season to taste, and serve.

CHICKEN AND TOMATO SOUP

Cut up a chicken, fry in butter with an onion, and a slice of ham chopped fine. Add two quarts of beef stock, two cupfuls of water, a small bunch of parsley, a tablespoonful of powdered sweet herbs, and salt and pepper to season. Add a can of tomatoes and cook until the meat falls from the bones. Remove the bones, chop the meat fine, reheat, and serve.

CREAM OF CHICKEN

Melt one tablespoonful of butter, add two tablespoonfuls of flour, and, when thoroughly blended, three cupfuls of chicken stock. Season to taste, add one cupful of boiling cream, and serve.

CREAM OF CHICKEN AND ASPARAGUS

Prepare Cream of Chicken according to directions given above, and add one cupful of cooked asparagus, which has been rubbed through a sieve. Add the asparagus tops, cooked separately, and serve with unsweetened whipped cream.

CREAM OF CHICKEN AND BARLEY

Prepare Cream of Chicken according to directions given above, and add one cupful of barley which has been cooked in chicken stock. Add more cream if too thick.

CREAM OF CHICKEN AND CELERY

Chop fine one head of celery, and boil until soft in four cupfuls of chicken stock. Rub through a sieve, reheat, thicken with two tablespoonfuls each of butter and flour, boiled in the soup, while stirring, season to taste, add two cupfuls of boiling cream, and serve.

CREAM OF CHICKEN AND NOODLES

Prepare Cream of Chicken according to directions given above, and add one cupful of cooked noodles. Season with grated Parmesan cheese.

CREAM OF CHICKEN AND OYSTERS

Prepare Cream of Chicken according to directions given above, and add one cupful of cooked oysters with their liquor. Season with minced parsley and lemon-juice.

CREAM OF CHICKEN AND SAGO

Prepare Cream of Chicken according to directions given above, and add one cupful of sago which has been cooked in chicken stock. Dilute with boiling cream if too thick, and serve with whipped cream in each plate.

CREAM OF CHICKEN AND VERMICELLI

Prepare Cream of Chicken according to directions given above, and add one cupful of broken vermicelli, which has been cooked in chicken stock. Season with minced parsley, and grated Parmesan cheese.

CREAM CHICKEN BOUILLON

Prepare Cream of Chicken according to directions given above, thicken with one tablespoonful each of butter and flour, add one cupful of boiling cream, and serve in cups with a tablespoonful of unsweetened whipped cream on each cup.

CREOLE CHICKEN GUMBO

Cut up a chicken, and fry brown in ham or bacon fat. Cover with three quarts of cold water, and boil until the chicken is tender. Add the corn cut from three large ears, or half a can of corn, two sliced tomatoes, two potatoes cut into dice, six pods of okra, and half a cupful of cold boiled ham chopped fine. Boil until the chicken falls to pieces, take out the bones, and serve.

EGG AND CHICKEN SOUP

Reheat six cupfuls of chicken stock, add half a cupful of cold boiled rice, and two hard-boiled eggs, chopped fine. Thicken with one tablespoonful each of butter and flour, rubbed smooth in the boiling soup, season with salt, pepper, and minced parsley, and serve.

GERMAN CHICKEN SOUP

Reheat six cupfuls of chicken stock, add one cupful of cooked tapioca, and one cupful of milk. Season to taste. Thicken with the yolks of two eggs beaten smooth with one cupful of cream, stir until eggs are cooked, and pour the hot soup over the whites of the eggs, beaten to a stiff froth.

GIBLET SOUP

Reheat four cupfuls of chicken stock. Add the finely minced cooked giblets of two chickens, and salt, pepper, and parsley to season. Thicken with two tablespoonfuls each of butter and browned flour, rubbed smooth in the boiling soup. Add two hard-boiled eggs, finely chopped, and serve.

HUNGARIAN CHICKEN SOUP

Chop fine, two cupfuls of cold roast chicken. Fry in butter, dredge with flour, add four cupfuls of chicken stock, one cupful of white wine, a bay-leaf, a sprig of thyme, and a small bunch of parsley. Simmer for an hour, rub through a sieve, and reheat. Add one-half cupful of chicken cut into dice, a shredded green pepper, which has been fried in butter, and a cupful of barley which has been cooked in chicken stock. Season to taste, and serve.

JELLIED CHICKEN BOUILLON

Cut up a large chicken and break the bones. Cover with cold water, and simmer for four hours. Cool, skim, and strain, season to taste, reheat, and add one-half package of gelatine, dissolved in cold water, for each quart of soup. Stir until the gelatine is thoroughly mixed with the hot liquid, strain through cheese-cloth, pour into cups, and set on ice.

MOCK CHICKEN GUMBO

Chop fine a quarter of a pound of cold cooked ham, and fry in butter with an onion. Add a can of chicken, half a cupful of stewed tomatoes, a can of okra, one cupful of chicken stock, and boiling water to cover. Boil for fifteen minutes, and thicken with a tablespoonful each of butter and flour, blended with a little cold stock. Season to taste, and serve with boiled rice.

CREAM SOUPS

CREAM OF ASPARAGUS

Prepare according to directions given for Cream of Celery, using two cupfuls of asparagus. Add a tablespoonful of whipped cream and a few of the cooked asparagus tops to each plate of soup.

CREAM OF BARLEY

Prepare according to directions given for Cream of Celery, using one cupful of cooked barley and an extra cupful of milk. Season with curry powder, celery salt, and minced parsley.

CREAM OF CELERY

Melt one-fourth of a cupful of butter, and add one-fourth of a cupful of flour. When thoroughly blended, add two cupfuls of cold milk, cook and stir until thick. Cook a large head of celery, cut fine, in boiling water until tender, and rub through a sieve. Measure the pulp and add enough of the water in which it was cooked to make two cupfuls. Add to the thickened milk, season with salt and pepper, and if too thick, dilute with boiling milk, or stock, to the proper consistency.

CREAM OF CLAMS

Prepare according to directions given above, using two cupfuls of minced clams with their liquor instead of the celery.

CREAM OF CORN AND TOMATO

Prepare according to directions given above, using one cupful each of corn and tomato pulp.

CREAM OF CRABS

Prepare according to directions given above, using two cupfuls of cooked crab meat. Season with lemon-juice and sherry.

CREAM OF MUSHROOMS

Prepare according to directions given above, using either fresh or canned mushrooms. Season with celery salt and parsley.

CREAM OF OYSTERS

Prepare according to directions given above, using two cupfuls of minced oysters with their liquor. Season with minced parsley.

CREAM OF PEAS

Prepare according to directions given above, using fresh or canned peas and enough of the water in which they were boiled to make two cupfuls. Put a tablespoonful of whipped cream into each plate.

CREAM OF TOMATO

Prepare according to directions given above, using two cupfuls of stewed tomatoes, and a small pinch of soda. Season with minced parsley and grated onion.

CREAM OF VERMICELLI

Prepare according to directions given above, using one cupful of cooked vermicelli, and an extra cupful of milk. Season with celery salt, curry powder, grated onion, and minced parsley.

FISH SOUPS

CLAM BROTH

Scrub the clams in cold water. Place over the fire in an iron kettle, and heat until the shells open. Strain the broth through two thicknesses of cheese-cloth, season to taste, and serve.

CLAM BOUILLON

Prepare according to directions elsewhere given for Oyster Bouillon, cooking a chopped onion and a bay-leaf with the clams.

CREAM CLAM BOUILLON

Prepare Clam Bouillon according to directions given above, and add one pint of boiling cream just before serving. Serve in cups, with whipped cream.

CLAM SOUP

Reheat one quart of clam broth, season with parsley, salt, red pepper, and grated onion. Add one cupful and a half of minced clams, and thicken with one tablespoonful of butter and two tablespoonfuls of flour, blended with a little cold broth. Stir while cooking. Add one pint of boiling cream, and serve.

CLAM AND OYSTER SOUP

Chop a pint of oysters. Heat with their liquor, add a pint can of minced clams, and one quart of milk. Thicken with two tablespoonfuls each of butter and flour, rubbed smooth in a little cold milk, season with salt and pepper, minced parsley, powdered mace, and grated onion. Serve with crackers.

CRAB GUMBO

Melt one tablespoonful each of butter and lard, add a minced onion, a clove of garlic, chopped fine, half a pound of minced raw veal or beef, half a cupful of chopped ham, a bay-leaf, and a small red pepper. Dredge with flour, add a quart of water, simmer for two hours, and strain. To the strained liquor add the meat of six crabs, one cupful each of rice and okra, and another quart of water. Simmer for an hour, adding more water if necessary, and serve without straining.

FRENCH FISH SOUP

Thicken three quarts of fish stock with three tablespoonfuls each of butter and flour. Stir while cooking. Add a tablespoonful of minced parsley, two wineglassfuls of sherry, a pinch of powdered mace, a grating of nutmeg, and white and red pepper to season. Add one pint each of cooked oysters and scallops, reheat, and serve immediately with croutons.

GERMAN FISH SOUP

Chop fine four onions, and fry brown in olive-oil. Add two cupfuls of canned tomatoes, three bay-leaves, a tablespoonful of powdered sweet herbs, a bunch of parsley, pepper and salt to season, and six cupfuls of stock. Boil for thirty minutes, rub through a sieve, and reheat. Add six small slices of fish, and simmer until the fish is firm. Season with curry powder, add a wineglassful of white wine, and thicken with four tablespoonfuls of flour rubbed smooth in a little cold stock. Serve with croutons.

OYSTER BOUILLON

Bring to the boil in their own liquor a quart of oysters. Skim out the oysters, chop fine, and return to the liquor. Add a quart of water, a teaspoonful of celery seed, and a tablespoonful of butter. Simmer for half an hour, strain through cheese-cloth, season with salt and pepper, and serve at once.

OYSTER SOUP

Scald one quart of oysters in their own liquor. Skim out the oysters, and set aside. Add one cupful of cream to the liquor, and three cupfuls of milk. Thicken with one tablespoonful of butter and one of flour, blended and rubbed smooth with a little cold milk. Stir while cooking. Add the oysters, season to taste, and pour, boiling hot, over the yolks of four eggs, well-beaten.

CREOLE OYSTER GUMBO

Fry a sliced Spanish onion brown in olive-oil, add a tablespoonful of flour, a chopped sweet pepper, and a pint of okra. Simmer for fifteen minutes, add one hundred oysters, with their liquor, and a tablespoonful of filè powder. Cook until the oysters ruffle, and serve with boiled rice. The Gumbo filè powder comes in bottles, and is sold by all first-class grocers.

OYSTER AND VEAL SOUP

Reheat two quarts of veal stock, season with salt, pepper, and celery salt, and add one quart of oysters, with their liquor. Cook until the edges of the oysters curl, and thicken with one tablespoonful each of butter and flour, cooked while stirring with a cupful of milk. Season with minced parsley, and serve with crackers.

SOUTHERN OYSTER SOUP

Drain the liquor from fifty oysters, add to it two cupfuls of cold water, and bring to the boil. Season with salt, pepper, and butter, and add two cupfuls of milk. Thicken with one tablespoonful of cornstarch, rubbed smooth in a little cold milk, stir while cooking, add the oysters, cook until the edges ruffle, and serve immediately.

SALMON SOUP

Simmer for fifteen minutes in boiling water either a pound can of salmon or a pound of the fresh fish. Rub through a sieve, and set aside. Bring to the boil two cupfuls each of milk and veal stock, thicken with one tablespoonful of butter and two of flour, stir while cooking, season with salt and pepper, add the salmon, reheat, and serve.

SPANISH SALMON SOUP

Cook together a quart of stock, a sliced onion, and half a can of salmon. Rub through a sieve, add a quart of boiling milk, season with salt, pepper, minced parsley, and celery salt, thicken with butter and flour, and serve with whipped cream.

SHRIMP SOUP

Chop fine two carrots and an onion. Fry brown in butter, with a tablespoonful of sugar, then add a quart of water, a sprig of thyme, two bay-leaves, four cloves, and two cans of shrimps. Simmer until the carrot and onions are soft. Rub through a sieve, reheat, add half a glassful of white wine, and serve with croutons.

FRENCH CREAM OF SHRIMPS

Chop fine two cans of shrimps, fry in butter, add a slice of stale bread, three anchovies, half a cupful of boiled rice, a sliced onion, and two quarts of veal stock. Simmer for two hours, rub through a sieve, season with salt and pepper, add a tablespoonful of sherry and serve hot.

SCALLOP STEW

Parboil one quart of scallops. Boil one quart of milk, season with butter, pepper, and salt, add the parboiled scallops, and one-half cupful of cracker crumbs. Reheat and serve.

HOFFMAN HOUSE CLAM CHOWDER

Chop fine one dozen large clams, one quart of tomatoes, and six large potatoes. Add one quart of milk, a tablespoonful of minced parsley, and the juice of the clams. Cook for forty-five minutes and add six crackers pounded fine. Season with pepper and serve.

CREOLE CORN CHOWDER

Fry brown in butter four large onions. Add five tomatoes, two sweet green peppers shredded, and two cupfuls of corn cut from the cob, or its equivalent of canned corn. Add boiling water to cover, season with salt, pepper, and sugar, and cook until the vegetables are done.

FRUIT SOUPS

CHERRY SOUP

Stone four cupfuls of sour cherries. Cover with a quart of cold water and bring to the boil. Add half a cupful of sugar, and when the cherries are soft, rub through a colander and return to the fire. Thicken with one tablespoonful of arrowroot, rubbed smooth with a little cold water. Bring to the boil once more, while stirring and when sufficiently thick take from the fire. Add the juice of half a lemon and serve very cold in sherbet cups with cracked ice.

CURRANT SOUP

Prepare according to directions given for Cherry Soup using currants instead of cherries.

GOOSEBERRY SOUP

Prepare according to directions for Cherry Soup, using gooseberries instead of cherries.

PRUNE SOUP

Soak one-half cupful of sago for an hour in cold water to cover. Add one quart of cold water and cook in a double boiler until transparent. Cook together, in water sufficient to cover, one cupful of soaked prunes, one-half cupful of soaked raisins, and one-half cupful of sugar. When the sago is clear, add the cooked fruit, and one-half cupful of currant-juice. Serve hot with croutons.

RAISIN AND SAGO SOUP

Simmer until transparent, in four cupfuls of water, two tablespoonfuls of well-washed pearl sago, adding a pinch of salt, and two inches of stick cinnamon. When the sago is done, take out the cinnamon, add one-half cupful of seeded and chopped raisins, and sugar to taste. Just before serving, add one cupful of orange-juice.

RASPBERRY AND CURRANT SOUP

Bring to the boil two cupfuls each of raspberry- and currant-juice. Sweeten to taste, thicken with three teaspoonfuls of arrowroot rubbed smooth in a little cold water, add one teaspoonful of sherry, and cool.

STRAWBERRY SOUP

Boil in six cupfuls of water one-half cupful of sago and one-half cupful of currant-juice. When the sago is transparent, add two cupfuls of strawberries and sugar to taste. Simmer for fifteen minutes, and serve cold.

MUTTON SOUPS

ASPARAGUS SOUP

Add to six cupfuls of mutton stock one cupful of cooked asparagus tips and half a cupful of parboiled sweet green peppers cut in shreds. Thicken with egg yolks and cream, if desired.

BAKED MUTTON SOUP

Arrange in an earthen jar half a dozen cold boiled potatoes, a sliced onion, a sliced turnip, three sliced tomatoes, a grated carrot, a cupful of green peas, and a cupful of cold boiled rice. Add two tablespoonfuls of butter, season with salt, pepper, and sweet herbs, and cover with cold mutton broth. Cover the jar tightly, and bake for two hours in a slow oven.

CLEAR MUTTON BROTH

Cut into bits one pound of lean mutton and break the bones. Cover with four cupfuls of cold water, and bring slowly to the boil. Add a large onion cut fine, and simmer until the meat is in rags. Strain, cool quickly, and when cold remove the fat. Return to the fire, season with salt, pepper, and curry powder, and add two tablespoonfuls of well-washed rice. Simmer until the rice is done and serve with croutons.

LAMB SOUP

Cut the breast of lamb into small pieces, and fry brown with an onion in butter. Dredge with flour and curry powder, add three quarts of boiling mutton broth, and half a cupful of raw ham chopped fine. Simmer until the meat falls from the bone. Take out the bones, and strain the soup, pressing the meat through a coarse sieve. Reheat, and thicken with the yolks of three eggs, beaten smooth with half a cupful of cream. Serve with dice of fried or toasted bread.

MUTTON AND CARROT SOUP

Cover the bones of cold roast mutton with two quarts of cold water. Add an onion which has been sliced and fried brown in butter, a potato and a turnip, and six medium-sized carrots cut fine. Simmer until the vegetables are tender, remove the bones, and strain through a sieve. Reheat, season, and thicken with one tablespoonful of flour and one of butter. Rub smooth with a little of the soup. Just before serving, add a cupful of hot cream.

NOODLE AND TOMATO SOUP

Cook a can of tomatoes for an hour in three quarts of mutton stock. Strain, reheat, season to taste, and cook a handful of noodles in the soup until tender. Serve with grated Parmesan cheese.

QUICK MUTTON SOUP

Chop together a pound of lean mutton and a small turnip, a carrot, a stalk of celery, and an onion. Cover with six cupfuls of cold water, bring to the boil, skim, and simmer forty-five minutes. Season with salt, pepper, and minced parsley, and serve with croutons.

VEAL SOUPS

AUSTRIAN VEAL SOUP

Reheat two quarts of veal stock and add one cupful each of cooked green peas and diced carrots. Thicken with butter and flour according to directions previously given.

CHIFFONADE SOUP

Chop fine two heads of lettuce, and fry brown in butter with a sliced onion. Season with salt and pepper, add six cupfuls of veal stock and one and one-half cupfuls each of peas, string beans, and asparagus tips. Simmer for forty minutes, and serve with croutons.

GREEN-PEA SOUP WITH RICE

Boil three pints of green peas with a carrot and an onion in two quarts of veal stock. Remove the onion and carrot and strain the soup through a fine sieve. Reheat, skim, season with salt, pepper, and sugar, add two cupfuls of boiled rice, and two teaspoonfuls of butter. Bring to the boil and serve.

ITALIAN VEAL SOUP

Cover a large knuckle of veal with three quarts of cold water, and simmer for three hours, skimming often. Strain, add a bay-leaf, a carrot, an onion, a turnip, a blade of mace, two cloves, a stalk of celery, and a small bunch of parsley. Boil for an hour, strain, and cool. When it has jellied, measure the jelly, and reheat with an equal amount of cream. Serve with dice of fried bread.

QUICK TOMATO SOUP

Add two cupfuls of stewed tomato to four cupfuls of veal stock. Strain, season to taste, and thicken with one tablespoonful each of butter and flour blended and cooked until thick in a little cold stock.

SOUP À LA DUCHESSE

Fry in butter two slices of carrot and two slices of onion. Add two blades of mace, and four cupfuls of veal stock. Simmer half an hour, strain, and add two cupfuls of boiling milk. Thicken with one tablespoonful of butter and two of flour, blended and cooked until thick with a little of the soup, season with salt and pepper, add one-half cupful of grated cheese, reheat, and serve with croutons.

SPRING SOUP

Cook in veal stock four young carrots, four young turnips, and two leeks cut fine. Add sufficient veal stock to make the desired quantity of soup, and one cupful of fresh green peas. Boil for fifteen minutes, season to taste, and serve.

VEAL BROTH

Break up three pounds of the neck of veal, cover with three quarts of cold water, add an onion and a turnip cut fine, and a small bunch of parsley. Simmer for three hours, take out the bones, and press the rest through a sieve. Cool, skim, and reheat. Add one cupful of washed rice, and simmer until the rice is done. Serve with croutons.

VEGETABLE SOUP

Put a knuckle of veal into four quarts of water, with a tablespoonful of salt and a pod of red pepper. Simmer for three hours, skimming as needed. Add one cupful of cabbage cut fine, two cupfuls of diced potatoes, a minced carrot, three large onions, and a head of celery cut fine. Simmer until the vegetables are done.

MISCELLANEOUS SOUPS

I

Cut up three pounds of the shin of beef, and break the bones. Cover with three quarts of cold water, add half a pound of lean ham, a turnip, an onion, a carrot, a quarter of a cabbage, and three stalks of celery, all cut fine. Simmer until the meat falls from the bones, skimming when necessary. Strain, cool, skim, reheat, and serve with dice of fried bread.

II

Put into a soup-kettle the bones and trimmings of a cold roast turkey, with a quarter of a pound of lean ham. Cover with cold water. Add a chopped onion, a stalk of celery, a tablespoonful of powdered sweet herbs, and pepper and salt to season. Simmer until the meat is in rags, strain, reheat, add half a can of corn, and a little of the turkey stuffing.

III

Take the bone of a rib roast of beef, the trimmings of beef steak, and the bones and trimmings of a cold turkey or chicken. Cover with four quarts of cold water, add two carrots, three turnips, and an onion, all cut fine, six cloves, and pepper and salt to season. Simmer for four hours, take out the bones, rub through a coarse sieve, cool, skim, and reheat. Thicken with one tablespoonful each of butter and flour, blended together and rubbed smooth with a little of the soup, season to taste, and serve with croutons.

IV

Break up a knuckle of veal, add a pound of lean ham cut fine, and a tablespoonful of powdered sweet herbs. Cover with cold water, simmer for five hours, cool, skim, reheat, season, and strain. Add a pinch of ground mace, and one-quarter of a pound of broken vermicelli, which has been cooked until tender in salted water. Serve with grated Parmesan cheese.

V

Break up a beef marrow bone, and cover with cold water. Add half a carrot, two stalks of celery, and an onion, all chopped fine. Simmer until the vegetables are very soft, take out the bone, cool, skim, rub through a sieve, and reheat. Add one cupful of cold mashed potato, a tablespoonful of minced parsley, a tablespoonful of butter, a pinch of soda, and one teaspoonful of cornstarch rubbed smooth in a cupful of cold water. Cook and stir until it thickens, and serve immediately with croutons.

VI

Chop fine two pounds of lean beef, cover with cold water, simmer until tender, cool, skim, and reheat. Add one cupful of sherry, two tablespoonfuls of made mustard, a teaspoonful of Worcestershire sauce, and a grating of nutmeg. Thicken with two tablespoonfuls of butter, blended with one tablespoonful of flour, and rubbed smooth with a little of the soup. Stir while cooking. Add one cupful of boiling cream, season to taste, and serve.

FIFTY WAYS TO COOK SHELL-FISH

CLAMS

CLAMS À LA MARQUISE

Cook a quart of opened clams with a cupful of white stock, a tablespoonful of butter, and pepper and mace to season. Skim out, drain, and slice the clams. In another saucepan blend together a teaspoonful each of butter and flour, add one cupful of the liquid, cook and stir for five minutes. Thicken with the yolks of two eggs, add the clams, and reheat. Fill small individual dishes with the mixture, sprinkle with crumbs, dot with butter, and bake until brown. Sprinkle with lemon-juice just before serving.

CLAMS IN THE CHAFING-DISH

Put a tablespoonful of butter in the blazer and when it froths add a green pepper and a very small onion, both chopped fine. Cook for five minutes. Add one-half cupful of clam-juice and season with red pepper. Add one cupful of clams finely chopped or one small can of minced clams, cook five minutes longer, and pour over hot buttered toast.

CLAM COCKTAIL

Put a dozen small clams into a cold bowl and pour over them a teaspoonful each of Worcestershire sauce, vinegar, lemon-juice, tomato catsup, and horseradish. Add a little salt, and a few drops of tabasco sauce. Serve very cold in small glasses.

CREAMED CLAMS

Chop fine two dozen hard clams. Make smooth in a saucepan two small spoonfuls each of butter and flour. When they cook through, add the clams and one-half cupful of the juice. Season with red pepper, simmer for ten minutes, then add the thickening and half a cupful of cream. Boil up once and serve.

CONNECTICUT CLAM PIE

Fill a buttered baking-dish with alternate layers of minced clams and thin slices of boiled potatoes, dredging each layer of clams with flour. Season with salt, pepper, grated onion, and minced parsley. When the dish is full, pour in one cupful of clam-juice, add three tablespoonfuls of strained tomato, cover with a pastry crust, and bake brown in a quick oven.

DEVILLED CLAMS

Chop fine two dozen clams, removing the hard parts. Mix with half the quantity of bread crumbs, a teaspoonful each of grated onion and parsley, and three tablespoonfuls of melted butter. Season highly with salt and pepper, and add a few drops of Worcestershire sauce. Put into buttered clam-shells, cover with crumbs, dot with butter, and bake until brown.

ESCALLOPED CLAMS

Clean the clams, scrub thoroughly, and heat until they open. Drain carefully. Strain the juice through linen and save a cupful of it. To one pint of clams allow one cupful of clam-juice, one cupful of milk, and two cupfuls of crumbs. Arrange the clams and crumbs in alternate layers in a baking-dish, seasoning with pepper and dots of butter, and having crumbs and butter on top. Pour over the hot liquid and bake in a brisk oven.

CRABS

BAKED CRABS

Butter a baking-pan and put a layer of seasoned crab meat in the bottom. Add a layer of finely chopped cooked ham, then a layer of crumbs. Dot with butter and repeat until the dish is full, having crumbs and butter on top. Add sufficient stock to moisten, and bake for half an hour in a moderate oven.

BAKED SOFT-SHELL CRABS

Clean the crabs, season with salt and pepper, dip in melted butter, and sprinkle thickly with dry bread-crumbs. Put into a dripping-pan and put into a very hot oven for five minutes. Serve with Tartar Sauce.

BROILED SOFT-SHELL CRABS

Clean carefully, dip into melted butter, season with pepper and salt, and broil. Serve on toast with melted butter and lemon-juice.

CRABS À LA CRÉOLE

Melt one tablespoonful of butter, add a clove of garlic, a sweet pepper, and a small onion chopped fine, one cupful of tomatoes, and salt and pepper to season. Cook for ten minutes, add one cupful of cooked crab meat, reheat, and serve on toast.

CRABS À LA ST. LAURENCE

To one and one-half cupfuls of minced cooked crab meat, add one cupful of white stock, one tablespoonful of sherry, one tablespoonful of grated cheese, and salt and pepper to season. Cook for ten minutes, pour over buttered toast, and sprinkle thickly with grated cheese. Put into a very hot oven until the cheese melts, and serve at once.

CRABS BAKED IN SHELLS

Chop fine two cupfuls of crab meat. Season with salt, red pepper, grated onion, mushroom catsup, lemon-juice, and a pinch of ginger. Heat with a tablespoonful of butter and half a cupful of stock until the liquid is nearly absorbed. Butter the empty shells, fill with the mixture, cover with crumbs, dot with butter, and brown in the oven.

CRAB CROQUETTES

Chop fine two cupfuls of boiled crab meat. Season with salt, pepper, and melted butter. Add half a cupful of cream and enough crumbs to make very stiff. Add one egg well-beaten, heat for a moment, and cool. Shape into croquettes, dip in egg and crumbs, and fry in deep fat.

DEVILLED CRABS

Melt one tablespoonful of butter, add one tablespoonful of flour, and cook thoroughly. Add one cupful of cream and cook until thick, stirring constantly. Season with salt, red pepper, and grated onion. Add two cupfuls of crab meat and two eggs well-beaten. Heat until it begins to thicken, then cool. Fill the crab-shells with the mixture, brush with beaten egg, cover with crumbs, dot with butter, and brown in the oven, or omit the butter and fry in deep fat.

CRAB FARCI WITH TOMATO SAUCE

Mix one cupful of cooked crab meat with half the quantity of bread-crumbs. Moisten with well-seasoned beef stock, season with salt, pepper, mustard, and melted butter, and add one-half cupful or more of stewed and strained tomato, to which a little chopped garlic and onion have been added. Fill the crab shells, cover with crumbs, dot with butter, and brown in the oven.

CRAB FRICASSEE

Prepare according to directions given for Creamed Crabs. Season with lemon-juice and add a pinch of soda dissolved in a little cream. Add the yolks of three eggs well-beaten just before serving.

FRIED SOFT-SHELL CRABS

Clean carefully, dip in egg and crumbs, and fry in deep fat. Drain on brown paper and serve with Tartar Sauce.

STUFFED CRABS

Boil large crabs. Take out the meat and rub the shells with oil. Add to the meat one-third the quantity of grated bread-crumbs and one chopped hard-boiled egg for each crab. Season with salt, paprika, grated nutmeg, and lemon-juice, and make to a paste with melted butter or cream. Fill the shells, cover with crumbs, dot with butter, and brown in the oven.

LOBSTER

BROILED LOBSTER

Split a boiled lobster lengthwise, rub the cut surface with soft butter, and broil with a slow fire.

BROWN LOBSTER CURRY

Melt three tablespoonfuls of butter and fry in it two small onions chopped fine. Dredge with one tablespoonful of flour and cook until brown. Add two cupfuls of stock, salt and pepper to season, the juice of a lemon, and one tablespoonful of curry powder rubbed smooth with a little cold water. Cook until thick, add the meat of a boiled lobster, reheat, and serve with boiled rice and ice-cold bananas.

DEVILLED LOBSTER

Pick out the meat from a boiled lobster, reserving the coral, and season with salt, mustard, cayenne, and mushroom catsup. Put into a buttered saucepan and heat thoroughly, adding enough hot water to keep the mixture from burning. Rub the coral smooth with the liquor, mix with a tablespoonful of melted butter, add to the lobster, keep hot five minutes longer, and serve.

ESCALLOPED LOBSTER

Cover the bottom of a baking-dish with fine bread-crumbs. Put in a layer of lobster and season with pepper and salt. Add another layer of crumbs and repeat until the dish is full, having crumbs and butter on top. Pour over enough milk to moisten, and bake about twenty minutes.

LOBSTER À LA NEWBURG

Put into a saucepan four tablespoonfuls of butter and when it melts add the meat of two boiled lobsters coarsely cut. Season with salt, pepper, and grated nutmeg, add two tablespoonfuls of sherry, and simmer for five minutes. Add the yolks of four eggs beaten smooth with one cupful of cream, cook for two minutes, and serve immediately.

LOBSTER IN CASSEROLE

Fry a chopped onion in a little butter, add one cupful each of chicken stock and strained tomato, season highly with salt and red pepper, and pour over the meat of a boiled lobster arranged in a casserole. Set into a hot oven for fifteen or twenty minutes and serve.

LOBSTER WIGGLE

Melt two tablespoonfuls of butter, add two small spoonfuls of flour, cook and stir thoroughly. Add one cupful of cream, and salt and pepper to season. Cook until thick, add one and one-half cupfuls of boiled lobster meat, and one teaspoonful each of lemon-juice and minced parsley. When hot, add half a can of French peas, bring to the boil, and serve on toast.

OYSTERS

BAKED OYSTERS

Put into a baking-dish one-half cupful of butter and one cupful of cream. Heat thoroughly, but do not boil. Add three tablespoonfuls of sherry, one teaspoonful of anchovy paste, a dash of red pepper, and a grating of lemon-peel. Dip out one-half cupful of the mixture and set aside. Put one quart of oysters into the baking-dish, sprinkle with salt, pepper, grated cheese, and dried bread-crumbs. Pour over carefully the remaining cream, sprinkle again with crumbs and cheese, and bake in a very hot oven. Serve immediately. If preferred, oysters may be baked this way in individual dishes.

BROILED OYSTERS ON TOAST

Drain three dozen large oysters, and wipe dry with a cloth. Season with salt and pepper, and fry briskly in butter for two minutes. Skim out, arrange on a buttered oyster-broiler, and broil brown on both sides. Arrange the oysters on thin slices of toast, pour over the hot butter, garnish with lemon and parsley, and serve.

CREOLE OYSTER LOAF

Cut the top from a baker's loaf and scoop out the crumb. Toast or fry the shell and lid. Fill with fried oysters, season with tomato catsup and sliced pimolas, put on the lid, reheat, and serve very hot.

CURRIED OYSTERS

Put into a saucepan one tablespoonful of butter and one teaspoonful of chopped onion. Fry the onion brown, add a heaping tablespoonful of flour and one teaspoonful of curry powder. Cook and stir until the mixture leaves the sides of the pan, add one cupful of cream, and salt and pepper to season. Stir constantly until the sauce is thick, add one quart of oysters with their liquor, and cook slowly until the edges of the oysters curl. Serve on toast.

DEVILLED OYSTERS

Parboil a pint of oysters, skim out, drain, and cool. Chop coarsely. Mix with two hard-boiled eggs, chopped fine, two tablespoonfuls of bread-crumbs, salt, red pepper, and lemon-juice to season, and enough cream to make the mixture a smooth paste. Fill buttered oyster-shells with this mixture, cover with crumbs, dot with butter, and bake in a hot oven until brown.

ESCALLOPED OYSTERS AND MACARONI

Break into inch pieces half a pound of macaroni. Put into salted boiling water, and boil for twenty minutes. Drain in a colander and pour fresh boiling-water through to remove superfluous starch. Butter a pudding-dish and put a layer of macaroni in the bottom. Cover with a layer of oysters, dot with butter, season with pepper and salt, and repeat until the dish is nearly full. Beat together two eggs, and one and one-half cupfuls of milk or cream. Pour over the oysters and macaroni, spread one cupful of cracker crumbs over the top, dot with butter, sprinkle with grated cheese, and bake about half an hour.

FRIED OYSTERS

Select large oysters and drain on a cloth. When dry, dip in beaten egg, then in dried bread-crumbs, sprinkle with salt and pepper, and set aside for two hours. Dip in eggs and crumbs again, fry brown in deep fat, drain on brown paper, and serve immediately.

OYSTERS IN BROWN SAUCE

Parboil a pint of oysters in their own liquor, skim out, and drain. Put into a saucepan one-quarter of a cupful of butter, and cook until brown. Add one-quarter of a cupful of flour, cook and stir until the mixture leaves the sides of the pan. Add one-half cupful of milk, one cupful of oyster liquor, one teaspoonful of anchovy paste, and salt and pepper to season. Cook until thick, add the oysters, reheat, and serve.

OYSTERS IN CASSEROLE

Toast small square slices of bread, butter thickly on one side, and put, butter-side down, into a casserole. Cover with oysters, dot with butter, sprinkle with red pepper and salt, cover the dish, and bake in a quick oven until the edges of the oysters curl. Serve with lemon quarters.

OYSTER COCKTAIL

Put into a glass two teaspoonfuls of lemon-juice, two drops of tabasco sauce, half a teaspoonful of Worcestershire, two teaspoonfuls of tomato catsup, a pinch of salt, and a saltspoonful of paprika. Mix thoroughly, add five or six small fresh oysters, let stand for five minutes, and serve very cold.

OYSTERS WITH DUMPLINGS

Make a light biscuit dough, roll thin, and cut into inch squares. Scald a quart can of oysters in their own liquor and when it boils, skim out the oysters and set aside. Add to the liquor two cupfuls of boiling water, a tablespoonful of butter, and salt and pepper to season. Cook and stir with a teaspoonful of flour rubbed smooth in a little cold milk. When boiling hot, put in the dumplings, cover closely, boil for forty minutes, add the oysters, reheat, and serve at once.

OYSTERS WITH GREEN PEPPERS

Put a tablespoonful of butter into a frying-pan and fry in it a sweet pepper and a small onion both chopped fine. Add a pint of oysters with their liquor, season with salt and paprika, and cook for five minutes. Serve on hot buttered toast.

OYSTER STEW

Drain one quart of oysters and put the liquor to heat in a saucepan. Add one cupful of cream, and salt and red pepper to taste. Bring to the boil, add two tablespoonfuls of butter, and thicken with one teaspoonful of flour rubbed smooth in a little cold milk. Cook and stir until it thickens, add the oysters, simmer until the edges curl, take from the fire, add the juice of half a lemon, and pour over thin slices of the buttered toast.

OYSTERS À L'INDIEN

Strain the juice from a quart can of tomatoes, and add enough water to make two cupfuls. Heat to the boiling point, add half a cupful of well washed rice, and cook for twenty minutes, stirring as needed. Add two tablespoonfuls of butter, two teaspoonfuls of curry powder, salt and pepper to taste, and two dozen large oysters. Cook until the oysters ruffle. Serve with thin brown bread sandwiches and bananas.

OYSTERS À LA MADRID

Butter individual baking-dishes. Put a layer of drained oysters in the bottom, season with salt and pepper, dot with butter, sprinkle with finely chopped pimentos, cover with crumbs, and repeat until the dish is full, having crumbs and butter on top. Bake in a quick oven.

SCALLOPS

FRIED SCALLOPS

Trim off the beards and black parts, rinse well, and drain. Sauté in hot lard, drain on brown paper, and serve at once. Or, dip in egg and crumbs and fry in deep fat.

PIGS IN BLANKETS

Parboil scallops, drain and dry on a cloth. Roll a thin slice of bacon around each one and fasten with a wooden tooth-pick. Fry until the bacon is crisp and serve on thin slices of buttered toast.

SHRIMPS

CREAMED SHRIMPS

Melt one tablespoonful of butter, add one tablespoonful of flour, and cook thoroughly. Add one cupful of milk, and cook until thick, stirring constantly. Add two cupfuls of shelled shrimps broken into small pieces, season to taste, reheat, and serve.

CURRIED SHRIMPS

Melt one heaping tablespoonful of butter, add one tablespoonful of flour and cook thoroughly. Add one cupful of boiling water and cook until thick, stirring constantly. Add a tablespoonful of curry powder and a teaspoonful of grated onion. Heat thoroughly and add a can of shrimps well-washed and drained. Cook for five minutes longer and serve with boiled rice and ice-cold bananas.

JELLIED SHRIMPS

Open a large can of shrimps and soak in ice-water for an hour. Dissolve half a box of powdered gelatine in cold water to cover, add to it one cupful of boiling water, the juice of two lemons and a pinch of salt. Strain into a ring mould and put in half the shrimps. Set on ice. When the jelly is firm, loosen from the mould by dipping for an instant in boiling water. Turn out on a round platter, and put the rest of the shrimps in the middle with the small hearts of lettuce. Serve with mayonnaise.

MAYONNAISE OF SHRIMPS

Prepare two cupfuls of shrimps, and break each one in two pieces. Mix with mayonnaise and serve with a border of lettuce leaves. A little finely cut celery may be added if desired.

SHRIMPS BAKED IN GREEN PEPPERS

Cut the stem ends from half a dozen green peppers and carefully remove the seeds and veins. Soak the green peppers in cold water for half an hour. Melt one tablespoonful of butter, add half a teaspoonful of mixed mustard and salt, pepper, celery salt, and grated nutmeg to season. Add one egg well-beaten and mix thoroughly. Add two cupfuls of shelled and broken shrimps and enough grated bread-crumbs to make a smooth paste. Fill the peppers, cover with crumbs, dot with butter, and arrange in a baking-pan with the open side up. Bake for twenty minutes.

SHRIMPS À LA CRÉOLE

Put into a saucepan two cupfuls of shelled shrimps, one heaping tablespoonful of butter, half a small onion chopped fine, and a bruised bean of garlic. Heat thoroughly, add one cupful of canned tomatoes, and salt and cayenne to season. Cook for ten minutes and add one-half cupful of French peas just before serving.

SHRIMP WIGGLE

Prepare according to directions given for Creamed Shrimps, using equal quantities of broken shrimps and French peas.

TOMATOES STUFFED WITH SHRIMPS

Take half a dozen large tomatoes, cut off the tops, and scoop out the pulp, leaving a thin shell. Melt a tablespoonful of butter, add the tomato tops and pulp and cook until thick, seasoning with salt, pepper, minced parsley, and grated onion. Add one small can of shrimps cut fine and enough crumbs to make a paste. Fill the tomato shells, cover with crumbs, dot with butter, and bake in the oven. Serve with a border of boiled rice.

SIXTY WAYS TO COOK FISH

COURT BOUILLON

Put into the bottom of the fish-kettle a thick layer of sliced carrots and onions, and a sliced lemon. Season with parsley, thyme, a bay-leaf, half a dozen whole peppers, and three or four whole cloves. Lay the fish on top of this and cover with equal parts of cold water and white wine, or with water and a little lemon-juice or vinegar. Put the kettle over the fire and let it heat slowly. The fish must always be put into it while cold and after boiling allowed to cool in the water.

BAKED BASS

Make a stuffing of one cupful of bread-crumbs, one teaspoonful each of melted butter, Worcestershire sauce, tomato catsup, minced parsley, minced onion, minced olives or pickles, and lemon-juice. Add salt, black pepper, and paprika to taste, and sufficient cold water to moisten. Sew up the fish and bake as usual. Serve withTartar Sauce.

BAKED BASS WITH SHRIMP SAUCE

Marinate the cleaned fish for an hour in oil and vinegar. Put into a baking-pan with slices of salt pork underneath and on top and sufficient boiling water to keep from burning. Add a teaspoonful of butter to the water and baste two or three times during the hour of baking. Strain the gravy and set aside. Melt one tablespoonful of butter, add one tablespoonful of flour, and cook until brown. Add one cupful of the liquid left in the baking-pan, making up the required quantity with boiling water if necessary. Cook until thick, stirring constantly; season with cayenne and lemon-juice, and add half a can of shrimps chopped fine. Bring to the boil, pour over the fish, and serve.

BOILED BASS

Clean the fish, put it into warm salted water, and simmer for twenty minutes.

BOILED SEA-BASS WITH EGG SAUCE

Boil the fish according to directions previously given. Melt one tablespoonful of butter, add one tablespoonful of flour, and cook thoroughly. Add two cupfuls of the water in which the fish was boiled, and cook until thick, stirring constantly. Season with salt, pepper, minced parsley, and lemon-juice, add three hard-boiled eggs coarsely chopped, pour over the fish, and serve.

COLD BASS WITH TARTAR SAUCE

Boil the fish in court bouillon and drain. Chop fine parsley, pickles, olives, and capers. Mix with a stiff mayonnaise and spread over the fish. Serve with a border of sliced cucumbers.

BAKED BLUEFISH À L'ITALIENNE

Score and scale the bluefish and put it into a buttered pan with three tablespoonfuls each of white wine and mushroom liquor, a tablespoonful of chopped onion, half a dozen chopped mushrooms, and salt and pepper to season. Cover with buttered paper and bake for fifteen minutes. Take out the fish and add to the sauce half a teaspoonful of beef extract, dissolved in half a cupful of boiling water. Add a wineglassful of white wine and thicken with one tablespoonful each of butter and browned flour. Pour the sauce over the fish, sprinkle with chopped parsley, and serve.

BAKED BLUEFISH

Clean, scrape, and split the fish and take out the backbone. Gash the flesh and insert a thin slice of salt pork under the skin. Make a stuffing of one cupful of bread-crumbs, two tablespoonfuls of chopped salt pork, and salt, minced parsley, chopped onion, red pepper, kitchen bouquet, and tomato catsup to season. Add one egg well-beaten. Fill the fish and sew up. Lay on thin slices of salt pork and bake, basting frequently with the fat. Garnish with cress and lemon.

STEAMED BLUEFISH

Season the fish with salt and pepper and pour over it a cupful of vinegar. Let stand for an hour, pour off the vinegar, and steam for twenty minutes. Serve with any preferred sauce.

BAKED CODFISH

Stuff the fish with seasoned crumbs and season with pepper and salt. Pour over two cupfuls of sherry and a tablespoonful of mushroom catsup. Add two cupfuls of stock, cover with buttered paper, and bake, basting often. When nearly done, sprinkle with bread-crumbs, dot with butter, and bake until brown. Take up the fish carefully, add a teaspoonful of beef extract and a little anchovy paste to the liquor in the baking-pan, strain, add two tablespoonfuls of butter and the juice of half a lemon, bring to the boil, pour over the fish, and serve.

CODFISH À LA CRÉOLE

Flake one pound of cooked codfish, add to it one cupful of boiled rice, half a can of tomatoes strained, a chopped onion, two tablespoonfuls of butter, and salt and pepper to season. Cook slowly for half an hour.

ESCALLOPED CODFISH AND MACARONI

Mix together equal parts of cooked and broken macaroni and flaked boiled cod. Mix with Cream Sauce. Fill a buttered baking-dish, sprinkle thickly with grated cheese, cover with crumbs, dot with butter, and brown in the oven.

BREADED CODFISH STEAKS

Season the steaks with salt, pepper, and lemon-juice, dip in egg and crumbs, and fry in deep fat. Serve with any preferred sauce.

BOILED FINNAN HADDIE

Divide into convenient pieces, cover with boiling water, add a teaspoonful of sugar, and boil for fifteen minutes. Take up on a hot platter, remove the skin, and dot with butter.

BROILED FINNAN HADDIE

Cut the haddie into small squares, skin and parboil it. Wipe dry, broil on a buttered gridiron and serve with melted butter.

CREAMED FINNAN HADDIE

Parboil, drain, and flake the fish. Reheat with shredded fried sweet peppers in a Cream Sauce. Canned pimentos may be used instead of the green peppers.

BROILED FROG LEGS

Soak the legs for half an hour in a marinade of oil and lemon-juice, seasoned with salt and pepper. Broil on a double-broiler, and serve with Maître d'Hôtel Sauce.

FROG LEGS À LA POULETTE

Season prepared frog legs with salt, pepper, and nutmeg, and fry brown in butter. Add two small spoonfuls of flour and two cupfuls of cream. Cook until thick, stirring constantly. Add a wineglassful of white wine, two tablespoonfuls of butter, a tablespoonful of minced parsley, and the yolks of four eggs beaten smooth with the juice of a lemon. Bring to the boil and serve.

HADDOCK RAREBIT

Cut the haddock into slices an inch thick. Free from bone and skin. Lay in a greased baking-dish, and season with salt and pepper. Grate sufficient cheese to cover, and season with salt, red pepper, and mustard. Make to a smooth paste with cream or beaten egg. Put into a hot oven and cook until the cheese melts and browns, and the fish is firm. Take up carefully on a platter, and pour one tablespoonful of Sherry over each slice.

HADDOCK AND OYSTERS

Clean and fillet a haddock. Cover the trimmings with water and add the liquor drained from a pint of oysters. Add a slice of onion, a pinch of powdered sweet herbs, and a slice of carrot; simmer to form a stock. Put a layer of sliced onion into a saucepan, and arrange upon it the fillets of fish and a pint of oysters; sprinkle with salt and pepper, add the juice of a lemon, cover with sliced onion, strain the stock over, cover and simmer until the fillets are tender. Arrange the fillets on a hot dish with the oysters, strain the liquid, thicken it with the yolks of four eggs, pour over, and serve.

HALIBUT À LA MAÎTRE D'HÔTEL

Soak two halibut steaks for an hour in lemon-juice, seasoned with salt, pepper, and minced parsley. Mix together two tablespoonfuls of butter, one tablespoonful of flour, and two cupfuls of boiling water. Cook until thick, stirring constantly. Put the slices of halibut into a buttered pan, cover with the sauce, and bake for twenty minutes, basting as required. Serve with any preferred sauce.

BAKED HALIBUT

Soak six pounds of halibut in salt water for two hours. Wipe dry and score the outer skin. Bake for an hour in a moderately hot oven, basting with melted butter and hot water. Add a little boiling water to the gravy, a tablespoonful of walnut catsup, a teaspoonful of Worcestershire sauce, salt and pepper to season, and the juice of a lemon. Cook while stirring with browned flour rubbed smooth with a little cold water.

HALIBUT STEAK À LA JARDINIÈRE

Soak halibut steaks for an hour in salt and water. Wipe dry and rub with melted butter. Butter a china baking-dish, sprinkle chopped onion on the bottom, and put in the steaks. On top put a boiled carrot cut into dice, half a dozen sliced tomatoes, a shredded green pepper, and half a cupful of green peas. Add enough salted boiling water to keep the fish from scorching, put a tablespoonful of butter on top, cover, and bake until done. Drain the liquor carefully from the pan, add three tablespoonfuls of white wine, and thicken with a teaspoonful of butter rolled in browned flour. Serve separately as a sauce.

FRESH BOILED MACKEREL

Clean the mackerel, sprinkle with vinegar, wrap in a floured cloth, and baste closely. Boil for three-quarters of an hour in salted water, drain, and take off the cloth. Strain a cupful of the water in which the fish was boiled, and bring to the boil with a tablespoonful of walnut catsup, a teaspoonful of anchovy paste, and the juice of half a lemon. Thicken with butter and browned flour.

PIKE BAKED IN SOUR CREAM

Clean a four-pound pike, cut into steaks, and free from skin and bone. Put into a buttered baking-dish with two small onions chopped and two bay-leaves. Season with salt and cayenne, add one cupful of sour cream, and bake. Put on a serving-dish, cover with crumbs and dots of butter, and brown in the oven. Add enough stock to the liquid to make the required quantity of sauce, thicken with butter and flour, season, add a dash of lemon-juice, pour around the fish, sprinkle with minced parsley, and serve.

BOILED SALMON WITH GREEN SAUCE

Boil a small salmon in salted and acidulated water. Take up carefully and reduce the liquid by rapid boiling to two cupfuls. Cook together one tablespoonful each of butter and flour, add the reduced liquid, and cook until thick, stirring constantly. Take from the fire, add two tablespoonfuls of chopped capers, one tablespoonful of chopped parsley, the juice of a lemon, and one tablespoonful of butter. Pour over the fish and serve.

BOILED SALMON À LA WALDORF

Boil a large piece of salmon in salted and acidulated water, seasoned with herbs and spice. Drain and keep warm. Add two cupfuls of the liquid in which the fish was cooked, one wineglass full of white wine, and two anchovies rubbed to a paste. Boil for fifteen minutes, then add in small bits a tablespoonful of butter. Serve the sauce separately.

BAKED SALMON

Rub a small cleaned salmon with olive-oil, sprinkle with salt and pepper, put into a buttered baking-pan, and add one cupful of boiling water and two tablespoonfuls of butter. Baste every ten minutes until done. Take up the fish and keep it warm. Thicken the gravy with a teaspoonful or more of cornstarch mixed with a little cold water. Season with grated onion, lemon-juice, and tomato catsup.

STUFFED SALMON

Clean, bone, and parboil a small salmon. Rub the inside with salt, pepper, and grated nutmeg. Stuff with chopped oysters, minced parsley, and seasoned crumbs. Fold together, put into a buttered baking-dish, and bake for half an hour, basting with its own dripping.

SALMON MAYONNAISE WITH CUCUMBERS

Steam salmon steaks until tender, remove the skin, and cool. Cover with thinly sliced cucumbers, mask with Mayonnaise, and serve with a border of lettuce leaves and sliced hard-boiled eggs.

SALMON CROQUETTES

Cook together one tablespoonful of butter and three tablespoonfuls of flour. Add one cupful of cream, and cook until thick, stirring constantly. Season with salt, red pepper, and minced parsley, take from the fire, add the juice of a lemon and a can of flaked salmon. Mix thoroughly and cool. Shape into croquettes, dip in egg and crumbs, and fry in deep fat.

SALMON LOAF

Mash a can of salmon, add the juice of a lemon, and half a cupful of fresh bread crumbs, three tablespoonfuls of minced parsley, four tablespoonfuls of melted butter, and four eggs beaten separately, folding in the stiffly beaten whites last. Put into a buttered mould and steam for an hour. Add to the oil drained from the salmon one cupful of boiling milk, one small spoonful of cornstarch rubbed smooth in a little cold milk, and a tablespoonful of butter. Cook until thick, stirring constantly, take from the fire, add one egg well-beaten, a teaspoonful of tomato catsup, and mace and pepper to season. Turn the mould out on a platter and pour the sauce around it.

FRICASSEED SALMON

Reheat a can of flaked salmon in a cupful of Drawn-Butter Sauce, adding half a cupful of cream, and salt, red and white pepper to season. Take from the fire, add one egg, well-beaten, pour over buttered toast, and sprinkle with parsley.

BAKED CREAMED SALMON

Cook together two tablespoonfuls of butter and one of flour, add two cupfuls of milk or cream, and cook until thick, stirring constantly. Add salt, pepper, and minced parsley to season, and a can of flaked salmon. Reheat and arrange in a baking-dish with alternate layers of crumbs and butter, having crumbs and butter on top. Bake in the oven until brown.

SALMON EN CASSEROLE

Chop a large onion and fry it in butter. Add a cupful of bread crumbs and one and one-half cupfuls of milk. Bring to the boil, add salt and pepper to season, a can of flaked salmon, and two eggs well-beaten. Pour into a buttered casserole, dot with butter, and bake brown. Sprinkle with minced parsley and serve.

BOILED SALMON-TROUT

Prepare and clean a salmon-trout, stuff with seasoned crumbs, and put on the grate in a fish-kettle. Sprinkle with salt, pepper, and grated nutmeg, add a bunch of sweet herbs, a clove of garlic, and two tablespoonfuls of butter. Add enough claret to cover and simmer until done. Drain the fish, strain the liquid, thicken if desired, and serve the sauce separately.

BAKED SARDINES

Marinate drained sardines in lemon-juice, then drain, sprinkle with cracker crumbs, and put into a hot oven for ten minutes. Cook together a heaping teaspoonful each of butter and flour, add one cupful of tomato-juice, and cook until thick, stirring constantly. Season with salt, pepper, grated onion, and sugar. Arrange the sardines on toasted strips of brown bread, pour the sauce over, and serve.

BROILED SHAD

Prepare and clean the fish, split, and remove the backbone. Season with salt and pepper, dip in oil, broil carefully, and serve with Maître d'Hôtel Sauce.

BONED FRIED SHAD

Remove the head and tail, then take out the back and side bones. Cut into convenient pieces for serving, season with salt and pepper, dip in egg and crumbs, and fry in deep fat. Serve with any preferred sauce.

BAKED SHAD

Bake a shad in a buttered baking-pan, adding enough boiling water to keep from burning. Baste while baking with melted butter and lemon-juice, seasoning with pepper and salt. Cook together a small spoonful each of butter and flour until brown. Add slowly a cupful of stock and cook until thick, stirring constantly. Take from the fire and add the yolks of two eggs beaten with the juice of half a lemon. Pour over the fish and serve.

BAKED SHAD STUFFED WITH OYSTERS

Rub a large cleaned fish with salt inside and out. Stuff with oysters and seasoned crumbs made very rich with melted butter, and bake, basting with melted butter and hot water. Thicken the gravy with flour browned in butter, adding a little hot water or stock if necessary, season with lemon-juice and catsup, and serve the sauce separately.

FRIED SHAD ROE

Parboil the roe for ten minutes in salted and acidulated water. Drain, plunge into cold water, and cool. Drain, dip in beaten egg, then in seasoned crumbs, and fry brown in deep fat. Serve with any preferred sauce.

SHAD ROE BAKED IN TOMATO SAUCE

Boil the roe, drain, cool, and skin. Cook together for ten minutes one cupful of canned tomatoes, one cupful of stock or water, a slice of onion, and salt and pepper to season. Cook together two tablespoonfuls of butter and one of flour, add the tomato, and cook until thick, stirring constantly. Rub the sauce through a strainer. Put the roe on a buttered baking-dish, season with salt and pepper, cover with the sauce, and bake. Serve in the dish in which it was baked.

SHAD ROE WITH BROWN SAUCE

Soak a shad roe in water for half an hour, scald, drain, cool, and cut in slices. Sauté in butter and drain. Cook a tablespoonful of flour in the butter, add one cupful of stock, and cook until thick, stirring constantly. Season with salt, paprika, Worcestershire, and curry powder; pour over the fish and serve.

BROILED SMELTS

Dip prepared smelts in lemon-juice and seasoned melted butter, then in flour; broil in a double broiler, and serve with Tartar Sauce.

BAKED SMELTS

Remove the heads, split, dip in melted butter, then in flour. Put into a buttered baking-pan, bake for ten minutes, sprinkle with cayenne and lemon-juice, and serve.

SMELTS AU BEURRE NOIR

Roll the cleaned smelts in flour, sauté in butter, and arrange on fingers of buttered toast. Brown half a cupful of butter, add a tablespoonful of vinegar, pour over the fish, and serve.

BROILED STURGEON STEAKS

Parboil sturgeon steaks for fifteen minutes, drain, wipe dry, season with salt and pepper, and broil. Serve with melted butter or Maître d'Hôtel Sauce.

BOILED TROUT

Tie a large trout in a cloth and boil it in salted and acidulated water to cover, adding an onion, a stalk of celery, and a bunch of parsley. When done, drain and keep warm. Stick blanched almonds into the fish, sharp side down, and pour over a Cream Sauce to which chopped hard-boiled eggs and parsley have been added.

BAKED TURBOT

Rub a small cleaned turbot with melted butter, sprinkle with minced parsley, powdered mace, and salt and pepper to season. Let stand for an hour and put into a buttered baking-dish. Brush with beaten egg, sprinkle with crumbs, dot with butter, bake, and serve with any preferred sauce.

TURBOT À LA CRÊME

Cook together three small spoonfuls each of butter and flour, add a quart of cream, and cook until thick, stirring constantly. Season with pepper, salt, minced parsley, and grated onion. Butter a baking-dish, put in a layer of cold cooked turbot flaked fine, cover with sauce, and repeat until the dish is full, having sauce on top. Sprinkle with crumbs, dot with butter, and brown in the oven. Sprinkle with chopped eggs and parsley.

BOILED WHITEFISH

Boil a large whitefish in salted and acidulated water, adding a bunch of parsley and a sliced onion to the water. Drain, and serve with any preferred sauce.

FRIED WHITEFISH

Clean and trim the fish and cut into convenient pieces for serving. Dip in seasoned flour and sauté in hot lard in a frying-pan.

BAKED WHITEFISH

Clean and split a large fish, remove the bone, and put in a buttered baking-pan skin side down. Season with salt, cayenne, and lemon-juice, sprinkle with crumbs, dot with butter, and bake. Serve with any preferred sauce.

STUFFED WHITEFISH WITH OYSTER SAUCE

Make a stuffing of two cupfuls of bread crumbs, half a cupful of chopped salt pork fried crisp, a chopped hard-boiled egg, half a cupful of vinegar, and salt, pepper, butter, sage, and mustard to season. Stuff the fish, place in a pie-tin, put into a steamer and steam until done. Pour over a Cream Sauce to which cooked oysters and a little lemon-juice and minced parsley have been added.

PLANKED WHITEFISH

Butter a fish-plank and tack a large cleaned and split whitefish on it, skin side down. Rub with butter, season with salt and pepper, and cook in the oven or under a gas flame. Put a border of mashed potato mixed with the beaten white of egg around the fish, using a pastry tube and forcing bag. Put into the oven for a few minutes to brown the potato, and serve with a garnish of lemon and parsley.

JELLIED WHITEFISH

Boil two pounds of whitefish in salted and acidulated water, with four bay-leaves, a tablespoonful of pepper-corns, and half a dozen cloves. Take out the fish, strain the liquid, and reduce by rapid boiling to a quantity barely sufficient to cover the fish. Add the juice of a lemon and two ounces of dissolved gelatine. Flake the fish with a fork, removing all skin, fat, and bone, mix with the liquid, pour into a fish-mould, wet with cold water, and put on ice until firm. Serve cold with Mayonnaise orTartar Sauce.

BAKED FISH

Prepare a Cream Sauce, seasoning with grated onion, minced parsley, and powdered mace. Take from the fire, add the yolks of two eggs, and salt and pepper to taste. Put a layer of cold, cooked, flaked and seasoned fish, into a buttered baking-dish, spread with the sauce, and repeat until the dish is full, having sauce on top. Sprinkle with crumbs, dot with butter, and brown in the oven. This may be baked in individual dishes if desired.

BOUILLABAISSE

Cut into pieces and remove the bones from three pounds of fish, add six shrimps or one lobster or two crabs, cooked, and cut into large pieces; add one-half pint of olive-oil; fry lightly, and add one lemon and two tomatoes, one onion, and one carrot, all sliced, one pinch of saffron—as much as lies on a ten-cent piece,—a bay-leaf, and some parsley. A bean of garlic is used, unless the casserole is rubbed with it before cooking. Stir for ten minutes, add one cupful of stock and one wineglassful of white wine or cider. Cook for fifteen minutes longer, pour out into a bowl, place slices of toast in the casserole, and cover with the fish and vegetables, allowing the sauce sufficient time to soak into the toast, and adding salt and pepper to taste.

FISH CHOPS

Mix cold cooked fish with a little very thick Cream Sauce, and season with lemon-juice and minced parsley. Shape into chops, dip in egg and crumbs, and fry in deep fat. Stick a small piece of macaroni in the small end of each chop to represent the bone. Serve with Tartar Sauce.

FISH À LA CRÉOLE

Chop an onion and a clove of garlic and fry in lard. Add three tablespoonfuls of flour, cook and stir until brown, and add one can of strained tomatoes. Have the fish cut into convenient pieces for serving, dredge with seasoned flour, and sauté in butter until brown. Pour the sauce over, simmer until done, and serve.

ONE HUNDRED AND FIFTY WAYS TO COOK MEAT AND POULTRY

BEEF

BROILED SIRLOIN STEAK

Have the steak cut thick and trim off the tough end. Broil carefully on a buttered gridiron, dot with butter, and serve.

BEEFSTEAK WITH FRENCH-FRIED ONIONS

Slice the onions thin, season with salt and pepper, and dredge thoroughly with flour. Put into a frying-basket and plunge into deep fat. Fry brown and crisp, drain, and serve with broiled steak.

STEAK BORDELAISE

Select a thick steak and broil carefully on a buttered gridiron. Chop a peeled clove of garlic very fine, or grate it. It cannot be too fine. Mix with three times the quantity of parsley finely minced and made to a smooth paste with melted butter. Spread over the steak and put in the oven for two minutes before serving.

BEEFSTEAK WITH OYSTER BLANQUETTE

Heat one quart of oysters with their own liquor, skim, and cook until the edges of the oysters curl. Thicken with flour cooked in butter, pour over a broiled steak, and serve very hot.

BEEFSTEAK WITH FRIED BANANAS

Broil the steak and put on the serving-platter. Dot with butter, sprinkle with minced parsley, and surround with bananas cut into quarters lengthwise and fried in butter. The bananas may be baked in the oven, basting with butter and sugar.

FRIED HAMBURG STEAK

Season chopped raw beef with grated onion, salt, minced sweet pepper and minced parsley. Mix with raw egg to bind and shape into flat cakes. Roll in crumbs, sauté in butter or drippings, and serve with Tomato Sauce.

SPANISH STEAK

Chop two large onions fine and fry brown in butter. Fry a flank steak in the same fat, seasoning with pepper only. Take up, put into a buttered baking-pan or casserole, sprinkle with salt, spread with onion, pour over a can of tomatoes, and add a green pepper seeded and shredded. Cover tightly and cook slowly for an hour or more. Thicken the remaining liquid with browned flour to make a gravy.

STEWED STEAK WITH OYSTERS

Have two pounds of rump steak cut into small squares. Fry brown in butter, take up the meat, and cook a tablespoonful of flour in the fat remaining in the pan. Add a cupful of water or stock and the liquor drained from one pint of oysters. Cook until smooth and thick, stirring constantly, and put the steak into the sauce. Cover and cook until the steak is tender, then add a pint of oysters and cook until the edges curl. Take from the fire, add a tablespoonful of lemon-juice, and serve.

BRAISED FLANK STEAK

Pound a large flank steak flat. Make a dressing of seasoned crumbs and chopped salt pork or suet, moistening with melted butter or beaten egg. Spread on the steak, roll up, and tie in shape. Cut fine a carrot, a turnip, an onion, and a small bunch of parsley. Spread the roll of meat thickly with butter, season with pepper and salt and pour over and cook slowly in a very hot oven. Rub the vegetables through a sieve, skim off the fat, and make gravy, adding more stock or water if required.

STUFFED FLANK STEAK

Pound a large flank steak flat. Make a stuffing of equal parts of sausage meat and bread crumbs, seasoning with minced onion and thyme. Roll up, tie into shape, brown in hot fat, cover with stock or water, and let simmer for two hours. Skim and strain the gravy, thicken with flour browned in butter or in a little of the fat, season with mushroom catsup, and pour over the meat or serve separately.

STUFFED PRESSED STEAK

Pound a large round steak flat and tender. Spread with highly seasoned stuffing, roll into shape, and sew tightly in cheese-cloth. Boil for three hours, in salted water, take out and press under a heavy weight until cold. Take off the cloth, cut in thin slices, and serve with horseradish or made mustard.

ROAST BEEF

Have a rib roast of beef cut standing—that is, with the bones left in. Put into a hot oven without seasoning and when the outside is seared enough to prevent the escape of the juices, reduce the heat and cook slowly until done, basting frequently with the dripping. During the last half hour of cooking, dredge with salt, pepper, and flour. Skim the drippings and thicken for gravy, adding more liquid if required.

POT ROAST

Put a round of beef into a deep pot, add a small onion sliced, and a cupful of boiling water. Cover and cook slowly, allowing ten minutes to the pound. Take up the meat, rub with butter, dredge with flour, and brown it in a hot oven. Strain the gravy left in the pan, season with salt, pepper, and mushroom catsup, and thicken with flour browned in butter. Pour over the meat and serve.

RÉCHAUFFÉ OF BEEF À L'ESPAGNOLE

Cook together a can of tomatoes, a chopped onion, half a dozen sweet green peppers, seeded and cut into rings, and a tablespoonful of butter. Simmer for an hour. Reheat in the sauce thin slices of rare roast beef and thicken with one or two beaten eggs.

CANNELON OF BEEF

Chop fine two cupfuls of cold roast beef, season with salt, pepper, and grated nutmeg, and moisten with beaten egg. Roll rich pie-crust into an oblong shape, spread with the meat, roll up, fasten the ends by pinching the pastry, rub with butter, and bake brown. Serve either hot or cold.

MACARONIED BEEF

Break macaroni into short lengths and cook in boiling salted water until tender. Drain, mix with Tomato Sauce and freshly grated Parmesan cheese. Reheat slices of rare roast beef in a little stock, season to taste, pour the macaroni over, and serve.

BEEF OLIVES

Cut rare roast beef into thin slices and wrap each one around a thin slice of bacon. Fasten with toothpicks, and reheat in beef-gravy or stock. If stock is used, thicken it with browned flour, and season to taste.

RAGOUT OF BEEF

Put into a stewpan a pound of rare roast beef sliced thin, add three onions sliced, and salt and pepper to season. Cover with boiling water and simmer until the meat is very tender. Add half a cupful of tomatoes, half a cupful of chopped mushrooms, and a few capers. Thicken with flour rubbed smooth in a little cold stock or water, season with curry powder, stir and simmer ten minutes longer. Serve in a casserole.

JELLIED TONGUE

Boil a beef tongue very slowly in water to cover. Let cool in the liquid, drain, skin, and cut into thin slices. Dissolve a package of gelatine in one cupful of water. Heat thoroughly two cupfuls of the cooking liquid, one cupful of stock, and three tablespoonfuls of vinegar. Add two teaspoonfuls of sugar, two teaspoonfuls of beef extract, and the dissolved gelatine. If there is not enough liquid to cover the tongue, add boiling water to make the necessary quantity. Strain through cheese-cloth. Wet a mould in cold water, pour in a layer of the jelly, and when set, add a layer of the tongue. Repeat until the mould is full. At serving time turn out and garnish with parsley.

STEWED TONGUE WITH RAISINS

Boil a tongue in water to cover until it is so tender that a straw will pierce it. Let cool in the water in which it was boiled, drain, and remove the skin. The next day reheat the cooking liquid and let it simmer for three hours with half a cupful of stoned raisins, and the juice and grated peel of a lemon. Half an hour before serving thicken the gravy with browned flour and simmer the tongue in it until serving time. Pour boiling water over half a cupful of raisins and when they have swelled, drain and add to the gravy. Pour the gravy over the tongue and serve. If the sauce is too sour, add a little sugar. This is a German recipe and well worth trying.

BEEF TONGUE À L'ITALIENNE

Cut a cold boiled tongue into strips. Chop fine three onions, fry in butter, dredge with flour, add two teaspoonfuls of lemon-juice and a cupful of mushrooms. Pour into a baking-dish, cover with crumbs, dot with butter, and brown in the oven. Serve with spinach or spaghetti.

SPANISH STEW

Use a pound and a half of the ribs of beef. Put into a saucepan with two quarts of cold water, bring to the boil, and cook for two hours. Add a can of tomatoes, three large onions chopped fine, half a dozen cloves, a pinch each of sage and celery seed, one-fourth of the peel of an orange, two bay-leaves, a pod of red pepper, and two cupfuls of boiling water. Cook for half an hour, strain, skim, and thicken the gravy, season to taste, pour over the meat, and serve.

BEEF STEW WITH TOMATOES

Use three pounds of the round of beef and cut into small slices. Cover with a can of tomatoes, add a chopped onion, and salt, pepper, and powdered cloves to season. Cook slowly covered until the meat is done, add a little mushroom catsup, and serve.

BEEF STEW WITH DUMPLINGS

Have three or four pounds of the neck of beef cut into convenient pieces. Cover with cold water and add three each of carrots and onions, sliced thin. Season with salt and pepper and minced parsley, cover, and cook until the meat is nearly done. Sift two cupfuls of flour with two heaping teaspoonfuls of baking-powder and a pinch of salt. Add an egg well-beaten in enough milk to make a stiff batter. Steam the dumplings in buttered patty pans in a steamer over boiling water. Take out the meat and dumplings, thicken the gravy with flour browned in butter, pour over, and serve.

TRIPE IN CASSEROLE

Cut a pound and a half of tripe into squares and put into a casserole. Slice an onion and a carrot and fry in butter. Put into the casserole with a clove, a bay-leaf, a sprig of thyme, a tablespoonful of minced parsley, two cupfuls of stock, and half a wineglassful of white wine. Cover and cook slowly until very tender. Serve in the casserole.

BRAISED BEEF

Use a solid piece from the round or shoulder and have it larded with thin strips of salt pork. Slice an onion, a turnip, and a carrot. Lay the meat upon the vegetables, add four cupfuls of boiling water, cover the pan, and put into a hot oven. Allow twenty-five minutes to the pound and when half done season with salt and pepper. Baste frequently, and when the meat is done, add enough water or stock to make the required quantity of gravy. Thicken with browned flour, season to taste, pour over the meat, and serve. Beef ribs may be used.

BREADED LIVER

Have fresh beef liver cut into thin slices, cover with boiling water, and let stand for ten minutes. Fry slices of bacon crisp and drain. Season the bacon fat with black and red pepper, dip the liver into it, then into bread crumbs, and fry in the bacon fat. Garnish the liver with the fried bacon, and sprigs of parsley. Add to the fat in the pan one tablespoonful of vinegar and two of tomato catsup. Pour over the meat and serve.

LIVER ROLLS

Have fresh beef liver cut into thin slices. Cover with boiling water, drain, wipe dry, remove the skin, and season with salt and pepper. Put a thin slice of salt pork or bacon on each slice of liver, roll up and fasten with a string. Brown in hot fat, dredge with flour, cover with boiling water or stock, and cook for half an hour. Take off the strings, season to taste, and serve, thickening the gravy more if required.

ROASTED BEEF HEART

Stuff the heart with highly seasoned crumbs, mixing with a beaten egg to bind. Season with salt and pepper, dredge with flour, and roast covered for an hour and a half, basting frequently with melted butter and water.

BEEF KIDNEY SAUTÉ

Chop an onion fine and fry brown in butter. Add a kidney which has been soaked for five minutes in boiling salted water and cut into squares. Cook for five minutes, sprinkle with flour, add a little stock, cook until the sauce is thick, and serve immediately, sprinkling with minced parsley.

STEWED BEEF KIDNEY

Cut the kidney into thin slices, season highly with pepper and salt, and brown in hot fat. Dredge with flour, add a little boiling stock or water, and when the sauce is smooth and thick, heat the kidneys in it. Season with minced parsley and serve.

BEEF À LA NEWPORT

Cut fine one cupful of dried beef and heat thoroughly with one cupful of canned tomatoes. Season with pepper, grated nutmeg, and chopped onion. Add half a cupful of grated cheese and three well-beaten eggs. Stir constantly until thick and smooth and serve on buttered toast.

DUTCH BEEF LOAF

Run twice through the meat-chopper a pound and a half of the round of beef and a quarter of a pound of fresh pork. Add half a cupful of stale bread crumbs soaked in stock or milk, half a cupful of canned tomatoes, and celery salt, minced parsley, salt, red pepper, and grated onion to season. Mix thoroughly, shape into a loaf, brush with beaten egg, sprinkle with crumbs, and bake, basting with melted butter and stock. Serve with Tomato Sauce.

SPICED BEEF LOAF

Chop fine three pounds of beef and half a pound of suet. Add two eggs well-beaten, four tablespoonfuls of cream, a tablespoonful of butter, two tablespoonfuls of summer savory, a teaspoonful of salt, and a little red pepper. Add enough bread crumbs to make a stiff mixture. Shape into a loaf, rub with butter, dredge with flour, and bake, basting frequently. Cook for two hours or less and serve either hot or cold.

CANNELON OF BEEF

Chop very fine two pounds of the round of beef. Season with grated onion, lemon-peel, nutmeg, minced parsley, salt, pepper, melted butter, and a pinch of powdered sweet herbs. Mix with a beaten egg and shape into a loaf. Dredge with flour, roll in buttered paper, and bake for half an hour, basting with melted butter and the drippings. Remove the paper and serve with Tomato Sauce.

FRICADELLES

Chop fine a pound of beef and a pound of sausage meat. Add a cupful of bread crumbs, two eggs well-beaten, two onions, finely chopped, and salt, pepper, and thyme to season. Mix thoroughly, shape into small flat cakes, sauté in hot fat, and serve with Tomato Sauce.

SPICED ROUND OF BEEF

Put into a buttered saucepan six pounds of the round of beef, two cupfuls of canned tomatoes, three sliced onions, half a dozen cloves, a stick of cinnamon, and a pod of red pepper. Cover the meat with thin slices of salt pork and pour over half a cupful of vinegar and one cupful of water. Cover and cook in a moderate oven for five hours, seasoning with salt when half done. Take up the meat, strain and skim the cooking liquid, and thicken with flour browned in a little of the fat.

BEEF À LA MODE

Have four pounds of the round of beef thickly larded. Brown in butter and season with pepper. Add two bay-leaves, two cloves of garlic, two shallots, three onions, and a calf's foot, split and cut into four pieces. Cover and cook slowly for two hours. Add two or three carrots cut into small pieces, and cook for an hour and a half longer. Ten minutes before serving, add two tablespoonfuls of claret. Arrange on a platter with the carrots around it and serve the gravy with it.

CREOLE HOT POT

Put two pounds of beef ribs into a saucepan with a tablespoonful of drippings or butter. Add two chopped onions, a chopped clove of garlic, half a dozen seeded and shredded green peppers, pepper and salt to season, a pinch of thyme, a tablespoonful of vinegar, a dozen raisins, a dozen olives, and a can of tomatoes. Cover and cook until the meat falls from the bones. Take out the bones, thicken with flour browned in butter, and serve on buttered toast.

BEEF PIE

Cut cold cooked beef into dice and reheat in gravy or in Brown Sauce. Season with grated onion, salt, pepper, and Worcestershire and add a few diced carrots. Line a buttered baking-dish with biscuit crust, put in the meat, cover with crust, gash, brush with beaten egg, and bake until thoroughly done. Serve very hot in the same dish.

CREAMED BEEF PIE

Reheat cold cooked chopped beef in a Cream Sauce, seasoning with chopped onion and minced parsley. Put into a baking-dish, cover with boiled rice or mashed potato, and bake. Serve very hot in the same dish.

GERMAN BEEF BALLS

Chop very fine cold cooked beef. Season with salt, cayenne, minced parsley, and grated onion. Add one-fourth the quantity of bread crumbs and enough beaten egg to bind. Shape into balls or small flat cakes, dredge with flour, and fry brown.

TURKISH BEEF STEW

Cut cold cooked beef into dice. Brown it in butter, take from the fire, add four tablespoonfuls of tomato catsup, a chopped onion, fried, a shredded green pepper, also fried, salt and black pepper to season, and enough stock or gravy to moisten. Heat thoroughly and serve in a border of boiled rice.

MUTTON AND LAMB

BROILED LAMB CHOPS

Trim the chops, put on a hot gridiron, and broil carefully. Serve with a border of green peas, or around a mound of mashed potatoes.

LAMB CHOPS IN CASSEROLE

Chop fine an onion, a small carrot, and a turnip. Fry brown in butter and put into a casserole. Cover with six or eight chops browned in butter, add a little stock or water, season to taste, cover tightly, and cook until tender. Thicken the gravy with browned flour and serve from the casserole.

LAMB PIE

Arrange tender lamb chops in a deep baking-dish with chopped mushrooms, half a cupful of canned tomatoes, half a dozen small onions fried brown in butter, and a can of peas. Thicken a sufficient quantity of stock with browned flour, pour in, cover with a rich crust, gash the top, cover, bake for half an hour or more.

BROILED MUTTON CUTLETS WITH CARROTS

Peel new carrots, cut into small pieces, and boil until tender in salted water. Drain and fry brown in butter, sprinkling with pepper and sugar. Squeeze in the juice of half a lemon, reheat, and serve with a border of broiled mutton cutlets.

ROAST LAMB WITH GARLIC

Trim a leg of lamb and remove the parchment-like skin. Separate the beans from a whole clove of garlic, peel and cut each one into four pieces. Make incisions in the surface of the meat with a sharp knife, stick the bits of garlic in, season highly with pepper and salt, and put into a hot oven until brown. Cover and roast slowly until done. Make a gravy of the drippings, skimming off the fat, thickening with browned flour, and adding stock or water if necessary to make the required quantity.

BRAISED LAMB WITH CELERY

Roast a leg of lamb in a quick oven until brown. Put into a saucepan with celery and carrots cut fine, a chopped onion, a bunch of sweet herbs, and enough chicken stock to cover. Add a little butter, cover, and cook slowly until done. Serve the vegetables with the meat. Cucumbers may be used instead of the carrots and celery.

BRAISED SHOULDER OF LAMB

Take the bone from a shoulder of lamb, lard it with small strips of bacon, tie in shape, and brown in butter. Add a dozen small peeled onions, a tablespoonful of minced parsley, and stock to cover. Simmer until the onions are tender. Take up the meat, remove the skin, thicken the cooking liquor with browned flour, pour over the meat, and serve with the onions as a garnish. The breast of lamb may be used.

STEWED BREAST OF LAMB

Cut a breast of lamb into convenient pieces for serving. Season with pepper and salt, and stew until tender in stock to cover. Thicken the sauce with flour browned in butter, add a wineglassful of vinegar. This may be cooked in a casserole.

FRICASSEE OF LAMB

Cut the breast of lamb into square pieces, sprinkle with salt, dredge with flour, and brown in butter. Cover with stock or water, add a sliced onion, and simmer until the bones can easily be removed. Take the lamb out, remove the bones, strain the liquid again, reheat, add one quart of shelled green peas, and simmer for fifteen minutes.

CURRIED LAMB

Cut the meat from two boiled breasts of lamb and brown in butter with a chopped onion. Add a tablespoonful of flour and two teaspoonfuls of curry powder. Mix thoroughly and add enough white stock or water to make the required quantity of sauce. Season with salt, pepper, minced parsley, and grated lemon-peel. Cover and simmer until done. Skim off the fat. Fill a well-buttered border mould with plain boiled rice, press firmly into shape, turn out on a hot platter, pour the lamb into the centre, and serve.

INDIAN MUTTON CURRY

Fry four chopped onions in butter, add a teaspoonful of curry powder, a teaspoonful of salt, and one cupful of chopped cooked apples. Add one cupful of cream or more and a tablespoonful of flour blended smooth with a little cold water. Simmer until thick, stirring constantly. Add two pounds of the breast of mutton cut in squares and browned in butter. Simmer until the meat is done, adding more cream if required. Serve very hot.

BLANQUETTE OF MUTTON

Divide a breast of mutton between the ribs. Put into a saucepan with a head of celery cut fine, a small onion, and a bay-leaf. Cover with boiling water or stock, bring to the boiling point, and boil rapidly for five minutes. Skim and simmer slowly for an hour. Take up the meat and reduce the liquid by rapid boiling to a pint. Strain, thicken while stirring with flour browned in butter, take from the fire, add the yolks of two eggs beaten smooth with a little cold water, season with salt and pepper, and pour over the meat. Sprinkle with minced parsley and serve with a border of mashed potatoes or boiled rice.

RAGOUT OF MUTTON

Have three pounds of the breast of mutton cut into squares. Brown in butter, dredge with flour, and add four cupfuls of water. Stir until the liquid thickens, then add a sliced onion and a diced turnip which have been browned in butter, pepper and salt to season, a bay-leaf, and a tablespoonful of minced parsley. Simmer for an hour and a half, take out the bay-leaf, and serve in a casserole.

BROILED LAMB'S KIDNEYS

Split and skin the kidneys, dip in olive-oil, season with salt, pepper, and grated nutmeg, fasten open with skewers, dip in crumbs, broil, and serve with any preferred sauce.

MUTTON KIDNEYS IN CASSEROLE

Brown the kidneys in butter and put into the casserole. Add a sliced onion fried, a slice of bacon, two potatoes, sliced, and two carrots finely minced. Add enough stock or water to cover, put on the lid, and bake slowly for three hours. Serve in the casserole.

KIDNEY BACON ROLLS

Peel and chop fine a small onion. Mix it with a cupful of bread crumbs, a tablespoonful of chopped parsley, the grated rind of half a lemon, and black pepper, paprika, and grated nutmeg to season. Make to a smooth paste with beaten egg, spread the mixture on thin slices of bacon, and place a small kidney on each. Roll up and fasten with toothpicks or skewers. Put the rolls in a hot oven and bake for twenty minutes. Garnish with parsley and sliced lemon.

DEVILLED KIDNEYS.

Parboil, skin, and split the kidneys, dip in melted butter, season highly with red pepper, and broil. Serve with melted butter and minced parsley.

LAMB STEW WITH DUMPLINGS

Have the lamb cut up into small squares. Cover with cold water, bring gradually to the boil, and cook slowly until it is nearly done. Add three slices of salt pork, cut into dice and fried crisp, two sliced onions, and two or three raw potatoes cut into dice. Cover and cook until the meat is tender. Sift two cupfuls of flour with a spoonful of baking-powder and a pinch of salt. Add enough milk to make a very stiff batter. Drop the dumplings into buttered patty pans, place in a steamer and steam over boiling water. Thicken the gravy with a little flour blended smooth with cold milk.

ENGLISH MUTTON STEW

Have three pounds of the breast of mutton cut into squares. Brown in butter with half a dozen onions chopped fine. Dredge with flour, add six cupfuls of stock or water, and cook until it thickens, stirring constantly. Season with salt, pepper, and grated nutmeg, add two chopped carrots, two chopped turnips, a bunch of sweet herbs, and a crushed clove of garlic. Cook for thirty minutes, add one cupful of lima beans, and cook until the beans are done. Skim the liquid, take out the parsley, and serve. This may be cooked in a casserole, after the meat has been browned.

IRISH STEW

Put trimmed loin mutton chops into a deep pot with alternate layers of seasoned and sliced raw potatoes. Add enough cold water nearly to cover and four each of turnips and onions, cut into small bits. Cover, and simmer slowly until the vegetables are soft, and nearly all the gravy has been absorbed.

STEWED LAMBS' TONGUES

Boil the tongues for an hour and a half. Plunge into cold water and remove the skins. Chop fine a large onion, two slices of carrot, and three slices of turnip. Fry brown in butter, dredge with flour, add two cupfuls of stock or water, and cook until thick, stirring constantly. Season with salt and pepper, a bay-leaf, a pinch of celery seed, and add the sliced tongues. Simmer for two hours. Thicken the gravy with browned flour if required, and remove the bay-leaf. Serve with a border of diced, cooked carrots, and turnips.

PICKLED LAMBS' TONGUES

Cook the tongues for two hours in salted and acidulated water to cover. Drain, put into an earthen jar, pour over boiling spiced vinegar, and let stand for three or four days before using.

FRICASSEE OF LAMBS' TONGUES

Boil five tongues for two hours in salted water. Cool in the water in which they were boiled, skin, and trim. Cut in two lengthwise, season with salt and pepper, dredge with flour, and fry in butter with a little minced parsley. Make a sauce of two tablespoonfuls of grated horseradish, one tablespoonful each of mustard, vinegar, and salad oil, and salt and pepper to season. Serve the sauce separately.

BOILED LEG OF LAMB

Soak the leg for an hour in salted and acidulated water to cover. Drain, wipe dry, dredge with flour, wrap in a cloth, tie firmly, and boil for an hour and a half in water to cover, seasoning with pepper and sweet herbs. When cooked, drain, take off the cloth, garnish with parsley and sliced lemon, and serve with Caper Sauce.

LAMB POT PIE

Cut three pounds of lean mutton or lamb into squares, removing fat and gristle. Cover with cold water, bring to the boil, and simmer for an hour. Add a cupful of salt pork cut into dice, and fried crisp, and stew half an hour longer. Season with salt, pepper, and kitchen bouquet. Sift together two cupfuls of flour, a pinch of salt, and a heaping teaspoonful of baking-powder. Add enough milk to make a soft dough, roll out, cut into small strips, and drop into the stew. Cover, cook for ten minutes, and serve very hot.

LAMB CROQUETTES

Chop fine a pound and a half of uncooked lamb. Peel and chop one large onion and mix it with the meat. Season with pepper and salt. Shape the mixture into small balls, cover with cold water, bring to the boil, and simmer slowly until done. Beat the yolks of four eggs with the strained juice of two lemons and a pinch of salt. Cook slowly over boiling water until it begins to thicken, then add slowly one cupful of the water in which the meat balls were boiled. Cook slowly for ten minutes longer, stirring constantly. Strain the sauce over the balls and serve very hot.

STUFFED SHOULDER OF LAMB

Remove the bone, fill with seasoned crumbs, and sew up. Cover the bottom of a deep pan with thin slices of salt pork and sliced onion. Sprinkle with chopped sweet herbs, lay the meat in, dredge with salt and pepper, and pour over a quart of stock. Cook slowly for two hours. When done, take up the meat, rub the gravy through a coarse sieve, reduce by rapid boiling, thicken with browned flour, pour over the meat, and serve with a border of green peas.

MUTTON BIRDS

Make a stuffing of bread crumbs seasoned with butter, salt, pepper, sage, and summer savory. Mix to a smooth paste with beaten egg. Spread thin slices of raw mutton with the mixture, roll up, and fasten with toothpicks. Brown in butter, then add a little hot water, and finish cooking in the oven, basting frequently. Thicken the gravy with browned flour and serve in a casserole.

CURRIED MUTTON

Chop a large onion fine and fry it in butter. Add one tablespoonful each of curry powder and flour, and a teaspoonful of salt. Stir until thoroughly mixed and add gradually two cupfuls of water or stock. Have ready two pounds of lean mutton, cut in small pieces. Fry brown in butter, add to the curry, and simmer until tender. Surround with a border of boiled rice and serve piping hot.

STUFFED CABBAGE LEAVES

Parboil and chop lean mutton, mix it with an equal quantity of boiled rice, and season with salt, pepper, and butter. Use the white leaves of cabbage. Lay a large spoonful of the meat and rice on each leaf, fold, and tie securely. Tie all the prepared leaves in cheese-cloth and boil slowly for half an hour in the water in which the mutton was boiled. Take off the cloth, remove the strings, and serve with melted butter.

LAMB IN MINT JELLY

Chop fine a bunch of mint, cover with vinegar, and add sugar to taste. Let stand over night. Rub through a fine sieve, and add enough white stock to make the required quantity of jelly. Tint green with color-paste if desired, and add soaked and dissolved gelatine in the proportion of one package to a quart. Add also a tablespoonful of finely chopped mint leaves. Pour a thin layer of jelly into a mould, cover with thin slices of lean, rare, cooked mutton, and let harden. Repeat until the mould is full. Set away to cool, turn out, garnish with fresh mint leaves, and serve with mayonnaise.

SHEPHERD'S PIE

Chop fine and season to taste cold cooked mutton. Put into a buttered baking-dish with enough stock or gravy to moisten. Cover with highly seasoned mashed potato to which a beaten egg has been added and bake until the potato is puffed and brown. Serve in the same dish.

PORK

SAUSAGE ROLLS

Prepare a good pie-crust, not too rich. Roll out half an inch thick, cut into strips, and roll a small sausage in each strip. Put the rolls into a baking-pan, and bake for half or three-quarters of an hour.

FRANKFURTERS

Drop the sausages into boiling water and boil slowly until they float. Drain, and rub with a mixture of butter, lemon-juice, and made mustard, heated very hot.

ROASTED SAUSAGES

Peel, core, and slice four or five tart apples. Make a syrup of one cupful each of sugar and water and cook the apples in it very slowly until tender. Prick the sausages with a fork, simmer in boiling water for fifteen minutes, then drain and brown in the oven. Put the sausages in the centre of a small deep platter, arrange the apples around in a border, and serve.

ROAST HAM WITH SHERRY

Soak a small lean ham in cold water for six hours, wipe dry, put into a saucepan, and cover with cold water. Add an onion, four sprigs of parsley, and six each of cloves and pepper-corns. Boil slowly for two hours. Let cool in the water, take up, skin, and sprinkle thickly with crumbs and sugar. Put into a roasting-pan with one pint of sherry. Bake for forty minutes, basting every ten minutes. Serve the ham hot with the gravy in a separate bowl, or cold if preferred.

BAKED HAM WITH NOODLES

Butter an earthen baking-dish and fill with alternate layers of cold cooked chopped ham and cooked and drained noodles. Have ham on top. Beat two eggs with a cupful of milk, pour over, cover with crumbs, dot with butter, and brown in the oven.

PORK CHOPS À LA MARYLAND

Dip the pork chops in beaten egg, then in seasoned crumbs, and put into a dripping-pan. Cover and cook in a very hot oven, adding a little boiling water if necessary to keep from burning. Serve with any preferred sauce.

JELLIED PIGS' FEET

Take two pounds of the pickled pigs' feet as they come from the market, and boil in water to cover, seasoning with salt, pepper, celery seed, and a little vinegar. Boil until the meat slips from the bones. Remove the meat, cut it into small pieces, and reduce the liquid by rapid boiling to a cupful. Put the meat into a mould, pour the liquid over, and set away to cool. Serve with potato salad.

BROILED PORK TENDERLOIN

Trim off all the fat and the sinew from two tenderloins of pork. Dip in seasoned oil and broil slowly. Chop fine one tablespoonful each of pickles and parsley and mix to a smooth paste with two tablespoonfuls of melted butter and one teaspoonful of vinegar. Pour over the sauce and serve.

BREADED TENDERLOINS

Split and trim the tenderloins, and marinate for an hour in lemon-juice and oil, seasoned with salt and pepper. Dip in fresh bread crumbs, broil, and serve with Piquante Sauce.

PORK TENDERLOINS WITH SWEET POTATOES

Wipe two pork tenderloins, put into a dripping-pan, and brown quickly in a hot oven. Sprinkle with salt, pepper, and powdered sage and bake for forty-five minutes, basting from three to four times. Have half a dozen sweet potatoes parboiled. Peel, cut in half, sprinkle with sugar, and put into the pan with the meat. Cook until soft, basting whenever the meat requires it.

MOCK DUCK

Split a large pork tenderloin, stuff with highly seasoned poultry stuffing, tie into shape, and roast. Baste frequently, take up, remove the string, and serve with gravy made of the drippings.

ROAST SPARERIBS

Trim off the rough ends, crack the ribs through the middle, rub with salt and pepper, fold over where cracked, stuff, sew or wrap with twine, put into dripping-pan with a pint of water, baste frequently and turn once. Should be a rich, even brown. Dressing: Three tablespoonfuls of bread crumbs, a finely chopped onion, same of apple, half a teaspoonful each of powdered sage, salt, and pepper, and two tablespoonfuls of chopped beef suet. Cook slowly in a little water.

ROAST LEG OF PORK

Score a leg of young pork, fill the slits with chopped onion and powdered sage, sprinkle with pepper, salt, and crumbs, and roast as usual, basting frequently. Serve with Cranberry Sauce.

GERMAN ROAST PORK

Boil the pork until tender, drain and roast in the oven with three onions and three carrots sliced thin, a little minced parsley, thyme, and two cloves. Add one cupful of boiling stock, and baste frequently for the first half hour. Then strain and skim the gravy and reduce by rapid boiling until there is just enough to coat the surface of the meat. Spread it upon the meat, sprinkle thickly with crumbs, dust with cinnamon and pepper, and bake brown. Serve with a Cherry Sauce made as follows:

Stone a pound of ripe cherries and simmer the kernels for fifteen minutes in water to cover. Strain the water, add to it the cherries, two cupfuls of water, half a dozen cloves, a wineglassful of claret, a slice of bread, and sugar to taste. Simmer for half an hour, rub through a sieve, and boil until thick. Serve very hot.

PORK ROASTED WITH SWEET POTATOES AND APPLES

Season a loin of pork and roast for two hours and a half, basting often with the drippings and hot water. About an hour before it is done, add peeled sweet potatoes cut in halves and sprinkle with sugar. Fifteen minutes later, add red cooking apples cored but not peeled. Bake until all are done, basting frequently. Thicken the drippings with flour for a gravy and serve separately.

MOCK GOOSE

Parboil a leg of pork and remove the skin. Put it in the oven to roast with a little water in the pan. Rub with butter, sprinkle with powdered sage, pepper, salt, bread crumbs, and finely minced onion. Insert poultry stuffing under the skin of the knuckle. Garnish the dish with balls of fried stuffing. Serve with gooseberry jam or tart apple sauce.

BAKED CHINE WITH SWEET POTATOES

The chine is the backbone with the meat attached. Rub with salt, pepper, flour, and sage, and put into a dripping-pan with a pint of water. Lay a dozen sweet potatoes peeled and cut into halves around the meat. Bake, basting with the dripping. Serve with the potatoes around the meats.

MOCK OYSTERS

Chop fine a pound and a half of fresh pork. Season with salt and pepper and minced onion. Add half the quantity of bread soaked until soft and squeezed dry, bind with two eggs well-beaten, shape into patties, and sauté in drippings. Garnish with sliced lemon and parsley.

VEAL

BROILED SWEETBREADS À LA MAÎTRE D'HÔTEL

Soak and parboil the sweetbreads, cut into slices, season with salt and pepper, dredge with flour, and broil, basting with melted butter. Serve with Maître d'Hôtel Sauce.

CALF'S LIVER IN CASSEROLE

Lard a whole liver with strips of salt pork. Brown in butter and drain off the fat. Brown a heaping tablespoonful of flour in fresh butter, add one cupful of white wine, and cook until thick and smooth, stirring constantly. Put the liver into a buttered casserole, pour over the gravy, add pepper to season, a bay-leaf, a small bunch of parsley, a bruised clove of garlic, two shallots, two onions, and a small carrot, sliced. Cover and cook slowly for an hour. Put the liver on a platter and strain the gravy over it. Return to the casserole, reheat, and serve.

VEAL LIVER PÂTÉ

Run twice through the meat-chopper one pound of calf's liver and half a pound of fat bacon. Season with salt, pepper, mace, and parsley, add two tablespoonfuls of finely chopped lean ham and a chopped onion which has been fried in fat. Mix with the yolks of two eggs and then fold in the stiffly beaten whites. Line a mould with thin slices of bacon, put in the meat, cover with bacon, and bake slowly in a moderate oven. When it can be pierced easily it is done. Let cool in the mould, turn out, and garnish with parsley and lemon.

BOILED CALF'S TONGUE

Soak for an hour in cold water. Cover with fresh cold water, bring quickly to the boil, and skim. Add for each tongue a carrot and turnip sliced and a small onion stuck with three cloves. Add sweet herbs to season and a little salt and pepper. Cook slowly for two hours. Drain, skin, and serve with a border of spaghetti or macaroni. If they are to be served cold, let them cool in the water in which they were cooked.

VEAL CHOPS À LA PROVENÇALE

Trim and clean veal chops and sauté in olive-oil with a finely chopped onion. Add a little brown stock, half a dozen chopped mushrooms, two minced beans of garlic, and a teaspoonful of minced parsley. Bring to the boil, thicken the gravy with browned flour cooked in butter, and serve.

BRAISED VEAL CUTLETS

Trim and clean convenient pieces of veal cutlet and lard with thin strips of bacon. Brown in a little butter, add a little clear stock with chopped onion, carrot, and turnip to season, and simmer until done. Drain and serve with string beans.

BAKED VEAL CUTLET

Butter a baking-pan, pour in a cupful of cold water, and lay in a thick slice of veal cutlet. Spread over the cutlet a dressing made of two cupfuls of bread crumbs, a chopped onion, a beaten egg, and salt, pepper and melted butter to season. Cover the pan, bake for half an hour, then take off the lid and brown.

VEAL BIRDS

Cut veal cutlets into convenient pieces and flatten with a potato-masher. Mix seasoned crumbs with chopped salt pork or bacon and make a stuffing. Roll up and tie into shape with strings. Brown in fat with a sliced carrot and a chopped onion. Add one cupful of stock, cover, and cook slowly for twenty minutes. This can be served in a casserole.

MOCK FRIED OYSTERS

Cut a veal cutlet into small pieces. Pound each piece until very tender. Dip in beaten egg, then in seasoned crumbs, and fry in deep fat. Serve with Tomato Sauce and shredded cabbage.

STEWED BREAST OF VEAL

Brown a breast of veal in butter. Add two cupfuls of hot water or stock, a bunch of sweet herbs, two onions, half a dozen cloves, the peel of half a lemon, a blade of mace, and salt and pepper to season. Cook slowly, take up the veal, remove the larger bones, and strain the cooking liquid. Cook together one tablespoonful each of butter and flour, add the veal stock and one cupful of cream. Cook until thick, stirring constantly. Take from the fire, add the yolks of two eggs well-beaten, the juice of half a lemon, and half a dozen parboiled oysters. Pour the sauce over the meat and serve.

VEAL STEW WITH DUMPLINGS

Cut three pounds of veal into strips, cover with cold water, boil, and skim. Add pepper, salt, and a little butter and a sufficient quantity of raw potatoes cut into balls with a French cutter. Make a batter of two eggs, half a cupful of milk, a pinch of salt, and enough sifted flour to make a batter that will drop from the spoon. Drop into the stew a spoonful at a time, cover, and boil for twenty minutes. Or steam the dumplings in oiled patty pans.

GERMAN VEAL STEW

Sprinkle a breast of veal with salt and ginger. Slice an onion and fry it in butter with a little parsley and two or three celery tops. When hot, put in the breast of veal. Cover tightly and brown the veal in the same fat. Add half a cupful of canned tomatoes and a very little hot water. Cover, and cook slowly for two hours, turning the meat frequently. Thicken the gravy with flour rubbed smooth in a little cold water, season with minced parsley or carraway seed, boil up once, and serve.

ROAST LOIN OF VEAL

Leave the kidney in. Unroll the loin and stuff with highly seasoned poultry stuffing, packing well around the kidney. Fold, tie firmly into shape, and roast, basting with the drippings and a little hot water. Before taking up, dredge with flour, and baste two or three times with melted butter. Take off the string and serve with a gravy made from the stuffing and thickened drippings.

STUFFED BREAST OF VEAL

Make a stuffing of stale bread crumbs and mix with a liberal quantity of finely chopped salt pork. Season with onion, salt, pepper, minced parsley, and melted butter. Fill the cavity under the thick part of the breast with as much stuffing as can be forced in and skewer into shape. Roast, basting frequently with melted butter and drippings.

ROAST SHOULDER OF VEAL

Have the knuckle removed from a shoulder of veal and roast the fillet, basting frequently with melted butter and the drippings. Garnish with quartered lemons and parsley and serve with Oyster Sauce.

ROAST VEAL À L'ITALIENNE

Bone a loin of veal, stuff with seasoned crumbs, and tie into shape. Season with salt and pepper, rub thickly with butter, and put it into a roasting-pan with half a cupful of water. Cover and roast for two hours, basting frequently. Drain the meat and brush it with the yolk of an egg, beaten smooth with half a cupful of stock. Sprinkle thickly with crumbs, grated cheese, and minced parsley, dot with butter, and brown in a very hot oven. Serve with mashed potatoes or potato croquettes.

BREAST OF VEAL BAKED

Rub a well-trimmed breast of veal with melted butter, season highly with salt and pepper, and brown quickly in a hot oven. Pour over two cupfuls of canned tomatoes and bake until the veal is well done. Serve with the tomatoes as a garnish for the meat.

VEAL LOAF

Chop fine three pounds of raw veal. Mix with three eggs beaten with three tablespoonfuls of cream or milk, four crackers rolled and sifted, and pepper, salt, and sage to season highly. Shape into a loaf and bake, covered in a little water, basting frequently with melted butter. Serve either hot or cold.

BRAISED KNUCKLE OF VEAL

Have a three-pound knuckle of veal larded and brown it in pork fat, seasoning with salt and pepper. Add stock to moisten and one cupful of partially cooked lima beans. Cook for forty-five minutes, and serve very hot.

VEAL IN CASSEROLE

Have lean veal cut into convenient pieces. Put into a buttered casserole and cover with milk. Add a teaspoonful or more of finely chopped parsley, cover, and simmer very slowly until done. It must not boil. Thicken with a little flour cooked in butter, season to taste, and serve.

JELLIED VEAL

Cover a knuckle of veal with cold water, bring to the boil, and simmer for two hours, skimming as needed. Add a slice of onion, a blade of mace, a dozen cloves, half a dozen pepper-corns, a pinch of allspice, and half a nutmeg grated. When the meat falls from the bones, take out the bones, shred the meat, and reduce the liquid by rapid boiling until there is barely enough to cover the meat. Wet a mould with cold water, put in the meat, add to the liquid the juice of a lemon and salt and pepper to season, and pour over the meat. Let stand overnight and serve cold.

KOENIGSBERGER KLOPS

Chop together three-quarters of a pound of veal and one-quarter pound of fresh pork. Soak three slices of stale bread in cold water, wring dry, and add to the meat. Add salt, pepper, and minced parsley to season. Shape into small balls, cover with cold water, bring to the boil, and simmer gently for half an hour. Strain the cooking liquor and reduce by rapid boiling to a pint. Cook together one tablespoonful each of butter and flour, add the cooking liquid, and cook until thick, stirring constantly. Take from the fire, add the yolks of two eggs well-beaten and two tablespoonfuls of capers with a little of the caper vinegar. Pour over the klops and serve.

VEAL AND OYSTER PIE

Cut into small pieces one pound of the neck of veal, cover with cold water, and cook slowly for an hour. Add two or three slices of salt pork cut into dice, a chopped onion, a tablespoonful of minced parsley, and salt and pepper to taste. Make a cupful of Cream Sauce in a separate pan, pour into the veal, and cook for twenty minutes longer. Pour into a baking-dish, cover the top with a layer of raw oysters, dredge with salt and pepper, cover with pastry, and bake for half an hour. Serve either hot or cold.

VEAL CROQUETTES

Chop fine cold cooked veal and season with salt, pepper, paprika, celery salt, grated onion, and minced parsley. Mix with a little very thick Cream Sauce and cool. Shape into croquettes, dip in egg and crumbs, and fry in deep fat. Serve with a border of green peas.

MOCK TERRAPIN

Reheat cold cooked veal, cut into dice, in Cream Sauce. Take from the fire and add an egg beaten with a tablespoonful of sherry. Add also two or three hard-boiled eggs coarsely chopped and a little minced parsley. Heat, but do not boil. Season with salt and red and white pepper, and serve.

CHICKEN

BROILED CHICKEN

Have young chickens cleaned and split down the back. Break the joints, season with salt and pepper, and rub with melted butter. Broil for twenty minutes and serve very hot.

FRIED CHICKEN

Clean and cut up two spring chickens, season with salt and pepper, and fry brown in butter with a chopped onion and a dozen fresh mushrooms. Pour over a wineglassful of white wine, and a cupful of stock. Add two cupfuls of canned tomatoes which have been rubbed through a sieve, and a tablespoonful of minced parsley. Thicken with flour browned in butter, heat thoroughly, season to taste, and serve.

FRIED CHICKEN WITH GREEN PEPPERS

Clean and joint two spring chickens, fry brown in butter, and put into the oven to finish cooking. Seed and shred six sweet peppers and boil in salted water until soft. Drain, and add to the chicken. Pour over two cupfuls of cream, bring to the boil, thicken with a little flour cooked in butter, and serve.

BREADED FRIED CHICKEN

Clean and cut up a young chicken, dip in beaten egg, then in seasoned crumbs, and fry brown in fat to cover. Serve with Cream Sauce to which minced parsley has been added.

CHICKEN STUFFED WITH OYSTERS

Fill a chicken with drained oysters which have been seasoned highly with salt, pepper, and melted butter. Sew the chicken up in cheese-cloth and boil, allowing twenty-five minutes to the pound. Take off the cloth, pour over a Maître d'Hôtel Sauce, and serve.

CHICKEN STEWED WITH ASPARAGUS

Clean and cut up a chicken, season with salt and pepper, and brown in butter. Dredge with flour and sprinkle with minced parsley. Boil two bunches of asparagus in salted water until tender but not broken. Put a lump of butter and a tablespoonful of cream into a saucepan and put half of the asparagus on it. Sprinkle with pepper, lay the pieces of chicken upon it, cover with the remainder of the asparagus, dot with butter, pour over a cupful of cream, and cook slowly until done. Serve with small squares of fried bread or with toast points.

SPANISH CHICKEN STEW

Clean and joint two spring chickens. Brown in butter and add five sliced onions, a can of tomatoes, four cloves of garlic, two tablespoonfuls of butter, a pod of red pepper without the seeds, and salt to taste. Cook slowly for forty-five minutes, adding stock or water if necessary to keep from burning. Take out the pepper and the garlic, add a can of peas, and simmer for fifteen minutes longer. Thicken the gravy with two tablespoonfuls of flour rubbed smooth with a little cold water and the yolk of an egg well-beaten.

FRICASSEE OF CHICKEN

Clean and cut up the chicken, and brown in butter with a sliced onion and a carrot. Season with salt and pepper, dredge with flour, add three cupfuls of stock or water, and cook until the sauce thickens, stirring constantly. Add a cupful of canned tomatoes and simmer until the chicken is done. Add a can of mushrooms cut in pieces, and a little minced parsley. Heat thoroughly and serve.

FRICASSEE OF CHICKEN WITH BISCUIT

Sift together four cupfuls of flour, four teaspoonfuls of baking-powder, and a pinch of salt. Work into it half a cupful of butter, and add enough milk to make a soft dough. Roll out, cut into biscuits, and bake. Cook two chickens, cleaned and cut up, in water to cover, seasoning with salt and pepper. When very tender, thicken the liquid with flour cooked in butter. Stir constantly. Split the biscuits and cover a serving platter with them. Pour over the chicken and serve.

CHICKEN PIE

Clean and cut up a chicken, boil until tender, cool, and remove the bones. Line a buttered baking-dish with a rich biscuit dough, and put in half of the chicken, seasoning with butter, pepper, and salt. Add a layer of hard-boiled eggs cut in slices, and the rest of the chicken. A few potato balls cut with a French vegetable cutter, and boiled until nearly done may be added. Add enough of the water in which the chicken was boiled to fill the dish, cover with a biscuit crust which has a large hole in the centre for the steam to escape, brush with the beaten white of egg, and bake for half an hour or more.

CHICKEN POTPIE

Clean and cut up the chicken. Put a small plate in the bottom of the kettle, put in the chicken, cover with hot water, and season with butter, pepper, and salt. Sift together three cupfuls of flour and three teaspoonfuls of baking-powder. Mix with enough milk or water to make a very thick batter. Drop the batter by spoonfuls into buttered patty pans, place in steamer, cover and steam over another pan of boiling water. Skim out the chicken, arrange on a platter, and thicken the gravy while stirring with flour blended with a little cold milk. Pour over the chicken and dumplings and serve.

ROAST CHICKEN

Stuff a chicken with highly seasoned crumbs to which a few chopped chestnuts have been added. Sew up, and lard the breast with thin strips of bacon. Roast and serve with Cream Sauce to which chopped cooked oysters have been added.

CURRIED CHICKEN

Clean and cut up a chicken and boil it until tender in water to cover. Drain the chicken and brown in butter with two small onions sliced. Sprinkle with two teaspoonfuls of curry powder, pour over the water in which the chicken was boiled, heat thoroughly, and thicken while stirring with a tablespoonful of flour rubbed smooth with a little cold water. Take from the fire, add the beaten yolk of an egg, and serve with a border of boiled rice.

CHICKEN À LA CRÉOLE

Clean and cut up a young chicken, season with salt and pepper, and fry brown in hot fat with two thinly sliced onions. Dredge with flour and add one cupful each of white stock and stewed and strained tomatoes. Cook until it thickens, stirring constantly, and simmer the chicken in it until tender, adding more stock if needed. Add a tablespoonful of tarragon vinegar, salt and pepper to season, and a cupful of cooked and broken macaroni. Serve very hot with a garnish of parsley.

CHICKEN À LA JEAN

181

Clean and disjoint the chicken. Fry brown in an iron kettle, using equal parts of butter and olive-oil for fat. When brown, season with salt and pepper, pour in a cupful of stock, cover, and cook slowly until done, adding more stock if required. Dredge with flour and turn the chicken slowly in the gravy until the gravy is thick. Take up the chicken, strain the gravy over it, garnish with parsley, and serve.

CHICKEN IN CASSEROLE

Put a small cleaned chicken into a casserole with a dozen peeled onions, two bay-leaves, a cupful of carrot cut into dice, a small turnip chopped fine, and two stalks of celery cut into small pieces. Fill the casserole half full of boiling stock, cover, and cook in a hot oven for an hour and a half, basting frequently. When the chicken is half done, add salt and pepper to season. Serve in the casserole. Either fresh or canned mushrooms may be added.

JELLIED CHICKEN

Have a chicken cleaned and cut up. Cook in boiling water to cover until the meat falls from the bones. Take out the bones, remove the skin, season with salt and pepper, and arrange in a mould. Reduce the liquid by rapid boiling and add to it a package of soaked and dissolved gelatine, pepper and salt to season highly, and the juice of a lemon. Pour over the chicken and cool on ice. Serve with a garnish of hard-boiled eggs and parsley.

MAYONNAISE OF CHICKEN

Clean and disjoint the chicken, and boil until tender in water to cover. Cool in the water in which it was boiled and remove the skin and fat and bones. Keep the pieces of chicken as large as possible. Arrange on a platter, and pour over a stiff mayonnaise dressing. Sprinkle with minced parsley, and garnish with lettuce leaves.

PRESSED CHICKEN

Have two chickens cleaned and cut up. Boil until the meat drops from the bones, then drain, and chop it fine. Reduce the liquid by rapid boiling to a cupful. Add to it a heaping tablespoonful of butter, a teaspoonful of pepper, a pinch of allspice, and an egg well-beaten. Mix thoroughly with the meat and press into a buttered mould. Cool on ice and serve cold, garnished with slices of hard-boiled eggs and parsley.

CHICKEN À LA WALDORF

Cut cold cooked chicken into dice. Reheat in two cupfuls of cream, seasoning with salt and pepper. Thicken with the yolks of two eggs beaten with two tablespoonfuls of Madeira. Mix thoroughly, and heat but do not boil. Take from the fire, add a heaping tablespoonful of butter, and serve.

CHICKEN CROQUETTES

Chop fine cold cooked chicken, and mix with a cupful of Cream Sauce. Add two eggs well-beaten, seasoning to taste, and enough bread crumbs to make the mixture very stiff. Cool, shape into croquettes, dip in egg and crumbs, fry in deep fat, and serve with any preferred sauce.

CHICKEN AND MACARONI

Shred cold cooked chicken very fine. Arrange it on a buttered baking-dish with alternate layers of cooked and broken macaroni, seasoning each layer with butter, pepper, and salt. Moisten with cream, cover with crumbs, dot with butter, sprinkle with cheese, and bake brown. Serve in the baking-dish.

DUCK

BRAISED DUCKS WITH OLIVES

Partly roast a pair of ducks and put them into a saucepan with two cupfuls of stock and two dozen pitted olives which have been rinsed in boiling water. Cover and cook in the oven for half an hour, basting frequently. Take up the ducks, skim off the fat, thicken the gravy with a little flour and butter cooked together, pour the sauce over the ducks, and serve.

ROAST DUCK

Rub a prepared and cleaned duck with butter, dredge with flour, season with salt and pepper, and roast, covered, in a hot oven. Make a gravy of the drippings, adding stoned olives to it, and surround the duck with a border of green peas.

GOOSE

ROAST GOOSE

Parboil for two hours, drain, and stuff with seasoned mashed potatoes. Roast in a covered roaster with two cupfuls of water in the pan. When done pour off the surplus fat, add enough water or stock to make the amount of gravy required, thicken with browned flour and a little butter cooked together, and season to taste.

TURKEY

JELLIED TURKEY

Put a tough turkey into cold water to cover, bring to the boil, and cook until the meat slips from the bones. Remove the meat, chop it fine, and return the bones to the stock. Simmer for two hours, and strain through cheese-cloth. There should be two cupfuls of the liquid. Add one package of gelatine that has been soaked and dissolved, and season with salt, pepper, grated onion, lemon-juice, and kitchen bouquet. Dip individual moulds in cold water, and put a slice of hard-boiled egg or pickled beet into the bottom of each one. Put in a little of the jelly, and let harden. Fill the moulds nearly to the brim with the minced and seasoned turkey, cover with the jelly, and set away to cool. Serve with mayonnaise.

ROAST TURKEY STUFFED WITH CHESTNUTS

Boil a quart of Spanish chestnuts, peel, chop, and mash them. Mix to a paste with melted butter, seasoning with salt and pepper, and stuff the turkey loosely. Roast as usual, in covered roaster and serve with Cranberry Sauce.

ROAST TURKEY STUFFED WITH OYSTERS

Make a stuffing of equal parts of bread and cracker crumbs rolled fine. Season highly with salt, pepper, and melted butter, and add a pint of raw oysters with their liquor. Add also two eggs well-beaten. Stuff the turkey loosely, truss, and roast, in a covered roaster. Turn over when brown on top. Make a gravy with the drippings, using browned flour to thicken.

TURKEY CROQUETTES

Chop cold cooked turkey fine, season to taste, and mix with very thick Cream Sauce. Season with salt, pepper, celery salt, and curry powder. When cool and stiff shape into croquettes, dip in egg and crumbs, and fry in deep fat. Serve with a border of green peas.

ESCALLOPED TURKEY

Reheat cold cooked turkey, cut small, in a Cream Sauce. Arrange in a buttered baking-dish in alternate layers with seasoned crumbs, having crumbs and dots of butter on top. Add also any bits of stuffing that may remain. Add stock or gravy to moisten, sprinkle with crumbs, dot with butter, and brown in the oven.

ESCALLOPED TURKEY AND SAUSAGE

Butter a baking-dish, and fill it with alternate layers of cold cooked minced turkey and sausage. Fill the dish with stock or gravy to moisten, cover thickly with crumbs, and pour over half a cupful or more of cream or milk with which a well-beaten egg has been mixed. Season with pepper and salt, dot with butter, and bake covered. Sprinkle with minced parsley before serving.

ESCALLOPED TURKEY AND OYSTERS

Reheat cold cooked turkey, cut fine, in a Cream Sauce, seasoning with salt, pepper, and grated nutmeg. Put into a buttered baking-dish with alternate layers of drained oysters and seasoned crumbs and dots of butter, and brown in the oven.

TURKEY LOAF

Chop fine the meat of a cold turkey, and to each cupful add one-third of a cupful of cracker crumbs and one egg. Mix thoroughly and add enough of the stuffing to season. Shape into a loaf, roll in cracker crumbs, dot with butter, and bake for half an hour.

PIGEON

PIGEON PIE

Clean and cut up the pigeons. Cook until tender in boiling water to cover, seasoning with salt, pepper, and chopped onion. Drain, and put into each pigeon a hard-boiled egg, with salt, pepper, thyme, and a little butter to season. Put into a deep baking-dish and strain over them the liquid in which they were cooked. Add one cupful of cream, one tablespoonful of butter, two tablespoonfuls of bread crumbs, one tablespoonful of minced parsley, and a pinch each of thyme and salt. Cover the pie with a rich crust, bake, and serve either hot or cold.

BROILED SQUABS WITH BACON

Clean the birds and split without detaching. Dip in seasoned oil, broil, and serve on toast. Pour over melted butter, seasoned with lemon-juice and minced parsley, and garnish with slices of fried bacon.

TWENTY WAYS TO COOK POTATOES

BOILED POTATOES

Peel potatoes of uniform size and soak for half an hour in cold water. Cover with boiling salted water and cook until tender but not broken. Drain thoroughly and keep hot, uncovered, until dry and mealy. Or, without peeling, let them stand in cold salted water for half an hour before cooking. Season with salt, pepper, and butter if desired. Minced chives or parsley may be added.

POTATO BALLS

Season a pint of hot mashed potatoes with salt, pepper, celery salt, minced parsley, and butter. Add a little onion-juice if desired or a beaten yolk. Moisten with a little milk or cream and add half of a beaten egg if the yolk has not been used. Shape into smooth round balls, brush with the remainder of the egg, and bake on a buttered tin until brown. Or, dip in egg and crumbs and fry in deep fat. The celery salt may be omitted.

BAKED POTATOES

Scrub potatoes of equal size, wipe dry, and bake for an hour in a hot oven. Break the skins that the steam may escape. Peel before baking if desired.

BAKED MASHED POTATOES

Mix together two cupfuls of hot mashed potatoes, half a cupful of cream or milk, two tablespoonfuls of butter, the yolk of one egg, and the whites of four, and salt and pepper to season. Beat very light, folding in the stiffly beaten whites last. Turn into a buttered baking-dish, brush with the beaten yolk of egg, and brown quickly. Or, arrange mashed potatoes in layers in a buttered baking-dish, alternating with lumps of butter and grated Parmesan cheese. Have cheese and butter on top. Brown in the oven and serve in the same dish.

BROWNED POTATOES

185

Peel and parboil potatoes of equal size. Drain and put into a baking-dish or into the pan with a roast and bake until brown, basting with butter or drippings. They may be dredged with flour before baking.

CREAMED POTATOES

Cover the potatoes with cold salted water, bring gradually to the boil, and cook slowly. Cool in the refrigerator. When ready to serve, peel and chop very fine, and reheat in hot butter, seasoning with salt, black pepper, and cream. Cover and let stand for ten minutes before serving.

POTATO CAKE

Mash boiled potatoes, season with salt and pepper, dredge with flour, and moisten with a very little milk. Butter a frying-pan, and shape into a flat cake to fit it. Cover and cook slowly until done, then dot the top with butter, and brown in the oven. The milk may be omitted and the potato shaped like an omelet. Fry brown, turning once.

POTATO CROQUETTES

Mix together two cupfuls of hot mashed potatoes, two teaspoonfuls of butter, one-third cupful of grated cheese, and salt, cayenne, and grated nutmeg to season. Add the yolks of two eggs beaten with two tablespoonfuls of cream, mix thoroughly, and shape into croquettes. Dip in flour, then in beaten egg, then in crumbs, and fry in deep fat.

DUCHESS POTATOES

Beat the yolk of an egg and add to it enough well-seasoned hot mashed potatoes to make a stiff mixture. Shape into balls, put into a shallow buttered baking-pan, brush with the well-beaten white of the egg, and brown in the oven.

POTATO FLAKES

Butter a baking-dish and press hot boiled potatoes into it through a colander or potato ricer, having first sprinkled the potatoes with salt and pepper. Put into the oven for a few minutes and serve. Or, sprinkle with crumbs, pour over a little melted butter, and brown in the oven.

POTATOES JULIENNE

Cut peeled and sliced potatoes into thin match-like shreds. Soak for an hour in cold water, drain, dry thoroughly, and fry in deep fat in a frying-basket. Sprinkle with salt and serve. These are sometimes called Shoestring Potatoes.

HASHED BROWN POTATOES

Peel and chop fine enough raw potatoes to make a pint. Heat two tablespoonfuls of beef drippings in a frying-pan, add the potatoes, sprinkle with salt and pepper, add two tablespoonfuls of stock or hot water, cover and cook slowly until soft, then more rapidly until brown. If more liquid is required, add a little stock or water or cream. When a crisp crust is formed, loosen at the edges, and turn like an omelet.

HASHED CREAMED POTATOES

Peel raw potatoes, chop fine, and put into a buttered baking-dish with alternate layers of well-seasoned Cream Sauce, sprinkling each layer of potatoes with salt, pepper, minced parsley, and onion-juice. Have sauce on top. Sprinkle with crumbs, bake for half an hour, and serve in the baking-dish.

LYONNAISE POTATOES

Slice two small onions and fry in butter. Reheat with six or eight boiled potatoes sliced thin or cut into dice. Season with salt and pepper, cook until brown, sprinkle with minced parsley, and serve. A few drops of vinegar or a teaspoonful of lemon-juice may be added.

MASHED POTATOES

Peel potatoes and soak for an hour in cold water. Drain, cover with fresh cold water, adding a teaspoonful of salt. Boil, put through a potato ricer, season liberally with butter, moisten slightly with milk or cream, and add pepper and salt to taste. If desired, add a little celery salt. Beat thoroughly and serve; or, put into the serving-dish, score the top into squares with a knife, pour over a little melted butter, and brown in the oven.

BOILED NEW POTATOES

Scrape off the skins, or rub off with a coarse cloth. Soak for an hour in cold water, drain, cover with cold salted water, and bring to the boil. Cook for half an hour, drain, sprinkle with salt, and dry for two or three minutes before serving. Add a little melted butter if desired. Or, pour over a cupful of cream or milk, which has been boiled with a heaping tablespoonful of butter. Or season with salt, pepper, minced parsley, melted butter and cream; a sprinkle of carraway seed may be added, or, serve withHollandaise Sauce.

CREAMED NEW POTATOES

Rub the skins from new potatoes with a coarse cloth. Cook until done in boiling salted water, pour over a Cream Sauce, and, if desired, sprinkle with minced parsley. Old potatoes, boiled whole, may be served in the same way.

POTATOES O'BRIEN

Cut boiled potatoes into dice and reheat in butter with canned red peppers cut into strips or fried green peppers, or both, and season with chopped onion fried in butter if desired. Or, prepare according to directions given for French Fried Potatoes, cutting into dice and frying with them the red or green peppers or both.

STUFFED POTATOES

Cut the top from each of six baked potatoes, scoop out the pulp, and mash to a smooth paste with three tablespoonfuls each of butter and cream, and salt and pepper to season. Add one-fourth cupful of grated cheese and cook to a smooth paste. Take from the fire, stir in one well-beaten egg, fill the skins, and bake.

POTATOES AND CHEESE

Peel and chop raw potatoes and cook, covered, very slowly in seasoned butter. When they are soft, drain and put into a baking-dish in layers, alternating with grated Parmesan cheese. Pour over a little melted butter and bake for half an hour in a slow oven. Serve in the same dish.

POTATOES À LA PROVENÇALE

Peel and slice the potatoes, wipe very dry, and sauté in oil. Cook slowly, adding a little minced garlic and onion towards the last. Finish cooking in the oven. Just before serving, drain and season with salt, minced parsley, and lemon-juice.

ONE HUNDRED AND FIFTY WAYS TO COOK OTHER VEGETABLES

BOILED ARTICHOKES

Cut off the tips of the leaves and round off the bottoms, removing the stalk and trimming away the under leaves. Soak for half an hour in salted water, washing thoroughly. Boil until tender in a large quantity of salted water. Drain, and remove the soft inside with a spoon. Put into a serving dish, dot with butter, heat until the butter is melted, and serve; or, serve with Béchamel or Hollandaise Sauce.

BOILED ASPARAGUS

Scrape and clean the asparagus and tie into bundles of five or six stalks each, taking care to have the heads even. Cook rapidly in boiling salted water until tender. Drain, and serve on toast with melted butter to which a little lemon-juice may be added. Drawn-Butter, Cream, Hollandaise, or White Sauce may be used instead. The tips may be cooked in the same way.

BAKED ASPARAGUS

Cut the tender parts of the asparagus into inch-lengths, boil until tender in salted water, and drain. Put a layer into a buttered baking-dish, season with pepper and salt, dot with butter, sprinkle with crumbs and hard-boiled eggs chopped fine. Repeat until the dish is full, having crumbs and butter on top. Bake for half an hour and serve in the same dish. A thin Cream Sauce may be poured over before sprinkling with the crumbs, and the eggs omitted. A little grated cheese may be used instead.

CREAMED ASPARAGUS

Boil the tender parts of asparagus until tender, drain, and chop. Reheat in a Cream Sauce to which a bit of baking-soda has been added. Season with salt and pepper and cool. Stir into it three eggs well-beaten with two tablespoonfuls of cream. Pour into a buttered baking-dish and bake covered for twenty minutes.

ESCALLOPED ASPARAGUS

Wash and cut up a bunch of asparagus, discarding the tough ends. Boil in salted water until tender, and drain. Boil three eggs hard, throw into cold water, remove the shells and, chop fine. Butter a shallow baking-dish, put in a layer of asparagus, cover with chopped eggs, sprinkle with grated cheese, and repeat until the dish is full, having asparagus on top. Pour over two cupfuls of Drawn-Butter or Cream Sauce, cover with crumbs, dot with butter, sprinkle with grated cheese, and bake until brown.

BOILED STRING-BEANS

Cut off the ends, remove the strings, and cut into two or three pieces. Wash in cold water, drain, and boil until tender in salted water. Drain, and serve with melted butter. A bit of bacon or ham, for flavor, may be boiled with the beans.

STRING-BEANS WITH CREAM

String the beans and boil until tender in as little water as possible. Without draining, add half a cupful of cream, a tablespoonful of butter, and pepper and salt to season.

STRING-BEANS WITH SOUR SAUCE

Remove the strings from a quart of beans, cut in pieces, boil with a pinch of soda until tender, and drain. Add a tablespoonful of butter blended with a teaspoonful of flour, a tablespoonful of vinegar, and salt and pepper to taste. Simmer for five minutes, while stirring add in a well-beaten egg, and serve immediately.

STRING-BEANS EN SALADE

Prepare according to directions given for Boiled String-Beans, changing the water once, and add a tablespoonful of butter after changing. Drain and pour over aFrench dressing to which a little chopped onion has been added. Serve hot. The onion may be omitted.

STRING-BEANS À LA BRETONNE

Prepare according to directions given for Boiled String-Beans. Cut two small onions into thin slices, fry golden brown in butter, dredge with flour, and add a little white stock. Cook until thick, stirring constantly, and seasoning with salt and pepper. Add the cooked beans to the sauce with a crushed bean of garlic, cook for ten minutes, sprinkle with minced parsley, and serve. The garlic and parsley may be omitted and one chopped onion used.

STRING-BEANS À LA PROVENÇALE

Prepare according to directions given for Boiled String-Beans and drain. Slice an onion, fry golden brown in oil with minced parsley, thyme, chives, and a bay-leaf. Remove the bay-leaf, add a little vinegar, pour over the beans, reheat, and serve. The juice of a lemon may be used instead of vinegar.

STEWED LIMA BEANS

Cover a pint of lima beans with a quart of boiling water and cook for thirty minutes. Drain off half the water, add a tablespoonful of chopped salt pork and a little grated onion and minced parsley. Add a pinch of salt and a cupful of hot milk and stew until the beans are tender. Thicken with flour cooked in butter and rubbed smooth in a little cold milk.

LIMA BEANS WITH ONIONS

Soak a pint of dried beans overnight, drain, and boil until tender in fresh water to cover. Drain and keep warm. Parboil and chop three small onions, fry in butter, and reheat the beans with the onions. Moisten with brown gravy or thickened stock.

LIMA BEANS À LA PHILADELPHIA

Prepare a pint of beans according to directions given for Stewed Beans and reheat in Cream Sauce, seasoning with salt, pepper, and a little grated onion. Take from the fire and add the yolks of two eggs beaten with a little cream. Serve very hot.

BOILED BLACK BEANS

Soak the beans in cold water for three hours, rinse thoroughly, and boil for three hours, or more if necessary. Fry three thin slices of bacon and add to it a little stock. Season with Chutney, mushroom catsup, and anchovy essence. Reheat the drained beans in the sauce.

FRIJOLES MEXICANA

Pick over and wash one pound of small red Mexican beans, cover with cold water, bring to the boil, and add a pinch of soda. Cook for five minutes, drain and rinse, then cover with cold water, and cook slowly until soft. Melt two or three tablespoonfuls each of drippings and butter. When sizzling hot drop in two or three cloves of garlic, peeled and crushed. Keep stirring until well browned, then add two or three chopped and seeded green peppers and a large onion, sliced. Stir until cooked, then add a few tablespoonfuls of the boiled beans, mashing a few of them to form a thickening gravy. Add the rest of the beans with a portion of the liquor in which they were cooked, and three or four tomatoes, peeled and cut up. Simmer for an hour. When ready to serve, grate one-half pound of Mexican or Parmesan cheese and stir into the beans. Serve very hot.

STEWED KIDNEY BEANS

Soak a cupful of beans overnight in cold water. Drain, cover with cold water, add a chopped onion and a carrot, three or four slices of bacon, and a pinch of soda. Simmer until the beans are tender, drain, season with butter, salt, and pepper, and serve hot.

KIDNEY BEANS À LA CRÉOLE

Soak overnight a quart of kidney beans and cook until tender in boiling salted water. Drain, put a layer into a baking-dish with half a pound of bacon in one piece which has been boiled until tender and skinned, and a chopped onion.

Cover with beans, season with salt and red pepper, fill the baking-dish with cold water, and bake slowly until the liquid is nearly absorbed.

BOSTON BAKED BEANS

Wash and pick over a quart of navy beans. Soak overnight in cold water to cover. In the morning drain, cover with fresh water, and heat slowly, keeping the water below the boiling point until the skins will burst when a spoonful is gently breathed upon. Drain the beans. Scald and scrape the rind of half a pound of fat salt pork, cut off one slice, and put into the bottom of the bean-pot. Fill the pot with the beans and bury the rest of the pork in it, scoring the rind deeply. Mix one teaspoonful of salt with one tablespoonful of molasses and three tablespoonfuls of sugar, add a cupful of boiling water, pour over the beans, and add more boiling water if necessary to fill the pot. Cover the bean-pot and bake in a slow oven for six or eight hours, adding boiling water as needed. During the last hour of cooking, remove the lid so that the top will be brown. A teaspoonful of mustard may be added with the other seasoning. This is the genuine Boston recipe. A sliced onion put in with the pork is considered by many to be an improvement.

BOSTON BAKED BEANS WITH TOMATO SAUCE

Prepare according to directions given for Boston Baked Beans. Chop an onion fine and cook it in a can of tomatoes for half an hour. Two hours before the beans are done, strain the tomato into the bean pot, adding a little at a time.

BEAN CROQUETTES

Boil two cupfuls of soaked beans until soft. Drain, press through a colander, season with salt and red pepper, and add one tablespoonful each of molasses, butter, and vinegar. Mix thoroughly, cool, shape into croquettes, dip in egg and crumbs, fry in deep fat, and serve with Tomato Sauce.

BOILED BEETS

Select small smooth beets and clean without cutting or scraping. Boil for an hour or two and cool. Remove the skins, cut into slices or quarters, and serve either hot or cold. Or, reheat in stock and melted butter, seasoning with salt, pepper, and vinegar. The stock may be omitted if desired and chopped onion and parsley added to the seasoning.

BUTTERED BEETS

Peel young beets, cut into dice, and cook slowly until tender in water to cover. Add a tablespoonful of butter, salt and pepper to season, and thicken with a teaspoonful of cornstarch rubbed smooth in a little cold water. Stir while boiling.

PICKLED BEETS

Wash small beets but do not cut. Cover with boiling water and boil until tender. Drain, rinse in cold water, peel, cut into slices, sprinkle with sugar, salt, and pepper, cover with vinegar, and let stand for several hours before using. Serve cold.

BOILED BRUSSELS SPROUTS

Wash and pick over the sprouts and boil until tender in water to which a little salt and baking-soda have been added. Drain, and reheat in melted butter with a little salt and pepper, but do not fry. Serve on buttered toast.

BRUSSELS SPROUTS SAUTÉ

Boil the cleaned sprouts for twenty minutes in salted water, drain, fry in butter, season with salt, minced parsley, and pepper, and serve. Grated nutmeg may be added.

BRUSSELS SPROUTS À LA PARMESAN

Boil the sprouts until tender in salted water and drain. Arrange in a baking-dish with alternate layers of grated Parmesan cheese. Season with salt, pepper, and melted butter, and serve very hot.

BOILED CABBAGE

Clean and quarter a firm cabbage and cover with boiling salted water to which has been added a pinch of baking-soda. Cook for fifteen minutes, drain, rinse and cover with boiling salted water. Cook until tender and drain, pressing out all the liquid. Chop fine and season with salt, pepper, and tomato catsup. Add a cupful of stock, heat thoroughly, add a tablespoonful of butter and a teaspoonful of lemon-juice and serve.

FRIED CABBAGE

Chop cold boiled cabbage and drain thoroughly. Mix with two tablespoonfuls of melted butter, four tablespoonfuls of cream, and pepper and salt to season. Heat in a buttered frying-pan and let stand long enough to brown slightly on the under side. Two well-beaten eggs may be added to the cabbage before heating; or, chop fine and fry brown in butter, seasoning with salt, pepper, and vinegar.

CREAMED CABBAGE

Chop or shred a cabbage fine and cover with boiling salted water to which a pinch of soda has been added. Boil until tender, drain, rinse in hot water, press out the liquid, and reheat in a Cream Sauce. Add a little grated cheese if desired.

HOT SLAW

Chop half a cabbage fine, pour over a tablespoonful of melted butter, and put into the oven. Beat together one tablespoonful each of mustard and olive-oil, add one teaspoonful of sugar and one egg well-beaten with three-fourths cupful of cream. Bring to the boil, season with salt and pepper, pour over the hot cabbage, and serve.

COLD SLAW

Shred a white cabbage fine and soak in ice-water. Make a dressing of the yolks of two hard-boiled eggs, one egg well-beaten, half a cupful of olive-oil, the juice of a lemon, and mustard, salt, and pepper to taste. Drain the cabbage thoroughly, mix with the dressing, and serve very cold.

CABBAGE WITH OYSTERS

Cut in two a small cabbage. Soak in cold water for an hour, drain, and cover with boiling water to which a teaspoonful of salt and a pinch of soda have been added. Boil for five minutes, drain, rinse, cover with fresh boiling water, and boil until tender. Drain, arrange on a platter, and moisten thoroughly with cream or melted butter. Cover with broiled oysters, season with salt, pepper, and curry powder, and serve.

CABBAGE WITH SOUR CREAM

Chop fine a small head of cabbage and cook in water enough to keep from burning, seasoning with salt and pepper. Beat together two eggs, one-half cupful each of sour cream and vinegar, and two tablespoonfuls of melted butter. Bring to the boil, pour over the cabbage, and serve.

SMOTHERED RED CABBAGE

Shred a red cabbage and cook until tender with a sliced onion and enough butter to keep from burning. When tender season with salt, pepper, and butter, add two tablespoonfuls of sugar and half a cupful of white vinegar.

STEWED RED CABBAGE

Shred a red cabbage very fine. Put into a kettle with five sour apples peeled and quartered, pepper and salt to season highly, one tablespoonful of sugar, and a pinch of powdered cloves. Add water to cover and boil until tender, adding more liquid as needed. There should not be over one cupful of water when done. Add a tablespoonful of butter, simmer for ten minutes, and serve.

RED CABBAGE À LA BABETTE

Slice a red cabbage very fine, sprinkle with salt, and add a peeled and sliced sour apple. Stew slowly with a tablespoonful of drippings, a chopped onion, and enough water to keep from burning. When tender, season with vinegar, brown sugar, and cinnamon. This is a Jewish recipe.

RED CABBAGE À LA HOLLANDAISE

Trim and shred a red cabbage and soak it in cold water for an hour. Parboil for five minutes, then drain. Fry a small chopped onion soft in butter, add the cabbage and four tart apples, peeled, cored, and chopped. Season with salt and pepper and cook uncovered for thirty minutes, stirring occasionally. Add half a cupful of cream, reheat, and serve.

BOILED CARROTS

Cook peeled and sliced carrots in salted boiling water to cover. Drain and serve with melted butter.

STEWED CARROTS

Parboil a bunch of carrots, drain, and cut into dice. Put into a saucepan with two small onions chopped, pepper, salt, and minced parsley to season, and enoughDrawn-Butter Sauce to moisten. Simmer half an hour and serve.

FRIED CARROTS

Clean and parboil the carrots, drain, cut into thin slices lengthwise, dip in egg and crumbs, and fry in deep fat.

SPRING CARROTS

Trim and scrape two bunches of spring carrots. Parboil for ten minutes in salted water to cover. Drain, and rinse in cold water. Put into a deep baking-dish with two tablespoonfuls each of butter and sugar and two cupfuls of well-seasoned beef stock. Cover and cook slowly until tender. Drain, reduce the liquid by rapid boiling, pour over the carrots, and serve.

CARROTS AND PEAS

Cook separately until tender diced carrots and green peas. Drain, mix, and reheat in White, Béchamel, or Cream Sauce, or season with salt, pepper, and melted butter.

CARROT CROQUETTES

Cook until very tender enough peeled and sliced carrots to make a pint. Mash through a sieve and add the yolk of one egg well-beaten, a tablespoonful of melted butter, and pepper and salt to season highly. Cool on ice, shape into croquettes or balls, dip in egg and crumbs, and keep on ice until firm. Fry in deep fat, drain, and serve very hot.

BUTTERED CARROTS

Cook peeled and sliced carrots until tender in boiling salted water. Drain and put into a saucepan with two tablespoonfuls each of butter and sugar, for each two cupfuls of carrots. Stir constantly until covered with syrup and colored a little. Sprinkle with lemon-juice and serve immediately.

BOILED CAULIFLOWER

Wash and trim a head of cauliflower and soak it for an hour in cold salted water, head down. Rinse thoroughly, cover with boiling salted water, and boil until done. Drain, and serve with any preferred sauce.

BAKED CAULIFLOWER

Prepare according to directions given for Boiled Cauliflower. Put into a buttered baking-dish, pour over a Drawn-Butter Sauce, sprinkle with crumbs, dot with butter, and add a little grated cheese if desired. Brown in the oven and serve in the baking-dish.

BUTTERED CAULIFLOWER

Boil two cauliflowers in salted water until tender. Drain, separate into flowerets, arrange in a serving-dish, and season with salt and pepper. Heat a cupful of butter in a frying-pan without browning, skim, and put in enough fresh crumbs to make a smooth thin paste. Spread over the cauliflower and serve.

CREAMED CAULIFLOWER

Prepare according to directions given for Boiled Cauliflower, adding a pinch of soda to the water. Cook slowly until done, drain, rinse in hot water, cut into convenient pieces for serving, pour over a Cream Sauce and serve, or break into flowerets, and reheat in Cream Sauce.

FRIED CAULIFLOWER

Clean a cauliflower and separate into flowerets. Parboil for five minutes, change the water, and cook until tender, adding a tablespoonful of salt to the water. Drain, dry, and, if desired, marinate in French dressing, dip in crumbs, then in an egg beaten with three tablespoonfuls of water, then in crumbs or batter. Fry in deep fat and serve with Tartar or Tomato Sauce.

CAULIFLOWER FRITTERS

Make a batter of a tablespoonful of melted butter, half a cupful of milk, the yolk of an egg well-beaten, salt and pepper to season, and a tablespoonful or more of flour. Separate freshly cooked cauliflower into convenient pieces. Dip in the batter and fry in deep fat.

ESCALLOPED CAULIFLOWER

Boil until tender, separate into small pieces, and pack stems downward in a buttered baking-dish, or use the cauliflower unbroken. Mix a cupful of bread-crumbs, two tablespoonfuls of melted butter, enough cream or milk to moisten, pepper and salt to season, and one egg well-beaten. Spread over the cauliflower, cover, and bake for six minutes, then uncover and brown. Serve in the same dish.

CAULIFLOWER AU GRATIN

Boil flowerets of cauliflower in salted water until nearly done and drain. Arrange in layers in a buttered baking-dish, with Cream Sauce between the layers and sprinkling each layer thickly with grated Parmesan cheese. When the dish is full, cover with sauce, sprinkle with cheese and crumbs, dot with butter,

196

and brown in the oven. Serve in the baking-dish. Or use milk, crumbs, and bits of butter between the layers instead of Cream Sauce.

CAULIFLOWER À LA PARISIENNE

Boil a large cauliflower until tender, drain, chop, and press hard into a mould. Turn out on a platter that will stand the heat of the oven. Cook together a tablespoonful each of butter and flour, add two cupfuls of stewed and strained tomatoes, and cook until thick, stirring constantly. Season with salt, pepper, and grated onion. Add enough cracker crumbs to make the sauce very thick. Spread over the cauliflower, put it into a hot oven for ten minutes, and serve.

BOILED CELERY

Cut cleaned and trimmed stalks of celery into short lengths and boil slowly in salted water to cover until tender. Drain and serve on slices of toast which have been dipped in the liquid. Pour over a little melted butter, season, and serve.

BRAISED CELERY

Trim bunches of celery, tie in bundles, parboil for ten minutes, drain, and cover with cold water. Let stand for ten minutes, drain, cover with white stock, and simmer for an hour. Drain, pour over Brown Sauce, and serve with a garnish of toast points or croutons.

FRIED CELERY

Parboil, drain, dry, and cool stalks of celery cut into short lengths. Dip into melted butter and fry brown, or dip into fritter batter, or in egg and crumbs, and fry in deep fat. Olive-oil or lard may be used for frying. Serve with melted butter or Brown Sauce, or with a sprinkle of grated cheese.

STEWED CELERY

Parboil eight heads of celery, drain, and finish cooking in stock to cover with a small slice of salt pork for each head of celery. Drain, skim the cooking liquid, and thicken with flour cooked in butter. Arrange the celery and pork alternately on the serving dish, pour over the sauce, and serve.

CELERY IN BROWN SAUCE

Clean and trim three heads of celery and cut into four-inch lengths. Cover with boiling water, let stand for ten minutes, drain, and rinse in cold water. Tie in bundles and put into a saucepan with three cupfuls of hot stock. Add one-fourth cupful of butter or drippings, half a carrot, half an onion, a teaspoonful of salt, and a little cayenne pepper. Cover and simmer until tender. Drain the celery, strain the liquid, skim off the fat, and thicken a cupful or more of the cooking liquid with flour browned in butter. Arrange the celery on toast, pour the sauce over, and serve.

CREAMED CELERY

Clean, trim, and cut the celery into short pieces. Boil until tender in salted water, drain, and reheat in a Cream Sauce. Diced cooked carrots may be added to Creamed Celery.

FRICASSEE OF CELERY

Clean and cut the celery into inch-lengths. Cover with cold water and soak for an hour. Drain, and cook until tender in stock to cover, with salt and paprika to season and a teaspoonful of grated onion. When tender, thicken the cooking liquid with flour browned in butter, and serve.

CELERY AU GRATIN

Cut two bunches of celery into inch-lengths and cook until tender in boiling salted water. Drain, mix with Cream Sauce, cool, and add two well-beaten eggs. Pour into a buttered baking-dish, cover with crumbs, dot with butter, and bake for half an hour.

CELERY À L'ITALIENNE

Trim off the tops and roots from four heads of celery. Cut the stalks into short lengths, parboil, and drain. Reheat with a cupful of white stock, a tablespoonful each of butter and chopped ham, and salt and pepper to season. When tender, strain the sauce and arrange the celery on pieces of toast. Add to the sauce a tablespoonful of grated cheese and the beaten yolk of an egg. Pour the sauce over the celery and bake until brown.

BOILED CORN

Strip off all the husks, remove the silk, and boil rapidly in water to cover, adding a tablespoonful of sugar; serve immediately with butter, pepper, and salt. Butter may be added to the water instead of sugar; it whitens and enriches the corn; or, boil in salted milk, drain, and serve with melted butter.

BAKED CANNED CORN

Pour a can of corn into a buttered baking-dish, season with salt and pepper, add one cupful of boiling milk or half a cupful of cream, and dot with two tablespoonfuls of butter broken into small bits. Bake for forty-five minutes in a moderate oven, and serve in the same dish.

CREAMED CANNED CORN

Reheat a can of corn with half a cupful of Cream Sauce and serve very hot, or reheat with enough cream to moisten and season with butter, pepper, and salt.

ESCALLOPED CORN

Butter a baking-dish and put in a layer of cracker crumbs, then a layer of canned corn, seasoning with salt, pepper, and bits of butter, cover with cracker crumbs and repeat until the dish is full, having crumbs on top. Pour in enough milk to fill the dish and bake for forty-five minutes.

INDIAN CORN CAKES

Grate from the cob on a coarse grater enough corn to make two cupfuls. Add a cupful of milk, half a cupful of sifted flour, one egg well-beaten, and salt and pepper to season. Bake on a griddle and serve with fried chicken.

CREOLE CORN CHOWDER

Slice three onions and fry brown in butter. Add three peeled and sliced tomatoes, three green peppers, seeded and chopped, and the corn cut from seven cobs. Cook for an hour, adding water as needed, and season with salt, sugar, and black pepper.

KENTUCKY CORN PATTIES

Four large ears of corn grated, two eggs, one cupful of milk, and one and one-half cupfuls of flour sifted with a teaspoonful of baking-powder and a pinch of salt. Mix thoroughly and fry in small flat cakes.

CORN STEWED WITH CREAM

Cut the corn from half a dozen ears with a sharp knife. Reheat in a cupful of Béchamel Sauce, adding a teaspoonful of butter and enough cream to make the stew of the proper consistency. Season with salt, pepper, and grated nutmeg. Serve very hot.

CORN SOUFFLÉ

Score each row of kernels deeply and press out the pulp with the back of a knife, using enough corn to make one cupful of pulp. Add one cupful of cream or top milk, a tablespoonful of butter, salt and pepper to season, and the yolks of three eggs well-beaten. Cook in a double boiler until smooth and creamy, stirring constantly. Take from the fire, cool, fold in the stiffly beaten whites of four eggs, turn into a buttered baking-dish, and bake for twenty minutes in a hot oven.

CORN PUDDING

Mix three cupfuls of milk with the corn cut from a dozen ears, and chopped fine. Add four well-beaten eggs, salt and pepper to season, and bake in a buttered baking-dish for two hours.

CORN OYSTERS

Score each row of kernels and press out the pulp from a dozen ears of corn. Season highly with salt and pepper and add four eggs beaten very light. Drop by spoonfuls on a griddle and fry carefully, turning once.

CORN FRITTERS

Mix thoroughly one egg, half a cupful of cream, one tablespoonful each of butter and flour, and two cupfuls of grated corn. Drop by spoonfuls into deep fat and fry brown.

CORN SUCCOTASH

Boil a pint of shelled lima beans for half an hour, or more, changing the water twice. Add an equal quantity of corn cut from the ear and cook until done. Season with salt, pepper, and butter, and serve. Add a little sugar and cream if desired, or moisten with Cream Sauce. The beans may be boiled with the corn-cobs, removing them when the corn is added. Twice as much corn as beans may be used.

ESCALLOPED CUCUMBERS

Peel and cut into dice six large cucumbers. Butter a baking-dish and put in a layer of the dice seasoning with grated onion and lemon-juice. Cover with crumbs, dot with butter, and season with paprika and celery salt. Repeat until the dish is full, having crumbs and butter on top. Cover and bake for an hour, then remove the cover, and brown. Serve with Sauce Piquante.

STUFFED CUCUMBERS

Peel and split large cucumbers lengthwise. Scoop out the pulp and fill with a stuffing made of cooked chicken chopped fine and mixed with soft crumbs seasoned nicely and moistened with a beaten egg or a little stock. Sprinkle with crumbs and put into a baking-pan with stock half an inch thick. Bake until the cucumbers are tender, basting frequently, and adding more stock if required. Thicken the gravy with a teaspoonful of cornstarch rubbed smooth in a little cold water and pour around the cucumbers when serving.

BROILED EGGPLANT

Peel and cut into thin slices and soak for an hour in cold salted water. Drain and dry thoroughly. Soak for half an hour in a marinade of olive-oil seasoned with salt and pepper. Add a little lemon-juice to the marinade if desired. Broil and serve with Maître d'Hôtel Sauce. The slices may be dipped in egg and crumbs before broiling.

BAKED EGGPLANT

Parboil, cut off the top, and scoop out the pulp. Mash the pulp and cook it in butter, seasoning with salt and pepper. Take from the fire, add the beaten yolk of an egg and enough bread crumbs to make a smooth paste. Mix thoroughly, refill the shell, and bake, basting with melted butter. A slice of onion, finely chopped, may be fried with the pulp. The egg may be omitted and the stuffing moistened with stock. Baste with stock when baking.

BAKED EGGPLANT WITH CHEESE

Cover two eggplants with boiling water and let stand for ten minutes. Drain, peel, slice thin, cut each slice in four, season with salt and pepper, and fry. Cook together one tablespoonful each of butter and flour, add one cupful of milk and half a cupful of stock, and cook until smooth and thick, stirring constantly. Season with salt and cayenne. Put the fried eggplant into a buttered baking-dish in layers, covering each layer with grated cheese and sauce. Have cheese on top. Sprinkle with crumbs, dot with butter, and bake for twenty minutes.

FRIED EGGPLANT

Peel and slice an eggplant and soak over night in cold salted water. Drain and cover with cold water for half an hour. Wipe dry, dip in seasoned flour, or in flour, beaten egg, and crumbs. Fry in deep fat. Grated cheese may be mixed with the crumbs. Serve with White, Cream, Tomato, or Caper Sauce.

EGGPLANT FRITTERS

Peel, slice, cover with cold water, boil until soft, and drain; or, put into boiling salted and acidulated water. Mash smooth, add salt and pepper to season, two eggs well-beaten, and enough flour to make a thick batter. Fry by spoonfuls in deep fat.

ESCALLOPED EGGPLANT

Boil a large eggplant until tender, peel and mash. Season with butter, pepper, and salt. Add two hard-boiled eggs chopped fine and half an onion grated. Add two tablespoonfuls of bread crumbs, put into a buttered baking-dish, cover with crumbs, dot with butter, and bake brown.

STUFFED EGGPLANT

Parboil a large eggplant for ten minutes, then plunge into salted ice-water and let stand for an hour. Make a forcemeat of half a cupful of minced boiled ham, a cupful and a half of bread crumbs, one egg well-beaten, and enough cream to make a smooth paste. Season with salt, pepper, minced parsley, and onion. Split the eggplant lengthwise, scrape out the pulp, and mix with the stuffing. Fill the shells, tie together, and put into a dripping-pan with a cupful of stock. Cover and bake for half an hour, remove the string, and serve.

EGGPLANT À LA CRÉOLE

Peel a young eggplant, cut it into dice, and simmer for ten or fifteen minutes in half a cupful of boiling water. Drain and press out the liquid. Chop fine two onions, fry in butter, add the eggplant, salt and pepper to season, and one tablespoonful each of minced parsley and vinegar. Add also two heaping tablespoonfuls of butter. Put into a baking-dish, cover with crumbs, dot with butter, and bake for twenty-five minutes.

BOILED HOMINY

Soak a cupful of hominy for three hours in warm water, drain, and cook in fresh boiling water until tender, adding a pinch of salt. Drain and reheat for fifteen minutes with a pint of milk, seasoning with salt and pepper. Cook for fifteen minutes, add a tablespoonful of butter, and serve.

CURRIED LENTILS

Chop fine three large onions, two green peppers, and a clove of garlic. Brown half a pound of washed lentils in butter, add the chopped mixture and cold salted water to cover. Boil until tender. Drain, add two sliced onions fried brown, two tablespoonfuls of butter, and a teaspoonful of curry powder. Serve with a border of boiled rice.

BUTTERED MACARONI

Boil a pound of macaroni until tender, drain, and put into a deep baking-dish. Spread over it half a cupful of butter broken into bits, and one-quarter of a pound of cheese, grated. Season with salt, and pepper, mix thoroughly, and bake, or serve without baking.

MACARONI AU GRATIN

Butter a deep baking-dish and fill with cooked macaroni, sprinkling each layer with grated cheese, and seasoning with pepper and dots of butter. Cover the top with cheese (Parmesan, which may be mixed with Swiss), dot with butter, and bake brown. Serve in the same dish. Milk or cream to cover may be poured over before baking.

MACARONI WITH BROWN BUTTER

Reheat cooked and drained macaroni in melted butter, cooking until the butter browns. Sprinkle with salt and pepper, season highly with grated Parmesan cheese, and serve.

MACARONI AND OYSTERS

Arrange in alternate layers in a baking-dish cooked, broken, and drained macaroni, and oysters, seasoning with dots of butter and pepper and salt. Beat together the liquor drained from the oysters, one and one-half cupfuls of milk, and two eggs. Pour over the macaroni, cover with crumbs, dot with butter, and bake for half an hour; or, spread over the top a beaten egg mixed to a smooth paste with crumbs.

MACARONI À LA GALLI

Rub through a fine sieve a large can of tomatoes and simmer for three hours or until as thick as jelly. Chop fine half a pound of salt pork and a large onion and fry brown and crisp. Mix with the tomatoes, season with salt and cayenne, and pour over cooked macaroni. Serve with grated cheese.

BROILED MUSHROOMS

Dip cleaned and peeled mushrooms into melted butter, put on ice for fifteen minutes, and broil. Serve with melted butter and lemon-juice; or, broil, basting with bacon fat. If the mushrooms are strongly flavored they may be soaked in cold salted water for a few minutes before broiling.

MUSHROOMS BAKED WITH CHEESE

Parboil two cupfuls of cleaned and trimmed mushrooms in salted water for ten minutes. Butter a baking-dish, put in the drained mushrooms, cover with a cupful ofCream Sauce, and sprinkle thickly with grated Parmesan or Swiss cheese. Cover with buttered crumbs and bake brown.

FRIED MUSHROOMS

Peel and trim very large fresh mushrooms and fry in oil or butter seasoned with pepper and salt. Serve on small thin slices of toast and put a teaspoonful of sherry or white wine on each mushroom, or use minced parsley and lemon-juice instead of wine.

NOODLES

Beat an egg slightly, with a pinch of salt, and add enough flour to make a very stiff dough. Roll out as thin as possible and dry on a cloth. Roll up tightly and slice downward into very fine strips. Toss lightly with the fingers to separate, and spread out on the board to dry. Keep in covered jars for future use.

BAKED NOODLES

Reheat boiled and drained noodles in milk to cover. Season with melted butter, grated Parmesan cheese, pepper, and nutmeg. Heat thoroughly, put into a baking-dish, sprinkle with crumbs, dot with butter, and brown in the oven. Serve in the same dish; or, arrange boiled and drained noodles in layers in a buttered baking-dish, seasoning each layer with salt, pepper, and grated nutmeg, and sprinkling thickly with grated cheese. Spread fried crumbs over the top, heat thoroughly, and serve.

NOODLES AU GRATIN

Boil half a pound of noodles for ten minutes in salted water to cover. Drain, and put into a saucepan with two cupfuls of milk or stock, a tablespoonful of butter, and salt, pepper, and grated nutmeg to season. Simmer slowly until the liquid has all been absorbed, then add half a cupful of cream or stock, a tablespoonful of butter, and a quarter of a pound of grated Parmesan cheese. Cook slowly until the cheese is melted and put into a buttered serving-dish. Sprinkle with crumbs and grated cheese and the yolk of a hard-boiled egg pressed through a sieve. Brown in the oven and serve.

BOILED OKRA

Boil the okra in salted water until tender, drain, season with salt, pepper, and butter, and serve very hot. A little cream may be added.

OKRA SAUTÉ À LA CRÉOLE

Chop fine an onion and a green pepper and fry soft in butter. Add two tomatoes peeled and cut up, three tablespoonfuls of Spanish Sauce or stock, and pepper and chopped garlic to season. Put in the required quantity of sliced okras, cover and cook for fifteen minutes. Sprinkle with minced parsley and serve.

BOILED ONIONS

Peel the onions under water. Boil until tender in salted water to cover, changing the water once. Drain, season with butter, pepper, salt, and hot cream, or reheat in White or Cream Sauce, or a well-buttered Velouté Sauce. A bunch of parsley may be boiled with the onions, and a little of the cooking liquid may be added to the sauce.

BAKED ONIONS

Peel and fry a dozen small onions, seasoning with salt, pepper, and sugar. When brown, add stock to cover, and bake until soft in a covered pan.

FRIED SPANISH ONIONS

Peel and slice two pounds of Spanish onions and put into a frying-pan with half a cupful of butter smoking hot, a small spoonful of salt, and a pinch of pepper. Dust with cayenne and cook until tender. Serve with the gravy they yield in cooking.

CREAMED ONIONS

Peel small onions and boil until tender, changing the water several times; or, slice large onions. Mix with well-seasoned Cream Sauce and serve. Drawn-Butter Saucemay be used instead.

STUFFED ONIONS

Boil fine white onions in salted water for an hour, changing the water three times. Drain, scoop out the centre, and fill with bread crumbs seasoned with salt, pepper, grated cheese, and catsup. Mash a little of the onion with the stuffing and moisten with cream or milk. Wrap each onion in buttered paper, twist the ends, put into a buttered pan, and bake for an hour. Remove the paper, pour over melted butter, and serve.

ROASTED ONIONS

Peel the onions and steam for an hour and a half. Bake, basting with drippings, and season with salt and pepper.

BOILED PARSNIPS

Boil cleaned parsnips until tender in salted water, adding a little butter if desired, drain, rub off the skins with a rough cloth, put into a hot dish, and serve with melted butter and parsley or Butter Sauce, seasoning with pepper and salt. White or Cream Sauce may be used instead.

BUTTERED PARSNIPS

Boil the parsnips until tender, scrape off the skin, and cut lengthwise in thin slices. Put into a saucepan with three or four tablespoonfuls of butter, and pepper, salt, and minced parsley to season. Shake over the fire until the mixture boils and serve with the sauce poured over. A little cream may be added to the sauce. Sprinkle the parsnips with minced parsley before serving.

CREAMED PARSNIPS

Boil parsnips in salted water until tender, drain, peel, cut into dice, and reheat, in a well-seasoned Cream Sauce. Sprinkle with minced parsley if desired, and add a little more butter.

ESCALLOPED PARSNIPS

Prepare Creamed Parsnips according to directions previously given, cutting the parsnips into dice. Put into a buttered baking-dish in layers, sprinkling each layer with chopped onion. Cover with crumbs, dot with butter, and bake for half an hour.

BOILED PEAS

Shell a peck of green peas and cook in boiling salted water until tender. Drain, season with salt, pepper, and butter or cream, and serve immediately. A small bunch of green mint or parsley or two or three young onions or a tablespoonful of minced onion may be boiled with them. A little sugar may be added to sweeten them.

CREAMED PEAS

Boil peas until soft in water to cover, adding a pinch of salt during the last fifteen minutes. Season with salt, pepper, and butter, and reheat in Cream or White Sauce. A little sugar may be added to the seasoning. Canned peas may be used.

BUTTERED PEAS

Cook a quart of green peas in salted water, using as little as possible and adding a tablespoonful of butter. Thicken with flour cooked in butter, then add more butter, a pinch of sugar, and a little grated nutmeg.

BROILED GREEN PEPPERS

Cut six green peppers into quarters, remove the seeds, and broil over a very hot fire, until the edges curl. Spread with butter, sprinkle with salt, and serve with broiled steak.

FRIED PEPPERS

Remove the stems and seeds, cut into rings, and soak for half an hour in cold water. Drain, dry, dip in flour seasoned with salt, and fry in fat to cover.

STUFFED PEPPERS

Make a stuffing of one cupful of bread crumbs and half a cupful of chopped boiled ham or tongue or sausage, seasoning with salt, pepper, and grated onion and moistening with melted butter. Stuff green peppers which have been seeded and soaked, and put into a buttered baking-dish. Pour over a cupful of stock, cover, and bake for fifteen minutes, then uncover and brown.

STUFFED PEPPERS À LA CRÉOLE

Make a stuffing of boiled rice and canned tomatoes, seasoning with salt and grated onion. Stuff half a dozen sweet peppers, brown in oil, then put into a baking-pan and finish cooking, basting with hot water.

BOILED SWEET POTATOES
Clean thoroughly, cover with boiling water, to which a little salt may be added, boil until soft, drain, peel, and serve. They may be peeled before boiling; or, cover with hot water, boil until done, dry in the oven, and peel just before serving.

BAKED SWEET POTATOES
Split lengthwise and steam or boil until nearly done. Drain and put into a baking-dish, flat side down, seasoning each one with pepper, salt, and sugar. Dot with butter and bake brown, basting with butter, or wash and trim and bake in a moderate oven until soft. They may be parboiled before baking. Serve in the skins.

BROWNED SWEET POTATOES
Boil sweet potatoes until soft in salted water to cover. Drain and mash, seasoning with butter, pepper, and salt. Put into a serving-dish, dot with butter, and bake until brown.

SWEET POTATOES IN CASSEROLE
Put one-fourth of a cupful of butter and two tablespoonfuls of sugar into a casserole. When hissing hot cover with peeled sweet potatoes, cut into thin slices lengthwise. Season with salt and pepper and cover with another layer of potatoes. Moisten with boiling water, cover, and cook until nearly done then uncover, and brown. Serve in the casserole.

CANDIED SWEET POTATOES
Peel and slice lengthwise four large sweet potatoes. Put into a covered saucepan with a tablespoon of butter, salt and pepper to season, and enough water to moisten. Steam until tender, drain, and put into a buttered baking-dish. Pour over one cupful of New Orleans molasses and bake until the molasses candies on the potatoes. Serve in the same dish.

ESCALLOPED SWEET POTATOES
Steam them until tender, peel and slice and put into a buttered baking-dish in layers, sprinkling each layer with a tablespoonful of sugar and bits of butter. Pour over a cupful of cream or milk and brown in the oven.

ROASTED SWEET POTATOES
Peel sweet potatoes of equal size and put into the pan with a roast or fowl an hour before taking up. Split if too large. Baste with the drippings. They may be parboiled before baking.

GLAZED SWEET POTATOES

Cut cold boiled sweet potatoes into slices an inch thick and season with salt and pepper. Dip in melted butter, sprinkle with sugar, and bake for twelve or fifteen minutes. Moisten with water if necessary.

BOILED RICE

Wash one cupful of rice in several waters, rubbing well with the hands. Drain, dry on a cloth, and boil for ten minutes in two quarts of boiling salted water. Drain, nearly cover with hot milk, and cook for ten minutes, covered, in a double boiler. Remove the cover and dry, tossing with a fork to allow the steam to escape.

BUTTERED RICE

Boil a cupful of well-washed rice, according to directions previously given, adding the juice of a lemon to the water. Drain, put into a buttered baking-dish, moisten thoroughly with clarified butter, cover, and put into a moderate oven for twenty minutes; or, sauté boiled rice in butter, keeping the grains separate. A little minced onion may be fried with it.

CURRIED RICE

Boil a cupful of rice in salted water, drain, and mix with a chopped onion fried in butter and two teaspoonfuls of curry powder dissolved in a cupful of stock or gravy.

CASSEROLE OF RICE

Boil rice in chicken stock and press firmly into a mould. Turn out on a serving-dish, brush with beaten yolk of an egg, sprinkle with grated Parmesan cheese, and brown in the oven. Serve with Tomato Sauce.

RISOTTO

Chop fine a small onion and three beans of garlic. Fry in butter, add half a cupful of boiling water, a teaspoonful of beef extract, and three or four dried mushrooms, soaked and chopped. Simmer for five minutes, pour over boiled rice, and season highly with grated Swiss and Parmesan cheese. Put in the oven until the cheese has softened, and serve.

SAVORY RICE

Cook half a cupful of rice in salted water until half done and drain. Cover with rich stock and simmer until the stock is absorbed. Season with salt and pepper, add three heaping tablespoonfuls of grated cheese, and serve.

RICE À LA CRÉOLE

Chop together a large onion, two seeded green peppers, and half a cupful of raw ham. Sauté in butter, then add a cupful of parboiled rice, three cupfuls of beef stock, one cupful of canned tomatoes, and a teaspoonful of salt. Cook very slowly until the rice is tender and the liquid nearly absorbed.

BOILED SALSIFY

Scrape a bunch of salsify and throw into cold acidulated water. Cut in pieces and boil until tender in salted water to cover. Drain, season with pepper, salt, and butter and, if desired, a little cream; or, serve with Maître d'Hôtel, Hollandaise, Onion, or Italian Sauce.

BAKED SALSIFY

Slice boiled salsify and put in layers in a buttered baking-dish, sprinkling each layer with crumbs and seasoning with salt, pepper, and butter. Have crumbs on top. Fill the dish with milk and bake until brown.

ESCALLOPED SALSIFY

Mash boiled salsify through a sieve, season with salt, cayenne, butter, and celery salt, and moisten with milk. Put into a buttered baking-dish, cover with crumbs, dot with butter, and bake in a pan of hot water until brown; or, use sliced boiled salsify alternately with Cream or Drawn-Butter Sauce and seasoned and buttered crumbs. Have sauce on top. Cover with crumbs, wet with cream, and bake brown.

FRIED SALSIFY

Prepare according to directions given for Boiled Salsify, drain, marinate in French Dressing, and sauté in very hot fat. Serve with Maître d'Hôtel Sauce if desired; or, boil, drain, dip in egg and crumbs or seasoned flour, and fry in deep fat.

SPAGHETTI À L'AMÉRICAINE

Cook spaghetti until tender, drain, and add a can of tomato paste. Simmer for twenty minutes, season to taste, add two tablespoonfuls of butter, and serve with grated cheese.

SPAGHETTI À LA TOMASO

Fry six pork chops brown with three sliced onions, adding a little butter or oil if the chops are not fat enough to fry. Pour over two cans of tomatoes and add three whole cloves of garlic peeled and sliced, and salt and paprika to season. A seeded and chopped green pepper is an improvement. Simmer slowly until the meat is in rags, adding boiling water if required. When the sauce is thick and dark, rub through a coarse sieve, pressing through as much of the meat pulp as possible. If it is not thick enough, simmer until it reaches the consistency of thick meat gravy. This sauce will keep for a day or two. Have ready a kettle of salted water at a galloping boil. Put in a handful of imported spaghetti without breaking, coiling it into the kettle as it softens. Cook for twenty minutes, or more if necessary, stirring to keep from burning. Drain in a colander, rinse thoroughly with fresh boiling water, and spread on a platter. Add olive-oil to moisten if desired. Mix with part of the sauce and sprinkle with freshly grated

Parmesan cheese. Pass sauce and cheese with it. Fried green peppers or fresh mushrooms may be mixed with the spaghetti, or a handful of soaked dried Italian mushrooms may be cooked with the sauce.

ESCALLOPED SPAGHETTI WITH OYSTERS

Put into a buttered baking-dish in layers drained oysters and boiled spaghetti cut into small pieces. Season each layer with salt, pepper, and dots of butter. Pour over enough Cream Sauce or milk to moisten, cover with crumbs, dot with butter, and bake until brown.

GREEK SPAGHETTI

Chop a small onion fine, fry in butter, and mix with a pound and a half of lean beef chopped fine and fried in butter, highly seasoned with black and white pepper. Fill a baking-dish with alternate layers of the meat and boiled spaghetti, seasoning each layer with grated Parmesan cheese. Bake until brown.

BOILED SPINACH

Cook a peck of well-washed spinach, uncovered, with a cupful of boiling water for ten minutes. Drain, pressing out all the liquid. Chop fine, rub through a sieve, season with salt, pepper, butter and sugar, and moisten with stock, gravy, Brown Sauce, or Cream Sauce. Garnish with hard-boiled eggs or croutons. It may be reheated without chopping and seasoned with salt, pepper, butter, and vinegar.

BUTTERED SPINACH

Cook two quarts of spinach according to directions previously given. Drain, and serve with melted butter; or, chop fine, press out all the liquid, reheat in Cream Sauce, season with a little grated nutmeg and at the last add two tablespoonfuls of butter.

BOILED SQUASH

Peel, remove the seeds, boil until tender, drain, and serve with melted butter or White Sauce; or, peel, seed, and quarter a squash, and cook in stock to cover, seasoning with salt, pepper, butter, and a little sugar. Or cook it in milk, seasoning with salt, pepper, and powdered mace.

BOILED SUMMER SQUASH

Cut into small pieces and cook for an hour in boiling water, then drain and mash, seasoning with salt, pepper, and butter. Moisten with a little cream, and serve.

CREAMED SQUASH

Steam or boil small pieces of squash, drain, and reheat in Cream Sauce.

FRIED SUMMER SQUASH

Cut the squash in slices, dredge with seasoned flour, and sauté in butter or dip in crumbs, then in egg and crumbs, and fry in deep fat. It may be parboiled for five minutes before frying; or, prepare according to directions given for Fried Eggplant.

ROASTED SQUASH
Peel and cut into long strips. Cook in the pan with a roast, basting with the drippings.

BROILED TOMATOES
Peel and slice large tomatoes, season with salt and pepper, and broil, basting with oil; or, dip in seasoned crumbs or corn-meal before broiling. Sprinkle with minced parsley if desired.

BROILED TOMATOES WITH SAUCE
Season Cream Sauce with a little mace, and salt and pepper to taste. When smooth and thick add a well-beaten egg and pour it over broiled tomatoes; or, serve broiled tomatoes with highly seasoned melted butter mixed with lemon-juice.

BAKED TOMATOES
Peel the tomatoes and put into a baking-dish. Sprinkle thickly with sugar and bake until the sugar has become a thick syrup; or, stuff tomato shells with seasoned crumbs, dot with butter, and sprinkle with sugar and bake.

BAKED TOMATOES À LA CRÉOLE
Peel and cut in two, three large tomatoes. Chop fine a green pepper and an onion and spread over the tomato. Sprinkle with salt, dot with butter, and bake, basting with the pan-gravy. Add half a cupful of cream or milk to the pan-gravy, thicken it with flour cooked in butter, and pour the sauce over the tomatoes. Serve on toast.

CREAMED BAKED TOMATOES
Make a Cream Sauce, seasoning with celery salt and onion-juice. Put a tablespoonful of the sauce into a ramekin, add a small peeled tomato, and cover with the sauce. Spread buttered crumbs over the top and bake in a pan of boiling water for half an hour. Serve in the ramekins.

CURRIED TOMATOES
Chop fine an onion and an apple and fry in butter, seasoning highly with curry powder. Moisten with stock or gravy and spread on fried or baked tomatoes.

DEVILLED TOMATOES
Mix together the mashed yolks of three hard-boiled eggs, a teaspoonful each of powdered sugar and made mustard, and a pinch each of salt and cayenne. Add three tablespoonfuls of butter and, gradually, three tablespoonfuls of vinegar or lemon-juice. Bring to the boil, add two eggs well-beaten, and cook in a double boiler until thick. Pour over fried or boiled tomatoes and serve; or serve with a Maître d'Hôtel Sauce made hot with mustard and cayenne.

ESCALLOPED TOMATOES

Put sliced tomatoes in layers in a baking-dish, seasoning with salt, pepper, and dots of butter, and onion-juice if desired, alternating with crumbs. Have the top layer of crumbs and butter. A cupful of stock may be poured over. Cover and bake until well done then uncover and brown. A little sugar may be added to the seasoning; or, season each layer of tomatoes with minced onion and grated cheese and have crumbs on top. Green tomatoes may be used, or drained canned tomatoes.

ESCALLOPED TOMATOES AND ONIONS

Fill a buttered baking-dish with alternate layers of sliced tomatoes and fried or parboiled sliced onions, seasoning each layer with salt, pepper, and butter, and sprinkling with crumbs. Cover with crumbs, dot with butter, and bake for forty-five minutes. Sprinkle with grated cheese if desired.

FRIED TOMATOES WITH CREAM

Cut six large tomatoes in half, and sauté the cut side in butter or drippings. Take up the tomatoes and cook a tablespoonful of flour in the fat. Add half a cupful of hot milk and cook to a thick sauce, seasoning with salt and cayenne. Pour over the tomatoes, and serve.

FRIED GREEN TOMATOES

Slice green tomatoes and soak for ten minutes in cold salted water. Drain, sprinkle with sugar, dip in corn-meal, and fry in hot fat. Season to taste.

FRIED TOMATOES WITH ONIONS

Slice onions and green tomatoes thin and fry in drippings.

FRIED TOMATOES AND PEPPERS

Seed and shred six green peppers and slice three tomatoes. Fry in olive-oil with a chopped onion and a bean of garlic and serve on toast.

STEWED TOMATOES WITH CHEESE

Stew fresh tomatoes and add a cupful of grated American cheese and three eggs well-beaten. It will be richer if the tomatoes are cooked in stock.

STEWED TOMATOES AND CELERY

Stew a can of tomatoes with two or three stalks of celery cut fine. Thicken with flour cooked in butter and season with salt, pepper, butter, sugar, and a little cinnamon or nutmeg.

STUFFED TOMATOES

Mix the scooped-out tomato pulp with bread soaked in milk and season with minced parsley, grated onion, salt, and pepper. Add a few chopped mushrooms if desired and a little chopped cooked meat. Fill the tomato shells, dot with butter, and bake.

SPANISH TOMATOES

Chop two onions fine and fry in butter, then add a can of tomatoes and a small can of Spanish peppers chopped fine. Cook for five minutes, season with salt, then pour into a baking-dish, cover with buttered crumbs, and bake for forty-five minutes. Green peppers may be used instead of the Spanish peppers.

BOILED TURNIPS

Peel and quarter young turnips and cook in boiling salted water to cover with four or five slices of bacon, changing the water once and adding a little sugar to the seasoned water. Reheat in Cream Sauce and serve with the bacon as a garnish.

BAKED TURNIPS

Peel and parboil small turnips, drain and put into a baking-pan with beef stock to reach to half their height. Sprinkle with salt, pepper, and sugar, dot with butter, cover, and bake until done basting occasionally with the stock.

BROWNED TURNIPS

Peel, slice, boil until tender, drain, and sauté in butter, sprinkling with salt, pepper, and sugar.

CREAMED TURNIPS

Cut boiled turnips into dice, reheat in a Cream or White Sauce, season with salt, pepper, and sugar, and serve on toast. Add a little grated nutmeg if desired. Brown Sauce may be used also.

TURNIPS AND CARROTS

Cook separately diced carrots and turnips, then, mix and season with salt, pepper, butter, and minced parsley; or, mix with Cream or White Sauce.

GLAZED TURNIPS

Boil small peeled turnips in rich stock to cover, adding a pinch of sugar. Drain, reduce the sauce by rapid boiling, and brown the turnips in the oven, basting with the stock.

TURNIPS IN BROWN SAUCE

Peel, slice, and boil until tender in salted water, drain, sauté in butter, and pour over a Brown Sauce. Season with salt, pepper, sugar, and mace.

BAKED BANANAS

Peel and quarter four bananas and put into a buttered baking-dish with eight tablespoonfuls of water, four of sugar, four teaspoonfuls each of melted butter and lemon-juice, and a sprinkle of salt. Bake slowly for half an hour, or less, basting frequently. The lemon-juice may be omitted.

FRIED BANANAS

Peel, slice lengthwise, season with salt, dredge with flour, and fry in oil or butter, or dip in egg and crumbs, or cut in two crosswise, dip in egg and seasoned crumbs, put on ice for two hours, and fry in deep fat. Sprinkle with lemon-juice if desired.

CURRY OF VEGETABLES

Mix one cupful each of cooked carrots and turnips cut into dice, one-half can of peas, and one cupful of cooked lima or kidney beans. Reheat in Brown Sauce, seasoning with minced onion, curry powder, a pinch of sugar, and a little vinegar. Add a cupful and a half of cooked potatoes cut into dice, simmer for twenty minutes, and serve in a border of boiled rice.

GNOCCHI

Bring to the boil a cupful of water and a tablespoonful of butter. Add sifted flour to make a batter and a pinch each of salt, pepper, and grated nutmeg. Add a heaping tablespoonful of grated Parmesan cheese and stir constantly until the mixture leaves the sides of the pan. Take from the fire and stir in one at a time three unbeaten eggs. Drop by spoonfuls into boiling water and simmer until firm. Drain, put into a buttered baking-dish, season with grated cheese and melted butter, and pour over aCream or Béchamel Sauce, thickened with the yolks of three eggs. Sprinkle with crumbs and grated cheese, bake until brown, and serve in the same dish.

CREAMED KOHLRABI

Peel, slice, and soak the kohlrabi in cold water for half an hour. Drain, cover with cold water, and cook until tender. Drain and pour over a Cream Sauce to which has been added the well-beaten yolk of an egg.

POLENTA

Boil a quart of white stock with two tablespoonfuls of butter and sprinkle in slowly, enough corn-meal to make a thick mush. Take from the fire, add four tablespoonfuls each of butter and grated Parmesan cheese and a tablespoonful of beef extract. Mould in small cups, turn out, sprinkle with crumbs and cheese, and bake, basting with melted butter.

INDIAN PILAU

Wash a cupful of rice thoroughly, throw into fast boiling water, boil for twenty minutes, and drain. A tablespoonful of butter may be added to the water. Season with salt and pepper, add a heaping tablespoonful of butter, and garnish with hard-boiled eggs and fried onions.

VEGETABLES À LA JARDINIÈRE

Mix half a can of French peas and one cupful each of diced cooked carrots and turnips. Reheat in a well-buttered Béchamel Sauce. Season with salt and pepper and add a little sugar if desired.

THIRTY SIMPLE SAUCES

ALLEMANDE SAUCE

Put two cupfuls of white stock into a saucepan with half a dozen mushrooms, chopped fine, a two-inch strip of lemon-peel, salt and pepper to season, and a teaspoonful of minced parsley. Simmer for an hour and strain. Thicken with a teaspoonful of flour rubbed smooth in a little cold stock or water, take from the fire, and add the yolks of three eggs beaten with the juice of half a lemon. Reheat, but do not boil. Take from the fire and add a tablespoonful of butter.

BÉARNAISE SAUCE

Bring to the boil two tablespoonfuls each of vinegar and water. Simmer in it for ten minutes a slice of onion. Take out the onion and add the yolks of three eggs beaten very light. Take from the fire, add salt and pepper to season, and four tablespoonfuls of butter beaten to a cream. The butter should be added in small bits.

QUICK BÉARNAISE SAUCE

Beat the yolks of four eggs with four tablespoonfuls of oil and four of water. Add a cupful of boiling water and cook slowly until thick and smooth. Take from the fire, and add minced onion, capers, olives, pickles, and parsley, and a little tarragon vinegar.

BÉCHAMEL SAUCE

Cook together two tablespoonfuls each of butter and flour, add two cupfuls of white stock and cook until thick, stirring constantly. Season with salt, pepper, and grated nutmeg.

BROWN SAUCE

Brown two tablespoonfuls of flour in butter. Add two cupfuls of milk or cream and cook until thick, stirring constantly. Season to taste.

BROWN BUTTER SAUCE OR BEURRE NOIR

Melt butter in a frying-pan and cook until brown, taking care not to burn. Take from the fire and add lemon-juice or vinegar, and salt and pepper to season. Serve hot.

BUTTER SAUCE

Beat the yolks of four eggs with half a cupful of cold water and two tablespoonfuls of vinegar or lemon-juice. Cook in a double boiler until thick, seasoning with salt, cayenne, and onion-juice. Add half a cupful of butter, cut into small pieces, take from the fire, and serve.

CAPER SAUCE

Add two or three tablespoonfuls of capers to two cupfuls of Drawn-Butter Sauce.

CHEESE SAUCE

Add half a cupful of grated cheese to two cupfuls of Cream or Drawn-Butter Sauce.

COLBERT SAUCE

Put into a saucepan one cupful of Espagnole Sauce, two tablespoonfuls of beef extract, the juice of a lemon, red and white pepper and minced parsley to season, and half a cupful of butter in small bits. Heat, but do not boil, and serve at once.

CREAM SAUCE

Cook together one tablespoonful of butter and two of flour. Add two cupfuls of cream or milk and cook until thick, stirring constantly. Season with salt and pepper.

CURRY SAUCE

Fry a tablespoonful of chopped onion in butter and add a tablespoonful of flour mixed with a teaspoonful of curry powder. Mix thoroughly, add one cupful of cold water, and cook until thick, stirring constantly. Take from the fire, season with salt and onion-juice, and serve hot.

DRAWN-BUTTER SAUCE

Cook to a smooth paste two tablespoonfuls of butter and two of flour. Add two cupfuls of cold water and cook until thick, stirring constantly. Season with salt and pepper.

DUTCH SAUCE

Cook together one tablespoonful each of flour and butter, add one cupful of white stock, and cook until thick, stirring constantly. Season with salt and pepper, take from the fire, and add the yolks of three eggs beaten with half a cupful of cream. Cook in a double boiler for three minutes, take from the fire, add a tablespoonful of lemon-juice, and strain.

DUXELLES SAUCE

Cook in butter one cupful of chopped mushrooms and one tablespoonful each of minced onion and parsley. Add to one pint of Spanish Sauce and serve.

EGG SAUCE

Add one-half cupful of sliced or chopped hard-boiled eggs to two cupfuls of Drawn-Butter Sauce or sufficient melted butter.

HOLLANDAISE SAUCE

Beat half a cupful of butter to a cream and add gradually the well-beaten yolks of two eggs, the juice of half a lemon, and pepper and salt to season. Cook over boiling water until it begins to thicken, beating with an egg beater. Serve as soon as it is of the proper consistency. Add a little boiling water if it is too thick.

ITALIAN SAUCE

Fry a chopped onion in butter with a teaspoonful of minced parsley and two tablespoonfuls of chopped mushrooms. Add one cupful of white stock and boil for ten minutes. Thicken with a small spoonful each of butter and flour cooked together, take from the fire, and add a tablespoonful of butter and a little lemon-juice.

MADEIRA SAUCE

Add four tablespoonfuls of mushroom liquor and a wineglassful of Madeira to Italian Sauce.

MAÎTRE D'HÔTEL SAUCE

Work into half a cupful of butter all the lemon-juice it will take, and add a teaspoonful or more of minced parsley; or, melt the butter without burning, take from the fire, add the juice of half a lemon and a teaspoonful of minced parsley.

MINT SAUCE

Chop fresh mint, or use dried mint, which is equally good. Cover with good cider vinegar and add enough granulated sugar to neutralize part of the acid. Let stand for several hours before using.

MUSHROOM SAUCE

Add the desired quantity of chopped canned mushrooms to White, Cream, Brown, or Drawn-Butter Sauce, using the can liquor for part of the liquid.

PARSLEY SAUCE

Boil two large bunches of parsley in water to cover for five minutes. Strain the water, and thicken with a tablespoonful each of butter and flour cooked together. Season with salt, pepper, and grated nutmeg, take from the fire, add the yolks of two eggs beaten with a little vinegar, three tablespoonfuls of butter in small bits, and a little minced parsley.

PIQUANTE SAUCE

Brown three small spoonfuls of flour in butter, add two cupfuls of stock, and cook until thick, stirring constantly. Season with salt and cayenne. Chop a small onion fine and cook it until tender in four tablespoonfuls of vinegar with a teaspoonful of sugar. Put into the sauce with two tablespoonfuls each of chopped capers and cucumber pickles. Heat thoroughly and serve.

REMOULADE SAUCE

Mix together the yolks of two hard-boiled eggs, the yolk of one raw egg, a pinch each of salt and pepper, and a teaspoonful of mustard. Set the bowl into a pan of ice and add gradually a cupful of olive-oil, beating constantly. When smooth and thick, add three tablespoonfuls each of tarragon or cider vinegar and a teaspoonful of minced parsley.

TARTAR SAUCE

Chop fine a teaspoonful each of pickles, parsley, olives, and capers. Mix with very stiff Mayonnaise. A little grated onion may be added if desired.

TOMATO SAUCE—I

Fry a chopped onion and half a clove of garlic in butter. Add half a cupful of water, a teaspoonful of beef extract, a cupful of canned tomatoes, and three or four dried mushrooms soaked and chopped. Simmer until smooth and thick, run through a sieve, and serve.

TOMATO SAUCE—II

Brown a tablespoonful of flour in butter, add a cupful of stewed tomatoes, and salt, pepper, grated onion, powdered cloves, and mace to season. Cook until smooth and thick, stirring constantly, rub through a sieve, and serve.

TOMATO SAUCE—III

Chop together capers, pickles, onion, and olives. There should be half a cupful in all. Add one-half cupful of stewed and strained tomatoes, a teaspoonful each of made mustard and sugar, and salt and cayenne to season highly. Serve very hot.

TOMATO CREAM SAUCE

Cook together for ten minutes one cupful of tomatoes, a slice of onion, two cloves, two pepper-corns, a stalk of celery, and a bit of bay-leaf. Rub through a sieve and thicken with three small spoonfuls of flour cooked in butter. Season with salt, paprika, and sugar, add one cupful of hot cream, bring to the boil, add a pinch of soda, and serve.

VELOUTÉ SAUCE

Cook together three small spoonfuls each of butter and flour, add one cupful of white stock and one quarter cupful of cream. Cook until thick, stirring constantly. Season with salt, cayenne, grated nutmeg, and minced parsley. Simmer for an hour, strain and serve.

VINAIGRETTE SAUCE

Beat together four tablespoonfuls of olive-oil and one tablespoonful of vinegar with salt and red pepper to season. Chop fine a little parsley, onion, and sweet pickle, or capers, and mix with the sauce. Serve with cold meat.

SALADS

SALADS AND DRESSINGS

FRENCH DRESSING

Put a pinch each of salt and paprika into a small bowl. Rub the inside of the bowl with cut garlic if desired. Put in four tablespoonfuls of the best olive-oil and stir until the salt is dissolved. Add one tablespoonful of vinegar and stir and beat until no separate globules of oil are visible. Cider vinegar or any of the flavored vinegars may be used. Sometimes three tablespoonfuls of oil are used to one of vinegar.

SEASONINGS FOR FRENCH DRESSING

To French dressing made according to directions given above may be added at discretion anchovy essence, anchovy paste, celery salt, celery pepper, chilli pepper, curry powder, pounded cardamon seed, minced chervil, minced chives, chutney, capers, grated cheese, caviare, minced garlic, onion, horseradish, mustard, either made or dry, Worcestershire Sauce, mushroom, walnut, or tomato catsup, mint, parsley, thyme, savory, sage, marjoram, tarragon, minced olives or pickles, shrimp essence, sardine paste, chopped truffles or pimentos.

FRENCH DRESSING FOR FRUIT SALADS

Prepare according to directions given for French dressing, using lemon-juice or wine instead of vinegar and omitting the paprika. Fruit-juice, claret, white wine, port, sherry, Madeira, Rhine wine, and lime-juice are all used in dressing for fruit salads. If additional seasoning is desired, add powdered cinnamon, nutmeg, ginger or mace, or chopped candied fruits. For some salads sweet wine may be used in the dressing.

MAYONNAISE

Put an earthen bowl into a larger one containing cracked ice. Break into it the yolks of two fresh eggs, add a pinch each of salt and paprika, and half a teaspoonful or more of dry mustard. Mix thoroughly and add oil drop by drop at first. A clear spot forming upon the egg is the test of the proper quantity of oil. Use a silver teaspoon for mixing and beat constantly. If the Mayonnaise should curdle, put it on the ice for an hour, or add a few drops of lemon-juice. When a cupful or more of oil has been used and the dressing is stiff enough to cut with a knife, add the juice of half a lemon, or more, according to taste. Cover with paraffine paper and keep on ice until ready to serve. For fruit salads, omit the mustard and pepper and at the last fold in a little cream whipped solid. Veal or chicken jelly may also be mixed with Mayonnaise. Chopped sweet herbs, pickles, olives, capers, onions, garlic, shrimp paste, horseradish and caviare are used to season Mayonnaise. Chopped olives, pickles, and capers, with a little onion or garlic, if desired, make Tartar Sauce when added to Mayonnaise.

BOILED DRESSING—I

Bring half a cupful of vinegar to the boil, with two teaspoonfuls of sugar, half a teaspoonful each of salt and mustard, and a dash of pepper. Thicken with one-fourth cupful of butter creamed with a teaspoonful of flour, and cook until smooth and thick, stirring constantly. Take from the fire, and add the yolk of an egg well-beaten. Cool, and if desired add a cupful of sweet or sour cream or buttermilk.

BOILED DRESSING—II

Beat the yolks of two eggs with a tablespoonful of sugar and a teaspoonful each of salt and mustard. Add gradually half a cupful of melted butter or oil, the beaten whites of the eggs, and half a cupful of lemon-juice or vinegar. Cook in a double boiler until it thickens, stirring constantly.

CREAM DRESSING

Beat two eggs until light, add a teaspoonful of sugar, a teaspoonful of butter, three tablespoonfuls of vinegar, with salt, mustard, and cayenne to season. Cook until thick in a double boiler, stirring constantly, and adding gradually four tablespoonfuls of boiling tarragon vinegar. Take from the fire, cool, and add a cupful of whipped cream just before serving.

SOUR-CREAM DRESSING

Mix one cupful of thick sour cream with two tablespoonfuls each of lemon-juice and vinegar, one tablespoonful of sugar, a teaspoonful each of salt and mustard, and pepper to taste.

EGG DRESSING

Beat three eggs, add gradually two tablespoonfuls of oil, a teaspoonful of sugar, and salt, white pepper, and cayenne to season. Add half a cupful of boiling vinegar, mix thoroughly, and cook in a double boiler until thick.

GERMAN SALAD DRESSING

Mix half a cupful of sour cream with a tablespoonful of sugar, a dash of pepper, a teaspoonful each of salt and mustard, two tablespoonfuls of bacon fat, and half a chopped onion cooked in half a cupful of boiling vinegar.

CLUB DRESSING

Chop very fine two hard-boiled eggs, two pimentos, half a small onion, a small bunch of chives, and one small root of garlic. It cannot be too fine. Rub to a paste with a spoon, add six tablespoonfuls of oil, two of tarragon vinegar, and salt and paprika to season.

CURRY DRESSING

Rub the yolk of a hard-boiled egg smooth with four tablespoonfuls of oil, one tablespoonful of tarragon vinegar, and a pinch of curry powder.

RAVIGOTE DRESSING

Put into a double boiler the well-beaten yolks of two eggs and a tablespoonful of butter. Cook until it begins to thicken, then add another tablespoonful of butter and cook to a cream. Season with minced chives, chervil, tarragon, and parsley.

FISH SALADS

ANCHOVY AND EGG SALAD

Rub a salad bowl with cut garlic and fill with crisp lettuce leaves. Put anchovies and sliced hard-boiled eggs on top and serve with French dressing.

ANCHOVY AND PEPPER SALAD

Skin and bone six anchovies and chop very fine. Mix with a Spanish onion sliced very thin, two shredded sweet Spanish peppers, and a slice of bread cut into dice. Mix with French dressing and serve on lettuce or cress, adding more bread if desired.

CLAM AND CELERY SALAD

Cut clams into small pieces, season with onion-juice, mix with shredded lettuce or celery, and serve on lettuce with French dressing or Mayonnaise. Either cooked or raw clams may be used.

SARDINE SALAD—I

Arrange on a bed of lettuce, sardines and shrimps, alternately. Season with minced onion, chopped pickle, capers, and hard-boiled eggs. Pour over French dressing, season with tomato catsup, and serve cold.

SARDINE SALAD—II

Bone and flake drained sardines and put on tissue paper until the oil is absorbed. Mix with three times the quantity of finely cut celery and marinate in French dressing. Drain and serve on lettuce or cress with Mayonnaise.

SHRIMP SALAD

Mix cooked flaked shrimps with finely shredded lettuce and French dressing. Garnish with spoonfuls of Mayonnaise.

SHRIMP AND ASPARAGUS SALAD

Mix two cupfuls of cold cooked asparagus cut into short lengths with one cupful of cooked flaked shrimps. Serve with French dressing to which the pounded yolks of three hard-boiled eggs have been added.

VEGETABLE SALADS

ARTICHOKE SALAD

Remove the chokes and inner leaves from boiled artichokes, sprinkle with minced parsley, and serve with French dressing.

ASPARAGUS SALAD

Mix cold cooked asparagus tips with diced or sliced cucumbers and serve on lettuce with Mayonnaise.

ASPARAGUS À LA VINAIGRETTE

Serve cold boiled asparagus or the bleached canned asparagus on lettuce with French dressing to which have been added chopped olives, pickles, and capers. Onion and mustard may be added to the seasoning.

BEAN SALAD—I

Season cold cooked beans with tomato catsup and mix with half the quantity of finely cut celery. Sprinkle with minced chives and capers and serve very cold on lettuce with French dressing.

BEAN SALAD—II

Mix equal quantities of finely cut celery and cooked wax beans and serve on lettuce with Mayonnaise.

BEAN SALAD—III

Mix cold cooked lima beans with crisp lettuce, sprinkle with chopped mint and serve with French dressing or Mayonnaise.

BEET SALAD—I

Slice six cold boiled beets and one Spanish onion. Serve on crisp lettuce with French dressing.

BEET SALAD—II

Fill a salad bowl nearly full of crisp lettuce and cover with sliced boiled beets and hard-boiled eggs. Season with grated onion and pour over a French dressing which has been seasoned with minced garlic and tomato catsup.

BRUSSELS SPROUTS SALAD

Chop separately onion, olives, walnuts, and capers. Mix and blend to a smooth paste with lemon-juice. Spread over cold cooked Brussels sprouts. Mix thoroughly and serve with Mayonnaise.

CABBAGE SALAD—I

Marinate shredded cabbage in French dressing, drain, and serve on lettuce with Mayonnaise.

CABBAGE SALAD—II

Mix two cupfuls of shredded cabbage with half as much celery and season with minced chives and tomato catsup or Tabasco Sauce. Serve on lettuce with French orMayonnaise dressing.

CARROT SALAD—I

Boil young carrots in water to which a little sugar may be added. Drain, cool, cut up, and serve on lettuce with French dressing or Mayonnaise.

CARROT SALAD—II

Mix diced cooked carrots with lettuce and serve with French dressing, sprinkling with minced cress, chervil, chives, or parsley.

CAULIFLOWER SALAD—I

Mix cooked cauliflower flowerets with Mayonnaise and serve in red-pepper shells on lettuce with Mayonnaise on top.

CAULIFLOWER SALAD—II

Marinate cooked cauliflower flowerets in French dressing, drain, and serve on lettuce with Mayonnaise. Garnish with diced cooked carrots or beets.

CELERY SALAD—I

Shred crisp celery very fine and serve with French dressing or Mayonnaise.

CELERY SALAD—II

Mix finely cut celery with sliced sour apple cut into small bits and serve on lettuce with Mayonnaise.

CELERY SALAD—III

Cut into small bits a large bunch of celery and three-fourths pound of blanched almonds. Serve on lettuce with Mayonnaise.

CHICKORY SALAD

Fill a salad bowl with well trimmed chickory and serve with French dressing seasoned with onion-juice.

CHIFFONADE SALAD

Mix one cupful each of shredded lettuce, celery, and chickory, and one teaspoonful each of chopped beets, onion, parsley, tarragon, and sweet red pepper. Serve with crisp lettuce and French dressing, garnishing with sliced tomatoes.

CRESS SALAD—I

Mix watercress, lettuce, sliced tomatoes, cucumbers, and onion with shredded green pepper and celery. Serve with French dressing and garnish with sliced hard-boiled eggs.

CRESS SALAD—II

Cut thin slices of sour apples and hard-boiled eggs into bits and mix with watercress. Serve with French dressing.

CUCUMBER SALAD—I

Slice cucumbers thin, and soak in cold salted water until wilted. Drain, rinse, wipe very dry, and serve with French dressing or with thick sour cream seasoned highly with black pepper.

CUCUMBER SALAD—II

Mix one cupful of diced cucumbers with two cupfuls of finely cut celery and half a can of drained mushrooms. Add three chopped hard-boiled eggs and serve on lettuce with Mayonnaise.

CUCUMBER SALAD—III

Cut three cucumbers into dice. Mix with one cupful of finely cut olives, three hard-boiled eggs, and three-fourths cupful of broken pecans or English walnuts. Serve on lettuce with Mayonnaise. Pickled nasturtium seeds or French peas may be added.

CUCUMBER JELLY SALAD

Slice two cucumbers and cook until soft in water to cover, with a slice of onion and salt and pepper to season. Take from the fire, and add half a package of soaked and dissolved gelatine. Line a mould with thin slices of cucumber, fill with the jelly, and chill. Serve on lettuce with either French dressing or Mayonnaise.

ENDIVE SALAD

Fill a salad bowl with small crisp leaves of endive and serve with French dressing or Mayonnaise. Sprinkle with minced chives if desired.

LETTUCE SALAD—I

Quarter crisp heads of lettuce and serve individually with Mayonnaise.

LETTUCE SALAD—II

Cut head lettuce in quarters, sprinkle with minced chives and parsley, and serve with French dressing which may be seasoned with onion or garlic.

MUSHROOM SALAD

Cut canned mushrooms into small pieces and serve on lettuce with French dressing, sprinkling with minced chives and parsley.

ONION SALAD—I

Slice peeled Spanish onions very thin, crisp in ice-water, drain, wipe dry, and serve on lettuce with French dressing, sprinkling with minced parsley if desired.

ONION SALAD—II

Mix sliced Spanish onion with twice the quantity of sliced and broken sour apples. Mix with Mayonnaise and serve on lettuce.

PIMENTO SALAD

Mix shredded pimentos with quartered hard-boiled eggs, sliced olives, and pearl onions. Serve on lettuce with Mayonnaise.

PEA SALAD—I

Mix cooked and drained peas with diced cooked carrots and finely cut celery. Serve on lettuce with Mayonnaise.

PEA SALAD—II

Mix cooked peas with cut walnut meats, marinate in French dressing, drain, and serve in lemon-cups on lettuce with a spoonful of Mayonnaise on top.

PEPPER SALAD—I

Chop a very small onion fine with twice the quantity of parsley. Add two small red peppers and eight sweet green peppers finely minced. Pour over a French dressing, seasoning with a pinch of powdered sugar and a teaspoonful of salt. Serve ice-cold on lettuce leaves.

PEPPER SALAD—II

Mix sliced Spanish onions with seeded and sliced sweet green peppers and serve on lettuce with French dressing.

PEPPER SALAD—III

Slice the tops from green peppers, remove seeds and veins, and soak in boiling water for fifteen minutes. Drain, chill, and fill with finely cut celery mixed withMayonnaise. Shredded cabbage may be used instead of the celery or mixed with it.

POTATO SALAD—I

Mix diced cooked potatoes with one-fourth the quantity of diced boiled beets. Serve on lettuce with French dressing or Mayonnaise, garnishing with anchovies and small pickles, or in a mould of aspic.

POTATO SALAD—II

Mix two cupfuls of diced boiled potatoes with half a cupful of finely cut celery and an apple. Marinate in French dressing and serve Mayonnaise separately if desired.

POTATO SALAD—III

Mix sliced cold potatoes with finely cut pickled walnuts and chives or onions. Serve with French dressing, seasoned slightly with sage.

POTATO SALAD—IV

Slice cold cooked potatoes and season with minced onion and parsley. Pour over a French dressing and let stand two hours on ice before serving. Serve very cold and pass Mayonnaise if desired.

POTATO SALAD—V

Mix half a cupful of vinegar, one-fourth cupful of cold water, two eggs well-beaten, one tablespoonful of sugar, and three tablespoonfuls of butter, with salt and pepper to season. Cook until thick in a double boiler, stirring constantly; take from the fire, cool, and mix with a little cream. An entire cupful of cream may be used if desired. Mix with sliced boiled potatoes, seasoned with chopped onion and parsley.

RADISH SALAD

Mix sliced radishes with bits of sour apple, marinate in French dressing, drain, and mix with Mayonnaise. Serve on lettuce.

RADISH SALAD—II

Slice crisp radishes and mix with minced chives or sliced spring onions and serve with French dressing.

SALSIFY SALAD

Cook sliced salsify in salted and acidulated water with a bit of onion and a bay-leaf and a sprig of parsley. Drain, marinate in French dressing, and serve on cress or lettuce with Mayonnaise. Garnish with minced parsley and sliced oranges.

SPINACH SALAD—I

Mould cold cooked spinach in small cups. Turn out on lettuce, garnish with hard-boiled eggs and bits of cooked ham or tongue. Serve with Mayonnaise or French dressing.

SPINACH SALAD—II

Season cooked chopped spinach with salt, pepper, oil, and lemon-juice, and mould in small moulds. Turn out on thin slices of cold boiled tongue and serve with Tartar Sauce.

TOMATO SALAD—I

Peel and quarter large tomatoes and serve on lettuce with Mayonnaise. Marinate first in French dressing if desired.

TOMATO SALAD—II

Fill a salad bowl with alternate layers of sliced tomatoes and cucumbers and serve with French dressing or Mayonnaise. Crisp lettuce may be added.

225

TOMATO SALAD—III

Mix sliced tomatoes with lettuce and fresh Roquefort cheese broken into small bits. Serve with lettuce and French dressing to which minced garlic has been added.

STUFFED TOMATO SALAD—I

Mix equal quantities of diced cucumber, tomato pulp, and cooked peas with a few capers and a little chopped pickle. Add a little cooked chicken, cut in dice, mix withMayonnaise, fill tomato-shells, and serve on lettuce.

STUFFED TOMATO SALAD—II

Chop cucumbers and mix with sweet green peppers, seasoning with grated onion. Mix with thick Mayonnaise, fill tomato-shells, and serve on lettuce with French dressing or Mayonnaise.

STUFFED TOMATO SALAD—III

Stuff tomato-shells with chopped celery and nuts, which may be mixed with Mayonnaise, and serve on lettuce with Mayonnaise.

TOMATO JELLY SALAD

Cook eight tomatoes with a slice of onion, six cloves, and salt and pepper to season. Rub through a sieve, and add half a package of soaked and dissolved gelatine. Mould in small cups, and serve on lettuce with Mayonnaise. Or, place small peeled tomatoes in moulds and fill with any desired aspic. Turn out and serve withMayonnaise. Yellow tomatoes may be used in the same way.

WALDORF SALAD

Mix finely cut celery and apples with broken English walnuts. Serve on lettuce with Mayonnaise, or fill bright red apples from which the pulp has been removed.

FRUIT SALADS

ALLIGATOR PEAR SALAD

Mix sliced alligator pears with sliced or quartered hard-boiled eggs and serve on lettuce with Mayonnaise.

APPLE SALAD—I

Slice the tops from large red apples and scoop out the pulp. Mix with finely cut celery, broken English walnuts, and Mayonnaise made without mustard. Fill the apple shells, put on the lids, and serve on lettuce leaves.

APPLE SALAD—II

Mix sliced boiled chestnuts with finely cut celery and apples. Serve on lettuce with French dressing made with lemon-juice.

APPLE SALAD—III

Mix bits of apple with an equal quantity of orange pulp and add a few sliced maraschino cherries. Serve in the orange shells with Mayonnaise made without mustard and whitened with whipped cream. Shredded pineapple may be added.

APPLE SALAD—IV

Mix finely cut apples, celery, and shredded green peppers with broken English walnuts, blanched almonds, or pecans. Serve on lettuce with Mayonnaise made without mustard to which whipped cream has been added.

APRICOT SALAD

Peel and split apricots. Fill the hulls with chopped maraschino cherries and nuts and serve on lettuce with French dressing made with wine.

BANANA SALAD—I

Peel one section from the skin of ripe bananas, take out the pulp, mix with French dressing made with lemon-juice, fill the shells and serve on lettuce, sprinkling with chopped nuts if desired. Mayonnaise may be used instead of French dressing.

BANANA SALAD—II

Remove one section of the banana peel and scoop out the pulp. Mix with shredded orange or grapefruit, seeded and peeled white grapes, and a few broken nuts. Stoned cherries may be added if desired. Mix with Mayonnaise made without mustard and serve on lettuce in the banana skins.

CANTALOUPE SALAD

Scoop out the pulp from ripe cantaloupes, drain, and mix with pounded ice. Serve in the shells immediately with French dressing made without mustard and whitened with whipped cream.

CHERRY SALAD—I

Stuff maraschino cherries or white California canned cherries or large sweet cherries with blanched hazel nuts, and serve ice cold on lettuce, with Mayonnaise made without mustard and whitened with whipped cream.

CHERRY SALAD—II

Mix sliced black or maraschino cherries with shredded pineapple and blanched hazel nuts. Serve on lettuce with Mayonnaise made without mustard and whitened with whipped cream.

GRAPE SALAD—I

Mix peeled and seeded white grapes with finely cut celery and broken walnut meats and serve on lettuce with French dressing made with lemon-juice, orMayonnaise made without mustard and whitened with whipped cream.

GRAPE SALAD—II

Mix peeled and seeded white grapes with orange pulp, finely cut celery, and broken nuts. Or, mix pineapple, celery, and pecans. Serve on lettuce with French dressing made with lemon-juice or wine, or with Mayonnaise made without mustard and whitened with whipped cream.

GRAPEFRUIT SALAD—I

Mix grapefruit pulp with broken English walnuts, hickory nuts, or pecans. Mix with Mayonnaise made without mustard, fill the grapefruit shells, and serve on lettuce.

GRAPEFRUIT SALAD—II

Mix the pulp of three grapefruits and one large orange with two sliced bananas and half a cupful of maraschino cherries. Serve with French dressing made with lemon-juice or orange-juice, or Mayonnaise made without mustard and whitened with whipped cream. Garnish with white grapes, or add peeled and seeded white grapes to the salad.

GRAPEFRUIT SALAD—III

Mix the pulp of one grapefruit with two cupfuls of diced apples and serve on lettuce with French dressing made with the grapefruit juice. Or, mix the drained grapefruit pulp with broken English walnuts and serve in the shell with French dressing made of the juice, or Mayonnaise made without mustard. Garnish either salad with white grapes and nuts.

MACEDOINE SALAD—I

Mix peeled and seeded white grapes with equal quantities of strawberries, raspberries, sliced bananas, oranges, and pineapples, any or all. Serve with French dressing made with wine, or Mayonnaise made without mustard, adding whipped cream if desired.

MACEDOINE SALAD—II

Mix sliced bananas with maraschino cherries and season with sherry, or mix pineapple, oranges, white grapes, and plums, and season with white wine. Serve on lettuce with French dressing made with lemon-juice, or Mayonnaise made without mustard and whitened with whipped cream.

MACEDOINE SALAD—III

Mix shredded pineapple and apples with finely cut strawberries, bananas, cherries, peeled and seeded white grapes, and bits of orange pulp. Add chopped almonds or peanuts and serve with French dressing made with lemon-juice.

ORANGE SALAD—I

Mix sliced oranges and bananas with broken English walnuts and serve on lettuce with Mayonnaise made without mustard and whitened with whipped cream. Or, use oranges, bananas, pineapple, and peeled and seeded white grapes.

ORANGE SALAD—II

Mix shredded pineapple, sliced bananas, orange pulp, and maraschino cherries. Season with sherry and serve on lettuce with Mayonnaise made without mustard and whitened with whipped cream. The cherries and bananas may be omitted.

ORANGE SALAD—III

Arrange thinly sliced oranges on cress, sprinkle with chopped nuts and serve with French dressing made with lemon-juice, or with Mayonnaise made without mustard.

ORANGE SALAD—IV

Arrange sliced oranges on lettuce and sprinkle with blanched and broken English walnuts. A little chopped celery may be added. Serve with Mayonnaise made without mustard and whitened with whipped cream.

PEACH SALAD—I

Peel and split ripe peaches, cover thickly with chopped almonds, and serve on lettuce with French dressing made with orange juice, or Mayonnaise made without mustard and whitened with whipped cream.

PEACH SALAD—II

Mix finely cut peaches with sliced bananas and serve on lettuce with Mayonnaise made without mustard and whitened with whipped cream.

PEAR SALAD

Mix sliced pears with chopped candied ginger and serve on lettuce with Mayonnaise made without mustard and mixed with a little whipped cream.

PINEAPPLE SALAD—I

Cut off the top of a ripe pineapple and scoop out the pulp carefully. Cut it fine, mix with sliced bananas and stoned cherries, and with stiff Mayonnaise made without mustard. Fill the pineapple shell and put on the top. Pass with it Mayonnaise whitened with whipped cream.

PINEAPPLE SALAD—II

Mix shredded pineapple with finely cut celery and broken English walnuts. Serve on lettuce with Mayonnaise made without mustard and whitened with whipped cream.

PINEAPPLE SALAD—III

Mix shredded pineapple with peeled and quartered tomatoes, figs soaked in sherry and cut into dice, and broken English walnut meats. Serve ice cold on lettuce withMayonnaise made without mustard and whitened with whipped cream.

EGG SALADS

EGG SALAD—I

Mix finely cut celery with the shredded whites of hard-boiled eggs. Mash the yolks to a smooth paste with sardines, moistening with oil, and shape into balls. Serve on lettuce with Mayonnaise, using the balls as a garnish.

EGG SALAD—II

Arrange quartered hard-boiled egg on lettuce and pour over Mayonnaise mixed with salmon which has been rubbed to a smooth paste with a little oil. Caviare, sardines, or anchovy paste may be used instead of the salmon.

EGG SALAD—III

Cut fine three hard-boiled eggs and four stalks of celery. Serve on lettuce with French dressing or Mayonnaise.

CHEESE AND NUT SALADS

CHEESE SALAD—I

Rub cottage cheese to a smooth paste with cream, butter, and salt. Rub a salad bowl with cut garlic and fill with chickory or endive. Add the cheese balls and quartered hard-boiled eggs, with onion-juice to season. Serve with French dressing.

CHEESE SALAD—II

Mix cottage cheese with chopped olives and make to a smooth paste with oil and lemon-juice, seasoning with salt and paprika. Shape into balls and serve on lettuce or endive with French or Mayonnaise dressing. Garnish with olives.

CHEESE SALAD—III

Mix one cupful of broken American cheese, three Neufchatel cheeses cut into small pieces, ten olives or pimolas sliced, and three finely cut pimentos. Season with salt and paprika, moisten with cream, and serve on lettuce with French dressing to which grated horseradish has been added. Garnish with pimentos cut in fancy shapes.

CHEESE SALAD—IV

Mix two cream cheeses to a smooth paste with chopped nuts and minced parsley and roll into small balls. Arrange in nests of crisp lettuce and serve withMayonnaise.

NUT SALAD

Mix equal parts of finely cut celery and apple with half the quantity of broken nuts, using almonds, peanuts, pecans, walnuts, or salted almonds or peanuts. Serve on lettuce with Mayonnaise made without mustard.

ALMOND SALAD

Stone and chop six olives. Add half a cupful of blanched almonds cut fine and half a cupful of finely cut celery. Serve on lettuce with Mayonnaise from which the mustard may be omitted, and to which a little whipped cream may be added.

CHESTNUT SALAD—I

Shell and blanch large chestnuts and cook until soft. Cool and serve on lettuce with French dressing made with lemon-juice, or with Mayonnaise made without mustard. Serve very cold. Broken English walnuts may be added if desired.

CHESTNUT SALAD—II

Shell, blanch, and boil until tender one pint of chestnuts. Drain, cool, and serve on lettuce with French dressing made with lemon-juice. Dust with hard-boiled egg yolks rubbed through a sieve, and garnish with shredded whites.

CHESTNUT SALAD—III

Mix boiled chestnuts with bananas and oranges, or English walnuts with cheese and celery, or with apples and figs, or with cream cheese and figs, or pecans with apples, celery, and cream cheese. Serve with French dressing made with wine or lemon-juice or with Mayonnaise made without mustard and whitened with whipped cream.

PEANUT SALAD

Chop peanuts fine and mix to a smooth paste with Mayonnaise. Spread on sliced tomatoes or fill tomato-shells and serve on lettuce.

PECAN SALAD

Mix half a cupful each of broken pecans and chopped olives with one and one-half cupfuls of finely cut celery, and half of a red or green pepper chopped fine. Serve on lettuce or in pepper-shells with Mayonnaise.

WALNUT SALAD—I

Mix equal quantities of finely cut celery and broken English walnuts or pecans and marinate in French dressing. Serve in a border of shredded lettuce and passMayonnaise if desired.

WALNUT SALAD—II

Mix two cupfuls of finely cut celery with the grated rind of an orange and a dozen chopped walnut meats. Mix with stiff mayonnaise made without mustard and serve in apple shells, adding some of the apple pulp if desired. Serve on lettuce and pass mayonnaise.

SIMPLE DESSERTS

BLANC MANGE

Thicken a quart of milk with four tablespoonfuls of cornstarch rubbed smooth with a little of it. Add a teaspoonful of salt, and sugar and flavoring to taste. Mould, chill, and serve with a sauce made of a cupful of jam or jelly thoroughly mixed with the whites of three eggs beaten to a stiff froth.

ALMOND BLANC MANGE

Thicken a quart of boiling milk with three tablespoonfuls of cornstarch rubbed smooth with a little cold milk. Add four tablespoonfuls of sugar, a pinch of salt, and a few drops of lemon extract. When smooth and thick, add half a cupful or more of split blanched almonds, mould, chill, and serve with whipped cream, sweetened and flavored to taste.

CHERRY BLANC MANGE

Stone a quart of cherries and stew, sweetening heavily. Thicken with one level tablespoonful of cornstarch rubbed smooth with a little cold water, and cook until smooth and thick, stirring constantly. Mould, chill, and serve with sugar and cream. Other fruits may be used in the same way.

CHOCOLATE BLANC MANGE

Thicken a quart of milk with four level tablespoonfuls of cornstarch rubbed smooth with a little of it, add a pinch of salt, a teaspoonful of vanilla, sugar to taste, and a square of bitter chocolate grated and cooked to a smooth paste in a little boiling water. Cook, while stirring, until smooth and thick, mould, chill, and serve with custard or whipped cream.

CREAM BLANC MANGE

Thicken one and one-half cupfuls of milk with two tablespoonfuls of cornstarch rubbed smooth with a little milk and add two tablespoonfuls of sugar and the stiffly beaten whites of two eggs. Take from the fire, flavor to taste, mould and chill. Make a custard of one and one-half cupfuls of milk, the beaten yolks of two eggs, two tablespoonfuls of sugar, and flavoring to taste. Serve with the custard poured around the pudding.

COFFEE BLANC MANGE

Mix a cupful of very strong coffee with two cupfuls of boiling cream, sweeten to taste and add half a package of gelatine which has been soaked and dissolved. Mould, chill, and serve with whipped cream.

FRUIT BLANC MANGE

Heat a quart of milk in a double boiler with half a cupful of cream and flavoring to taste. Add a package of gelatine which has been soaked and dissolved, and mould in layers, alternating with preserves or jam or crushed and sweetened fresh fruit. Chill and serve with a border of the fruit. Cover with whipped cream if desired. Cherries, peaches, strawberries, bananas, or pineapples may be used.

PEACH BLANC MANGE

Thicken two cupfuls of boiling milk with one tablespoonful of cornstarch rubbed smooth with a little cold water. Add two tablespoonfuls of sugar, boil for five minutes, while stirring, take from the fire, add a tablespoonful of butter and the yolks of four eggs well-beaten. Butter a baking-dish, put in a pint of canned peaches, pour the cornstarch over and bake in a quick oven for half an hour. Take from the fire and cover with a meringue made of the whites of eggs beaten to a stiff froth, and sweetened to taste. Serve cold. Apples, apricots, cherries, figs, gooseberries, plums, pears, pineapples, quinces, rhubarb, and berries may be used in the same way.

VANILLA BLANC MANGE

Sweeten a quart of boiling cream with a little syrup, add half a package of gelatine which has been soaked and dissolved, mould, chill, and serve with whipped cream.

BLUEBERRY CAKE

Cream a tablespoonful of butter with a cupful of sugar, add an unbeaten egg and mix thoroughly. Add a cupful of milk, and two and one-half cupfuls of flour sifted with three teaspoonfuls of baking-powder. Add a pinch of grated nutmeg and stir in lightly three cupfuls of blueberries. Turn into buttered pans and bake for thirty-five minutes in a hot oven.

BLUEBERRY TEA-CAKES

Sift two cupfuls of flour with a pinch of salt and two teaspoonfuls of baking-powder. Work into it a tablespoonful of butter, add the yolk of an egg beaten with half a cupful of sugar, and one cupful of milk. Fold in the stiffly beaten white of the egg and add a heaping cupful of blueberries, which have been dredged with flour. Bake for half an hour in muffin pans. Sour milk may be used with half a teaspoonful of soda instead of the baking-powder.

CHOCOLATE CAKE

Beat the yolks of six eggs, add a cupful of sugar, and the grated rind and juice of half a lemon. Sift in half a cake of grated bitter chocolate, a teaspoonful of baking-powder, with a pinch each of cinnamon, and clove, and enough flour to make a thin batter. Fold in the stiffly beaten whites of the eggs and bake in layer-cake pans. Put together with currant jelly. Ice with frosting made of a beaten egg, a cupful of powdered sugar, and half a teaspoonful of vanilla.

CHOCOLATE CREAM CAKE

Cream half a cupful of butter with one cupful of sugar, add the stiffly beaten whites of four eggs, and sift in one and one-half cupfuls of flour with a teaspoonful of baking-powder. Flavor with vanilla. Bake in a square tin. Boil one and one-half cupfuls of sugar with half a cupful of milk until the syrup makes a soft ball when dropped in cold water. Flavor with vanilla, stir until thick, spread on the cake and pour melted chocolate on top.

COCOANUT CAKE

Cream half a cupful of butter with two cupfuls of sugar, add the beaten yolks of five eggs, a teaspoonful of vanilla, one cupful of milk and four cupfuls of flour sifted with a teaspoonful of soda and two teaspoonfuls of cream tartar. Fold in the stiffly beaten whites of the eggs, add a cupful of shredded cocoanut soaked soft in milk, and bake in a moderate oven. Spread with boiled frosting, sprinkling thickly with grated cocoanut.

CREAM CAKE

Beat three eggs with one and one-half cupfuls of powdered sugar, add a tablespoonful of lemon-juice and half a cupful of cold water. Sift in two cupfuls of flour and two teaspoonfuls of baking-powder. Bake in layer-cake tins. Heat one and one-half cupfuls of milk in a double boiler. Beat together one tablespoonful of flour, two-thirds cupful of sugar, two eggs, and a pinch of salt. Add gradually to the boiling milk, stir, and cook for fifteen minutes. Flavor to taste, cool, and put the cake together with the filling. Ice with any preferred frosting.

COFFEE CREAM CAKE

Cream together half a cupful of butter and a cupful of sugar. Add half a cupful of milk and sift in half a cupful of cornstarch, one and one-fourth cupfuls of flour, half a teaspoonful of cream tartar and a pinch of soda. Fold in the stiffly beaten whites of three eggs and bake in buttered layer-cake tins for half an hour. Cook in a double-boiler one cupful of milk, one cupful of strong coffee, and a cupful of sugar. Thicken with the yolks of three eggs and three tablespoonfuls of flour rubbed smooth with a little cold milk. Stir while cooking. Take from the fire, add two tablespoonfuls of butter, and cool. Spread between the layers and ice with confectioner's sugar moistened with coffee.

CREAM PUFFS

Bring to the boil one cupful of water, half a cupful of lard or butter, and a pinch of salt. Add enough sifted flour to make a smooth thick paste, sifting it in gradually and stirring it constantly. Take from the fire and add one at a time five unbeaten eggs, beating thoroughly each time. Drop by spoonfuls on a buttered tin sheet and bake for twenty minutes in a moderate oven. Thicken a pint of milk and two beaten eggs in a double-boiler with half a cupful of sifted flour rubbed smooth with a little cold milk. Sweeten and flavor to taste. When the puffs are cold, split with a sharp knife and fill with the cream. Sprinkle the puffs with powdered sugar and serve.

DEVIL'S FOOD CAKE

Boil together until thick one-half cupful each of grated chocolate, milk, and sugar, then cool. Cream one-half cupful of butter with a cupful of brown sugar, add two eggs well-beaten, two-thirds cupful of milk, and a teaspoonful of vanilla. Add the cooked mixture and sift in two cupfuls of flour with a heaping teaspoonful of baking-powder. Bake in layers and put together with chocolate frosting or boiled frosting.

FIG LOAF CAKE

Cream a cupful of butter with two cupfuls of brown sugar, add four eggs well-beaten, one teaspoonful each of cinnamon and nutmeg, half a teaspoonful of powdered cloves, and a cupful of water. Sift in three cupfuls of flour with two teaspoonfuls of baking-powder and add half a pound of finely cut figs and two cupfuls of raisins, dredging the fruit with flour. Bake for two hours in a moderate oven.

FRUIT CAKE

Cream a cupful each of butter and sugar, add the yolks of four eggs well-beaten, a pinch of grated nutmeg, and a cupful of flour sifted with a teaspoonful of baking-powder. Fold in the stiffly beaten whites, add half a cupful each of currants and blanched and shredded almonds, and, gradually, half a cupful of sherry. Put into a buttered tin in layers, alternating with shredded candied orange-peel and citron. Bake in a moderate oven for three hours and ice with boiled frosting.

HONEY TEA-CAKE

Mix one cupful of honey, half a cupful of sour cream, two eggs well-beaten, half a cupful of butter, melted, and two cupfuls of flour sifted with half a teaspoonful of soda and a teaspoonful of cream tartar. Bake for half an hour in a moderate oven.

MARGUERITES

Blanch and chop a pound of almonds and mix to a stiff paste with the stiffly beaten whites of two eggs. Beat the white of another egg to a stiff froth and add enough powdered sugar to make a thick icing. Spread crackers with the icing, then with the chopped nuts, and bake golden brown in a cool oven.

NUT CAKE

Cream a cupful each of butter and sugar, add two eggs well-beaten, a cupful of milk, a teaspoonful of vanilla, and two cupfuls of flour sifted with two teaspoonfuls of baking-powder. Add a cupful each of blanched and chopped nuts and stoned raisins dredged with flour and bake in a deep buttered pan in a moderate oven.

RASPBERRY TEA-CAKE

Beat together one cupful of sugar and one tablespoonful of butter, melted, add two eggs well-beaten, a pinch of salt, a grating of nutmeg, one cupful of milk, and two cupfuls of flour sifted with three teaspoonfuls of baking-powder. Bake in two layers and put together with butter and raspberry jam. Serve hot.

SPICE CAKE

Beat an egg and add to it two-thirds cupful each of sugar, melted butter, and molasses. Add a cupful of milk in which a teaspoonful of soda has been dissolved, and sift in two and one-half cupfuls of flour with a teaspoonful of cream tartar. Add a tablespoonful each of lemon-juice and mixed spice, turn into a shallow pan, and bake for twenty minutes in a moderate oven.

SPONGE CAKE

Mix two beaten eggs with a cupful of sugar, add one-third cupful of water, a teaspoonful of lemon or vanilla, and fold in lightly one cupful of flour sifted with a teaspoonful of baking-powder. Bake in a square pan.

TEA-CAKE

Cream a tablespoonful of butter with a cupful of sugar, add one egg well-beaten and three-fourths cupful of milk. Add three-fourths cupful of currants or raisins which have been dredged with flour and sift in one and one-half cupfuls of flour and a teaspoonful of baking-powder. Bake in a buttered tin or in patty-pans.

CHARLOTTE RUSSE

Line charlotte-russe moulds or dessert glasses with lady-fingers, split and trimmed to fit. Fill with cream whipped solid and sweetened and flavored to taste.

ALMOND CHARLOTTE RUSSE

Arrange six small sponge cakes in a serving-dish and spread thinly with jelly or jam. Stick blanched and split almonds into the cake and pour over a custard made of a cupful of milk and two tablespoonfuls of sugar, thickened with one egg well-beaten. Flavor with almond.

APPLE CHARLOTTE

Steam a quart of sliced sour apples until soft. Put into a baking-dish with alternate layers of bread crumbs, sprinkling the apples with sugar and cinnamon. Have crumbs on top. Beat the yolk of an egg with two cupfuls of milk, add two tablespoonfuls of melted butter, a pinch of salt, and two eggs well-beaten. Pour over the apples, bake until the milk is absorbed, and serve with sugar and cream.

BLACKBERRY CHARLOTTE

Make a boiled custard with one quart of milk, the yolks of six eggs, three-fourths cupful of sugar, and grated lemon peel to flavor. Line a serving-dish with slices of sponge cake dipped in cream and fill with alternate layers of cakes and blackberries crushed and sweetened. Pour the cold custard over, cover with meringue, and decorate with blackberries.

CREAM CHARLOTTE

Line a mould with lady-fingers. Whip a pint of cream to a stiff froth, sweetening and flavoring to taste and adding one-half package of soaked and dissolved gelatine. Pour into the mould, chill, and serve.

COFFEE CHARLOTTE

Thicken a cupful of milk with the yolks of four eggs beaten with a cupful of sugar and add a cupful of very strong coffee. Add half a package of gelatine which has been soaked and dissolved, and when cool but not set, fold in two cupfuls of cream whipped solid. Turn into a mould lined with lady-fingers, chill, and serve.

ORANGE CHARLOTTE

Soak and dissolve half a package of gelatine, using as little water as possible. Add the juice of a lemon, one cupful each of sugar and orange-juice, and a little of the grated orange peel. When cool but not set, fold in a pint of cream whipped solid and turn into a mould lined with slices or sections of oranges.

PEACH CHARLOTTE

Rub through a sieve enough canned peaches to make a cupful. Add the juice of a lemon, a cupful of sugar and half a package of gelatine which has been soaked and dissolved in as little water as possible. When cool but not set, fold in the stiffly beaten whites of three eggs, mould, chill, and serve with whipped cream. Pears or other fruits may be used in the same way.

VICTORIA CHARLOTTE

Trim the frosting from a loaf of angel-food and cut it into squares. Arrange in a serving-dish, cover with split marshmallows, minced candied fruit, and chopped nuts, and pile high with whipped cream sweetened and flavored to taste.

APPLE COBBLER

Sift together four cupfuls of flour, two heaping teaspoonfuls of baking-powder, one teaspoonful of salt, and one tablespoonful of sugar. Work into it half a cupful of butter and add enough milk to make a dough that will roll. Line a deep buttered baking-dish with the dough rolled thin, fill with peeled, cored, and quartered apples sweetened and sprinkled with spice, cover the pan with the rest of the dough rolled into a crust, and steam for two hours and a half, or bake. Serve with a sauce made of syrup thickened with cornstarch, seasoned with lemon-juice, grated peel, butter, and grated nutmeg or other spice. Apricots, plums, and peaches or berries may be used in the same way.

FRUIT COBBLER

Fill a deep buttered baking-dish with fresh or stewed fruit—apples, peaches, apricots, rhubarb, plums, or gooseberries being commonly used—and cover with a crust made as follows: Sift together two cupfuls of flour and two teaspoonfuls of baking-powder. Rub into it half a cupful of butter and add one egg beaten with a cupful of milk. Spread over the fruit which has been previously sweetened to taste and bake until the crust is done. Serve either hot or cold with cream or any preferred sauce.

COMPOTE OF APPLES

Peel and core the apples and cook until soft in syrup to cover, flavoring with lemon or spice if desired. Drain, fill the cores with jelly, reduce the syrup by rapid boiling, pour around the apples and chill. At serving time cover with whipped cream and sprinkle with chopped nuts.

COMPOTE OF FIGS

Soak a pound of figs over night in cold water to cover, and simmer over a slow fire until tender. Add half a cupful of sugar and the juice of half a lemon. Turn into a serving-dish, cool, and cover with whipped cream slightly sweetened and flavored with vanilla.

ALMOND CREAM

Soak and dissolve a package of gelatine. Make a custard of six cupfuls of milk, four eggs well-beaten, a pinch of salt, and a few drops of almond extract. Add two-thirds cupful of sugar, and, when cool, the gelatine. Add a few blanched and shredded almonds, mould and chill.

APPLE CREAM

Peel, core, and quarter six or eight apples and cook until soft in a thin syrup to cover, flavoring the syrup with lemon-juice and spice. Drain, reduce the syrup by rapid boiling, pour over the apples, arrange in a serving-dish, and chill. Cover with whipped cream just before serving.

BANANA CREAM

Peel five bananas and rub through a sieve with five tablespoonfuls of powdered sugar and a tablespoonful of lemon-juice. Add half a package of gelatine which has been soaked and dissolved in a little milk, and when cool, but not set, fold in a cupful of cream whipped solid. Mould, chill, and serve with whipped cream.

BAVARIAN CREAM

Soak half a package of gelatine in a cupful of cream and dissolve by gentle heat. Rub through a sieve enough canned or fresh fruit to make a cupful. Sweeten heavily and mix with the dissolved gelatine. Whip a cupful of cream solid and when the fruit mixture is cool but not set, fold it gradually into the cream. When it begins to stiffen, mould, chill, and serve with whipped cream if desired. Observing the same proportions, Bavarian Creams may be made of apples, apricots, bananas, cherries, chestnuts, cocoanut, figs, preserved ginger, gooseberries, plums, huckleberries, oranges, pears, peaches, pineapple, quinces, raspberries, strawberries, chopped nuts, chocolate syrup, maple syrup, coffee,—indeed almost anything. When almonds are used, a little more cream should be added. There should be one cupful of cream and gelatine, two cupfuls of whipped cream, and one cupful of fruit pulp. Half a cupful of chocolate dissolved in a little cold water and cooked to a paste will be sufficient. In using coffee or maple syrup put in only enough to flavor. Pineapple Bavarian Cream should be served as soon as possible after making, as the pineapple contains a ferment which softens the gelatine.

CHESTNUT CREAM

Peel, boil, drain, and mash thirty large fresh chestnuts. Rub through a sieve and cook for ten minutes with half a cupful each of sugar and water. Arrange in a circle on a serving-dish and fill the centre with whipped cream sweetened and flavored to taste.

GINGER CREAM

Add a package of soaked gelatine to a cupful of hot milk and dissolve by gentle heat. Whip a cupful of cream solid, sweetening with powdered sugar, add a tablespoonful of ginger syrup, a few drops of essence of ginger, and a little preserved ginger chopped very fine. When the gelatine is cool but not set, fold in the cream carefully and beat until it begins to stiffen. Mould and chill. Serve with whipped cream flavored with ginger syrup.

ITALIAN CREAM

Mix two cupfuls of cream, two-thirds cupful of sugar, and two wineglassfuls of white wine. Add the juice of two lemons, a little of the grated peel, and a package of gelatine which has been soaked in cold water and dissolved in a pint of hot cream. Mould and chill. Nuts or candied or preserved fruit may be added if desired.

MACAROON CREAM

Thicken a pint of cream with one tablespoonful of cornstarch rubbed smooth with a little cold milk. Stir while cooking. Cool, flavor with vanilla, and pour over macaroons arranged in a serving-dish. Chill and garnish with bits of bright jelly or candied fruit.

MARSHMALLOW CREAM

Cut marshmallows into quarters and mix with whipped cream sweetened and flavored to taste. Serve in dessert glasses and sprinkle with chopped nuts or garnish with marshmallows or candied cherries.

ORANGE CREAM

Heat in a double boiler the juice of six oranges and the grated rind of two. Add to it one cupful of sugar and half a package of gelatine which has been soaked and dissolved. Take from the fire, add the well-beaten yolks of six eggs, and stir until cool. When cool but not set, fold in two cupfuls of cream whipped solid. Mould and chill.

PEACH CREAM

Mash through a sieve enough fresh peaches to make a cupful. Whip a cupful of cream solid, add two tablespoonfuls of powdered sugar and the peach pulp. Serve immediately in dessert glasses. Other fruits may be used in the same way.

PINEAPPLE CREAM

Drain the juice from a pint can of pineapple and add to it the juice of one orange. Season with grated lemon-peel and add half a package of soaked gelatine. Heat over boiling water until the gelatine is dissolved. Take from the fire and when cool, but not set, fold in gradually one cupful of cream whipped solid and the pineapple cut fine. Mould and chill.

RASPBERRY CREAM

Rub a pint of raspberries through a sieve, sweeten to taste, and add a package of gelatine which has been soaked and dissolved in a cupful or more of water. Mix in a few drops of vanilla and when cool, but not set, fold in a cupful of cream whipped solid. Mould, chill, and serve with whipped cream.

SPANISH CREAM

Soak half a package of gelatine in cold water to cover, and dissolve by gentle heat. Beat together the yolks of three eggs, three tablespoonfuls of sugar, and a pinch of salt. Pour into a double boiler, add a pint of hot milk and cook until thick, stirring constantly. Take from the fire, add the dissolved gelatine and fold in the stiffly beaten whites of the eggs. Mould, chill, and serve with any preferred sauce.

TAPIOCA CREAM

Soak half a cupful of tapioca over night in cold water and cook until soft in a double boiler with a quart of milk and a pinch of salt. Add the yolks of four eggs beaten with a cupful of sugar, cook for ten minutes, then fold in the stiffly beaten whites of the eggs, and flavor to taste. Turn into a serving-dish, cool, and drop a few teaspoonfuls of currant jelly upon the pudding when serving. Three eggs may be used instead of four.

APPLE CUSTARD

Sweeten four cupfuls of stewed and mashed apples with half a cupful of sugar, two tablespoonfuls of butter, and the juice and grated rind of a lemon. Add half a cupful of water, two eggs well beaten, and two cupfuls of bread crumbs mixed with one tablespoonful of flour. Add a cup of milk, heat well, turn into a buttered baking-dish, and bake for forty minutes in a moderate oven. Serve with Hard Sauce or with sugar and cream.

CARAMEL CUSTARD

Brown half a cupful of sugar, add half a cupful of hot water, and simmer for fifteen minutes. Add to a pint of milk beaten slightly with four eggs and a pinch of salt; turn into a baking-dish and bake in a slow oven for forty minutes. Serve cold.

CHOCOLATE CUSTARD

Dissolve four heaping tablespoonfuls of grated bitter chocolate in a quart of hot milk. Add the yolks of six eggs beaten with a cupful of sugar and a teaspoonful of vanilla, take from the fire, pour into custard cups, set into a baking-dish, with an inch of hot water and bake slowly until set. Cover with meringue, return to the oven until puffed and brown, and serve cold.

COFFEE CUSTARD

Thicken six cupfuls of boiling milk with the yolks of eight eggs beaten with eight tablespoonfuls of sugar, and add a cupful of strong black coffee. Strain into custard cups, put into a pan of water to reach to half their height, and simmer for twenty minutes. Serve cold.

CREAM CUSTARD

Heat a cupful of cream with two tablespoonfuls of sugar, boil for fifteen minutes, and flavor to taste. Take from the fire, fold in the stiffly beaten whites of four eggs and chill. Or, put into a baking-dish, sprinkle with sugar, bake until puffed and brown and serve hot.

FRENCH CUSTARDS

Add to a pint of rich boiled custard half a cupful of blanched chopped almonds and a little shredded citron. Serve cold.

MAPLE CUSTARD

Beat five eggs with a tablespoonful of flour, a cupful of maple sugar and a pinch each of salt and grated nutmeg. Mix with three pints of warm milk, turn into a baking-dish or custard cups, set the dish into a pan of hot water and bake in a moderate oven until the custard is set.

MARQUISE CUSTARD

Thicken four cupfuls of boiling milk with the beaten yolks of eight eggs and the whites of five, adding a pinch of salt, and sugar and flavoring to taste. Cool, turn into a serving-dish, and beat the whites of three eggs to a standing froth. Beat into the whites four tablespoonfuls of raspberry or strawberry jam and drop by tablespoonfuls upon the custard. Serve immediately.

NUT CUSTARD

Beat the yolks of four eggs with two cupfuls of milk, add half a package of soaked gelatine, dissolve by gentle heat, add sugar to taste, and strain. Add half a cupful of chopped nuts, stir until it begins to stiffen, then mould and chill.

RASPBERRY CUSTARD

Beat together the yolks of two eggs, two cupfuls of milk, two tablespoonfuls of sugar, and a tablespoonful of cornstarch, rubbed smooth with a little milk. Cook slowly in a double boiler until smooth and thick, stirring constantly. Put a pint of red raspberries into a serving-dish, mash lightly with a spoon, sprinkle with powdered sugar, pour over the custard and cool. Make a meringue of the beaten whites and a tablespoonful of powdered sugar and tint it pink with berry juice. Spread over the custard and serve. Other fruits may be used in the same way.

RICE CUSTARD

Mix a pint of milk with a cupful of cream, a heaping tablespoonful of ground rice, two tablespoonfuls of rose-water, and half a cupful of sugar. Bring to the boil, stirring constantly, take from the fire, add the beaten yolks of three eggs, turn into a serving-dish, sprinkle with powdered sugar and grated nutmeg, and chill.

DOUGHNUTS

Cream one cupful of butter with two cupfuls of brown sugar, add six eggs well-beaten, half a cupful of milk, and enough flour with baking-powder to make a moderately stiff dough. Roll thin, cut out, and fry in deep fat. Drain, and sprinkle with powdered sugar.

APPLE DUMPLINGS

Rub a tablespoonful of lard into a pint of flour sifted with a pinch each of salt and soda and a teaspoonful of cream tartar. Mix to a stiff dough with milk, roll thin, cut into squares, and put in the centre of each a peeled and cored sour apple. Fill the cavity with butter and sugar creamed together and season lightly with spice. Wrap the dough around the apple, pinching firmly, and steam or bake. Serve hot with sugar and cream or Hard Sauce.

PEACH DUMPLINGS

Peel and stone peaches, enclose in pastry, brush with beaten egg, and bake. Serve either hot or cold with sugar or sweet sauce. Pears or almost any other fruit may be used in the same way.

FRITTER BATTER

Beat one egg light, add a cupful of milk and one cupful of flour which has been sifted with a teaspoonful of baking-powder and a pinch of salt. Beat hard for three minutes, then dip prepared fruit into the batter and fry brown in deep fat.

APPLE FRITTERS

Peel, core, and quarter small apples, sprinkle with sugar and nutmeg, dip in fritter batter, fry in deep fat, drain, and serve with any preferred sauce. Other fruits may be used in the same way. Sprinkle with powdered sugar if desired.

VIENNA FRITTERS

Cut stale sponge cake into thin rounds and fry in butter. Drain, spread with jam or jelly, and serve with cream.

FROZEN DAINTIES

APRICOT ICE

Rub through a sieve enough peeled apricots to make a cupful, sweeten with syrup, add two cupfuls of water, and, if desired, the white of one or two unbeaten eggs. Freeze. Canned apricots may be used.

BANANA ICE-CREAM

Heat a pint of cream in a double boiler with a cupful of sugar and stir until dissolved. Cool, add eight bananas mashed through a sieve, add another pint of cream, and freeze.

CAFÉ PARFAIT

Thicken a cupful each of milk and strong coffee with the yolks of eight eggs beaten with ten tablespoonfuls of sugar. Cool, strain, and fold in a cupful of cream whipped solid. Turn into a mould and bury in ice and salt for four hours.

CARAMEL ICE-CREAM

Cook half a cupful of sugar until dark brown with a tablespoonful of water, stirring constantly. Heat a quart of milk with half a cupful of sugar and thicken, while stirring, with three small spoonfuls of cornstarch rubbed smooth with a little cold water. Add a pinch of salt, three eggs well-beaten, and the caramel. Bring to the boil, strain, cool, and freeze. Chopped nuts may be added if desired.

CEYLON ICE

Make a quart of strong Ceylon tea, sweeten heavily while hot, and add the juice of a lemon. Cool, strain, freeze, and serve in glasses.

CHERRY ICE

Stone a pound of black cherries and cut into bits. Sweeten the juice heavily with syrup, add the juice of half a lemon and three cupfuls of water, and freeze. If a pink ice is desired, add the unbeaten whites of one or two eggs.

CHOCOLATE ICE-CREAM

Scald six cupfuls of cream with sugar to sweeten heavily and add half a cake of chocolate grated. Add also a package of soaked and dissolved gelatine, and two teaspoonfuls of vanilla. Strain and freeze.

COFFEE ICE-CREAM

Mix two cupfuls of cream with one cupful of very strong coffee, sweeten heavily, add the unbeaten white of an egg, and freeze.

GRAPE ICE-CREAM

Cook a cupful of grape juice to a thick syrup with a cupful of sugar, mix with two cupfuls of cream, and freeze. The cream will be lavender in color. A little less sugar may be required for some tastes.

LEMON ICE

Mix two cupfuls of lemon-juice with three cupfuls of water and sweeten heavily with thick syrup. Freeze. The unbeaten whites of two eggs may be added if a frothy ice is desired.

LEMON ICE-CREAM

Make a syrup of a cupful of sugar, half a cupful of water, and the juice and grated rind of two lemons. Strain, add to three pints of cream, and freeze.

MACAROON ICE-CREAM

Dry half a pound of macaroons in the oven, cool, roll, and sift. Mix with cream, allowing three cupfuls of cream to each cupful of crumbs. Sweeten heavily and freeze.

MAPLE ICE-CREAM

Mix a cupful of maple syrup with two cupfuls of cream and freeze. A beaten egg may be added.

ORANGE SHERBERT

Mix two cupfuls of orange juice, the grated yellow rind of an orange, and the juice of a lemon. Add two cupfuls of sugar and four cupfuls of water, let stand for two hours and freeze.

PEACH ICE-CREAM

Peel and mash through a sieve enough peaches to make two cupfuls. Add a cupful and a half of sugar and a few drops of lemon or almond extract. Let the fruit stand for an hour, then add a quart of cream, and freeze.

RASPBERRY ICE

Mix three cupfuls of raspberry-juice, with one cupful of water sweetened heavily and add if desired the juice of half a lemon. Let stand for an hour and freeze. Cherries, strawberries, currants, and pineapple may be used in the same way. The unbeaten white of an egg or two may be added.

STRAWBERRY ICE

Mix two cupfuls of strawberry-juice with three cupfuls of thin syrup and the juice of a lemon. Freeze, adding the unbeaten white of one or two eggs, if desired.

STRAWBERRY ICE-CREAM

Rub through a fine sieve enough strawberries to make a cupful, add a cupful of sugar, the juice of a lemon, two cupfuls of cream, and freeze.

JELLIED DESSERTS

COFFEE JELLY

Sweeten heavily three cupfuls of strong hot coffee and add half a package of gelatine which has been soaked and dissolved. Mould in a border mould and at serving-time fill the centre with whipped cream sweetened and flavored to taste.

CHOCOLATE CREAM JELLY

Melt half a cake of bitter chocolate in a quart of milk and thicken with yolks of seven eggs beaten with ten tablespoonfuls of powdered sugar and a teaspoonful of vanilla. Add half a package of gelatine which has been soaked and dissolved. Strain, mould, and chill.

CUSTARD JELLY

Heat a pint of milk with a pinch of soda, add a cupful of sugar, the yolks of three eggs well-beaten, and a teaspoonful of vanilla. Cook until smooth and thick, stirring constantly, then add half a package of gelatine which has been soaked and dissolved. When cool but not set, fold in the stiffly beaten whites of the eggs, mould, and chill.

JELLIED APRICOTS

Rub a can of apricots through a sieve and cook to a smooth paste with half a cupful of maraschino, the juice of two lemons, and half a cupful of sugar, add a package of gelatine which has been soaked and dissolved, mould, chill, and serve.

JELLIED FRUIT

Cut fine two oranges and four bananas, sweeten to taste, and add a little wine. Pour over one-half package of acidulated gelatine which has been soaked and dissolved, and chill. Cut into squares and serve with whipped cream or boiled custard. Other fruits may be used in the same way.

JELLIED RHUBARB

Cut a pound and a half of rhubarb into inch-lengths and cook slowly until tender, sweetening with brown sugar. Add a package of gelatine soaked and dissolved, using as little water as possible. Mould and chill.

JELLIED WHITE CURRANTS

Cook a pint of white currants until soft in thin syrup to cover. Add the juice of a lemon and a package of gelatine soaked and dissolved in two cupfuls of water. Mould, chill, and serve.

LEMON JELLY

Make a strong hot lemonade, and, if desired, add a little of the grated peel. Stiffen with gelatine which has been soaked and dissolved, allowing half a package to each scant quart of liquid.

WINE JELLY

Soak a package of gelatine in a cupful of cold water and dissolve by gentle heat. Add to four cupfuls of wine heavily sweetened, mould, and chill. Coffee or fruit-juice may be used instead of the wine and the stiffly beaten whites of four or five eggs may be folded in just before the mixture begins to set. Strawberry, raspberry, cherry, lemon, orange, maraschino, kirsch, chocolate, pineapple, and numberless other jellies may be made in the same way. Fresh or preserved fruit, small sponge cakes, or candied fruit may be moulded in these jellies.

VANILLA CREAM JELLY

Thicken a quart of boiling milk with the yolks of eight eggs beaten with ten tablespoonfuls of powdered sugar. Strain, flavor with vanilla, and add half a package of gelatine which has been soaked and dissolved. Mould, chill, and serve with whipped cream.

PIES

PLAIN PIE CRUST

Cut together with a knife one quart of sifted flour, half a cupful each of lard and butter, a teaspoonful of salt, and a tablespoonful of sugar. Add gradually three-fourths cupful of ice-water, turn out on a floured board, roll, chill, and use as desired.

APPLE PIE

Make a rich crust of half a pound of butter, a pound of flour, and a pinch of salt. Work with the fingers until it is like meal, and add ice-water to mix. Roll out, pat into shape, and line a pie-tin with the crust. Peel, core, and cut up good cooking apples, fill the pie, dot with butter, sprinkle with sugar and spice, cover with the other crust and bake. Sprinkle with powdered sugar before serving.

APRICOT PIE

Cut fine a can of apricots and mix with half a cupful of sugar and the beaten yolk of an egg. Bake with one crust, cover with meringue, and return to the oven until puffed and brown.

CHOCOLATE PIE

Line a deep pie-tin with pastry and bake. Heat a cupful of milk with half a cupful of sugar and a teaspoonful of butter. Add two tablespoonfuls of grated chocolate, the beaten yolks of two eggs, and thicken with one and one-half small spoonfuls of cornstarch rubbed smooth with a little cold milk. Cook until smooth and thick, stirring constantly, add half a teaspoonful of vanilla, fill the pastry shell, and cool. Serve with whipped cream.

COCOANUT CUSTARD PIE

Soak half a cupful of shredded cocoanut in a cupful of milk, add two tablespoonfuls of melted butter, one cupful of sugar, and two eggs well-beaten. Bake with one crust, and after the pie is done, cover with meringue and return to the oven until puffed and brown.

CRANBERRY PIE

Stew cranberries in just enough water to cover until they burst. Mash, smooth, sweeten well, turn into a pie-plate lined with pastry, lay strips of pastry across the pie, and bake in a moderate oven.

CREAM PIE

Beat together two cupfuls of milk, half a cupful of sugar, two teaspoonfuls of flour, and the yolks of three eggs. Flavor with grated nutmeg, vanilla, or lemon, and boil, while stirring, for twenty minutes. Turn into a pie-tin lined with pastry which has been baked, and bake until done. Make a meringue of the whites of the eggs and three tablespoonfuls of powdered sugar. Spread on the pie and bake until puffed and brown.

CURRANT PIE

Line a buttered pie-tin with pastry, fill with stemmed currants, dredge with sugar, sprinkle with flour, cover with crossbars of pastry, and bake.

GOOSEBERRY PIE

Line a deep pie-tin with pastry and fill with stewed gooseberries sweetened to taste and flavored with grated nutmeg. Cover with crust, bake, and sprinkle with powdered sugar in serving.

LEMON CREAM PIE—I

Line a pie-tin with pastry and bake. Make a syrup of one cupful of sugar and two-thirds cupful of water. Thicken with a teaspoonful of flour beaten with the yolks of two eggs and add the grated rind and juice of a lemon. Cook until smooth and thick, stirring constantly, fill the crust, bake for five minutes, then cover with meringue and bake until puffed and brown.

LEMON CREAM PIE—II

Mix the juice of two lemons with the grated rind of one, a cupful each of water and sugar and bring to the boil in a double-boiler. Thicken while stirring with one tablespoonful of cornstarch rubbed smooth in a little cold water, take from the fire, add a teaspoonful of butter, and three eggs well-beaten. Turn into pie-tins lined with pastry and bake. Cover with meringue and return to the oven until puffed and brown.

PEACH PIE

Line a deep pie-tin with rich pastry and fill with peeled and split peaches. Sprinkle with two tablespoonfuls of cracker crumbs, and one cupful of sugar, fill with cream and bake for thirty minutes.

PRUNE CREAM PIE

Stew, stone, and rub through a sieve enough prunes to make a cupful of pulp. Add one cupful of milk or thin cream, cooked with a teaspoonful of cornstarch rubbed smooth in a little cold milk, the yolks of two eggs well-beaten, and one-third cupful of sugar. Line a pie-tin with pastry, fill with the mixture, and bake quickly. Cover with meringue and brown. Serve either hot or cold.

PUMPKIN PIE

Mix a pint of stewed and strained pumpkin with a pint of milk, two eggs well-beaten, one cupful of sugar, one teaspoonful of cinnamon, one-half teaspoonful each of ginger and nutmeg, and the grated peel of half a lemon. Bake for half an hour with an undercrust only.

RHUBARB PIE

Line a deep pie-tin with pastry and fill with chopped rhubarb stewed soft in a little water, sweetened to taste and mixed with a well-beaten egg. Sprinkle with flour, cover with crust, and bake.

STRAWBERRY PIE

Line a pie-tin with pastry, fill with fresh strawberries, dot with butter, sprinkle with powdered sugar, cover with crossbars of pastry, and bake.

APPLE PUDDING

Peel and grate six sour apples. Add the juice and grated rind of a lemon, the well-beaten yolks of four eggs, and two tablespoonfuls of butter creamed with half a cupful of sugar. Season with spice, fold in the stiffly beaten whites of the eggs and bake in a buttered baking-dish. Serve cold with cream.

APPLE SAGO PUDDING

Soak four tablespoonfuls of sago over night in a pint of water and cook slowly in a double boiler until transparent, adding more water if necessary, and sugar to taste. Fill a baking-dish with peeled and cored apples, pour the sago over them, cover and bake until the apples are tender. Cool, and serve with sugar and cream.

APRICOT PUDDING

Sweeten hot boiled rice and arrange in a border on a serving-dish. Fill the centre with stewed apricots or canned apricots drained, and sprinkle with grated lemon-peel. Cover with whipped cream and sprinkle with chopped nuts. Almost any other fruit may be used instead of apricots.

BALTIMORE PUDDING

Butter a baking-dish and line it with stale sponge cake cut in thin slices. Fill nearly full with stewed peaches or cherries, cover with cake and spread with a meringue made of the stiffly beaten whites of two eggs and two tablespoonfuls of sugar. Bake until puffed and brown and serve cold with cream.

BIRD'S NEST PUDDING

Peel and core eight apples and put into a buttered baking-dish, filling the cores with brown sugar seasoned with grated nutmeg. Cover and bake until the apples are done. Beat the yolks of four eggs, add two cupfuls of flour sifted with three teaspoonfuls of baking-powder and a pinch of salt, two cupfuls of milk and the stiffly beaten whites of the eggs. Pour the batter over the apples, bake for an hour in a moderate oven, and serve with any preferred sauce.

BLACKBERRY PUDDING

Stew a quart of blackberries with sugar and pour hot over thin slices of buttered bread, making alternate layers, and having fruit on top. Cover with a plate, chill, and serve with sugar and cream. Cherries and other fruits may be used in the same way.

BLUEBERRY PUDDING—I

Sift together two cupfuls of flour, a pinch of salt, two heaping teaspoonfuls of cream tartar and a teaspoonful of soda. Add a pint of berries and enough milk to mix to a stiff batter. Turn into a buttered mould, cover and steam for an hour and a half. Serve with a sauce made by creaming half a cupful of butter with a cupful of sugar and two teaspoonfuls of flour and cooking until thick with a cupful of boiling water. Flavor with nutmeg or vanilla.

BLUEBERRY PUDDING—II

Sift together three cupfuls of flour, a pinch of salt, and two teaspoonfuls of baking-powder. Add one cupful of milk, one egg well-beaten, and two cupfuls of blueberries. Turn into a deep buttered mould, leaving room for the pudding to swell. Steam for two hours and serve hot with any preferred sauce. Apples, apricots, blackberries, cherries, currants, figs, preserved ginger, plums, oranges, peaches, pears, pineapples, raspberries, and strawberries may be used in the same way.

BREAD AND APPLE PUDDING

Fill a buttered pudding-dish with alternate layers of thin buttered slices of bread and sliced apples which have been peeled and cored, seasoning the apples with sugar and spice. Add enough water to moisten, cover and bake slowly for two hours. Serve hot or cold with cream or Hard Sauce.

CABINET PUDDING

Butter a mould and line it with raisins or currants and bits of citron. Fill the mould nearly full with alternate layers of stale sponge cake and candied fruit or raisins and citron. Pour over a custard made of three eggs beaten with a pint of milk and sweetened to taste. Put the mould in a pan of boiling water to reach to one-third its height and bake for an hour in a moderate oven.

CALIFORNIA PUDDING

Beat three eggs with one and one-half cupfuls of milk and half a wineglassful of claret. Add a few drops of almond extract. Cook until it thickens, stirring constantly. Put small pieces of stale sponge cake into a baking-dish and sprinkle with chopped citron. Pour over the custard and let stand for half an hour. Cream half a cupful each of butter and sugar, spread over the pudding, bake for an hour, and serve either hot or cold.

CARAMEL PUDDING

Make a custard of one cupful of milk beaten with the yolks of four eggs and the white of one, and a tablespoonful of sugar. Brown half a cupful of sugar in an iron pan, add half a cupful of water and simmer until it is a thick syrup. Line a mould with the caramel, turning rapidly from side to side, strain in the uncooked custard, cover and steam for half an hour.

CHERRY PUDDING

Soak three cupfuls of stale bread crumbs until soft in milk to cover. Add a teaspoonful of salt, a tablespoonful of sugar, grated nutmeg to flavor, and flour to make a batter sifted with two teaspoonfuls of baking-powder. Add three eggs well-beaten, and as many stoned cherries as can be incorporated in the batter. Fill a buttered tin, leaving room for the pudding to rise one-third, steam for two hours and a half and serve hot with any preferred sauce.

CHOCOLATE PUDDING

Heat two cupfuls of milk and add slowly one-half cake of grated chocolate, one heaping tablespoonful of sugar and one tablespoonful of cornstarch rubbed smooth with a little cold milk. Cook until smooth and thick, stirring constantly, take from the fire, add a few drops of vanilla, mould, chill and serve with cream and sugar.

CHOCOLATE CREAM PUDDING

Cook to a smooth paste two squares of grated bitter chocolate, four teaspoonfuls of sugar, and four tablespoonfuls of hot water. Add half a cupful of cream and one-fourth cupful of milk. Bring to a boil, add the yolks of two eggs beaten with a little milk, and cook until it thickens, stirring constantly. Fold in the stiffly beaten whites, add a pinch of salt, and vanilla or cinnamon to flavor. Cover and let stand in a double boiler until light and spongy. Turn into a serving-dish, sprinkle with powdered sugar, and serve cold with whipped cream.

CHRISTMAS PUDDING

Open a pint can of mince meat and add to it the yolks of six eggs well-beaten. Add enough sifted flour to make a stiff batter and fold in the stiffly beaten whites of the eggs. Pour into a buttered mould, leaving room to swell, cover tightly, put into boiling water and boil rapidly for five hours. Serve with Wine Sauce.

CRACKER PUDDING

Roll six crackers to crumbs. Add a cupful of milk and the grated rind of half a lemon and cook to a smooth paste. Add three tablespoonfuls of softened butter, two heaping tablespoonfuls of sugar, a tablespoonful of sherry, and four eggs well-beaten. Pour into a buttered dish, cover and steam for half an hour. Serve with Hard Sauce.

CORNSTARCH PUDDING

Heat two cupfuls of water and thicken with three tablespoonfuls of cornstarch rubbed smooth with a little cold water. Cook for ten minutes, stirring constantly, add the juice and grated rind of a lemon, half a cupful of sugar, the yolks of two eggs well-beaten, half a cupful of milk, and two tablespoonfuls of butter. Take from the fire, mix thoroughly, turn into a buttered baking-dish, bake for half an hour, cover with meringue and return to the oven until puffed and brown. Serve either hot or cold.

COTTAGE PUDDING

Cream together one cupful of sugar and two tablespoonfuls of butter. Add two eggs beaten separately and a cupful of milk. Sift in two cupfuls of flour and three teaspoonfuls of baking-powder, beat thoroughly, turn into a buttered baking-dish, sprinkle thickly with powdered sugar, and bake in a moderate oven for forty minutes. Serve hot with Lemon Sauce.

CURRANT PUDDING

Fill a small buttered baking-dish with thin slices of baker's bread, buttered, and alternate layers of fresh currants, stewed and sweetened to taste. Have fruit on top. Cover and bake for half an hour in a moderate oven, cool, and serve with sugar and cream. Blackberries, blueberries, raspberries, gooseberries, and strawberries may be used in the same way.

CUSTARD PUDDING

Heat a pint of milk in a double boiler and thicken with a tablespoonful of cornstarch rubbed smooth in a little cold milk. Add a pinch of salt, half a cupful of sugar, half a teaspoonful of powdered cinnamon, take from the fire, cool, and add three eggs well-beaten. Turn into a buttered baking-dish and bake until a knife thrust into the centre of the pudding comes out clean. Serve very cold. Any other flavor may be used instead of cinnamon.

DATE PUDDING

Chop fine one cupful of suet. Add the yolks of two eggs beaten with a cupful of milk, a teaspoonful of cinnamon, a pinch of salt and half a nutmeg grated. Sift in three cupfuls of flour and a teaspoonful of baking-powder. Add a pound of washed, stoned, and and chopped dates dredged with flour, turn into a buttered mould, and steam for three hours. Serve hot with Hard Sauce.

DATE CUSTARD PUDDING

Thicken a pint of milk with one tablespoonful of cornstarch rubbed smooth with a little cold milk, add the yolks of three eggs well-beaten with two tablespoonfuls of granulated sugar, and a teaspoonful of lemon extract. Take from the fire, add a tablespoonful of butter, turn into a buttered baking-dish, and bake brown. Cover with chopped dates and almonds or English walnuts, then with meringue flavored with lemon, and return to the oven until puffed and brown. Serve cold.

DANISH PUDDING

Wash a cupful of tapioca and soak it over night in six cupfuls of cold water. In the morning cook for an hour in a double boiler, stirring frequently. Add a pinch of salt, half a cupful of sugar, and one cupful of jelly. As soon as the jelly is melted mould, chill, and serve with whipped cream.

FARINA PUDDING

Cook three tablespoonfuls of farina in a double boiler with a quart of milk and a teaspoonful of salt. At the end of an hour add a cupful of currant jelly and, if desired, a little more sugar. Mould, chill, and serve with whipped cream.

FRUIT PUDDING

Mix one cupful of chopped beef suet, one cupful of molasses, one cupful of sour milk, one teaspoonful of salt and one-half cupful of raisins or currants. Sift in three cupfuls of flour, one teaspoonful of soda and half a nutmeg grated. Turn into a buttered mould and steam for three hours.

FRUIT AND RICE PUDDING

Boil a cupful of washed rice until soft in salted water to cover, and drain. Spread upon a buttered pudding cloth and fill the centre with preserved or fresh fruit sweetened to taste. Tie up, steam for two hours, and serve hot with any preferred sauce.

GINGER PUDDING

Mix one cupful of stale cake crumbs with a cupful of freshly grated cocoanut. Add two cupfuls of hot sweetened cream and let stand until the crumbs are soft. Add four eggs well-beaten and turn into a buttered mould lined with thin slices of preserved ginger. Steam for two hours and serve with the syrup drained from the ginger.

LEMON PUDDING

Grate half a loaf of bread, pour over a cupful of boiling milk, and cool. Add the grated peel of two lemons, half a cupful of butter beaten to a cream, powdered sugar to sweeten, and three eggs well-beaten. Fill a buttered baking-dish or small buttered cups and bake for twenty minutes in a moderate oven. Serve hot with any preferred sauce.

LEMON CUSTARD PUDDING

Make a pint of Lemon Jelly and add to it the beaten yolks of four eggs. When cool, but not set, fold in the stiffly beaten whites of the eggs, mould, chill, and serve with sugar and cream.

NEW ENGLAND INDIAN PUDDING

Sift a cupful of corn-meal slowly into four cupfuls of boiling milk and cook in a double boiler for half an hour, stirring frequently. Take from the fire, add a scant cupful of molasses, four cupfuls of milk, one teaspoonful of salt, two tablespoonfuls of butter, and one egg well-beaten. Pour into a deep earthen dish, and bake slowly for four hours. Serve hot with Hard Sauce flavored with vanilla.

ORANGE PUDDING

Peel, seed and quarter six oranges, put into a baking-dish and sprinkle with sugar. Thicken a quart of milk with two tablespoonfuls of cornstarch rubbed smooth with a little of it, add a pinch of salt, a teaspoonful of butter, and the yolks of three eggs beaten with half a cupful of sugar. Add a little grated orange peel, and cook until smooth and thick, stirring constantly. Pour the custard over the oranges, bake for twenty minutes, then cover with meringue made of the beaten whites of the eggs and two tablespoonfuls of sugar, sprinkle with sugar and bake until puffed and brown. Serve cold with cream.

PEACH PUDDING

Thicken three cupfuls of boiling milk with two tablespoonfuls of cornstarch rubbed smooth with a little cold milk. Cook until smooth and thick, stirring constantly, then take from the fire, add a tablespoonful of butter and the yolks of three eggs beaten to a cream with a cupful of sugar. Drain a can of peaches, put into a baking-dish, pour the custard over and bake for ten minutes, then cover with meringue and return to the oven until brown.

PEACH BLOSSOM PUDDING

Blanch and shred a cupful of almonds, add to a cupful of cream and sweeten heavily. Add half a package of gelatine which has been soaked and dissolved in as little water as possible, and a few drops of almond extract. Tint pink with color paste and when cool but not set, fold in a cupful of cream whipped solid. Mould, chill, and serve with whipped cream.

PEACH AND RICE PUDDING

Wash half a cupful of rice and soak it for two hours in cold water to cover. Drain and cook in a double-boiler with two and one-half cupfuls of milk, one cupful of sugar, and a pinch of salt. Cook for two hours, then put into a buttered baking-dish in layers with stewed or preserved peaches, having rice on top. Dot with butter, sprinkle with sugar and spice, bake brown, and serve hot or cold with any preferred sauce.

PINEAPPLE PUDDING

Soak half a package of gelatine in cold water to cover, add half a cupful of milk and dissolve by gentle heat. Heat two cupfuls of milk in a double boiler, add a cupful of sugar, a pinch of salt, and the beaten yolks of six eggs. Cook until it thickens, stirring constantly, then add three cupfuls of grated canned pineapple, bring to the boil, take from the fire, and when cool but not set fold in the stiffly beaten whites of the eggs. Mould, chill, and serve with whipped cream.

PRUNE PUDDING

Stone a cupful of stewed prunes and rub through a sieve. Beat the whites of five eggs to a stiff froth, add five tablespoonfuls of powdered sugar, a pinch of cream tartar, and a few grains of salt. Add the prunes gradually, turn into a deep buttered baking-dish, and bake in a slow oven for twenty minutes. Serve either hot or cold, with Boiled Custard.

QUINCE PUDDING

Peel, core, and quarter five quinces and simmer until softened in water to cover. Rub through a sieve, add a cupful of sugar and the yolks of four eggs beaten with a pint of milk. Line a deep baking-dish with pastry, turn in the quince, and bake for forty-five minutes. Cover with a meringue made from the beaten whites of four eggs and six tablespoonfuls of sugar. Return to the oven until puffed and brown and serve cold.

RASPBERRY PUDDING

Fill a buttered baking-dish with alternate layers of raspberries and dry bread crumbs, sweetening each layer of berries with sugar. The top layer should be crumbs. Dot with butter, sprinkle with sugar and bake for half an hour. Serve with cream.

RED SAGO PUDDING

Wash a cupful of sago and soak over night in four cupfuls of cold water. Cook in a double boiler in the water in which it was soaked until the sago is transparent. Add a pinch of salt, two cupfuls of raspberry, cherry, strawberry, or currant-juice, and sugar to taste. Cook for half an hour, turn into a wet mould, chill, and serve with whipped cream. This pudding may be made with jelly instead of fruit juice. Grape juice made tart with lemon-juice may also be used.

RICE PUDDING—I

Wash half a cupful of rice thoroughly, soak in cold water for two hours, and drain. Add two tablespoonfuls of sugar, a teaspoonful of salt, a little grated nutmeg, four cupfuls of milk, and half a cupful of raisins. Bake for two hours, stirring occasionally, then add a cupful of milk and bake for an hour longer. Serve in the baking-dish.

RICE PUDDING—II

Boil a cupful of rice in milk to cover, add two well-beaten eggs, sugar, and flavoring to taste, with a little cream. Bake in buttered cups and serve hot with sauce.

RICE PUDDING—III

Boil a cupful of rice until tender in milk to cover, adding a pinch each of salt and sugar, and flavoring to taste. Take from the fire, add the yolks of three eggs well-beaten, turn into a buttered baking-dish and cover with a meringue made of the stiffly beaten whites of the eggs, two tablespoonfuls of sugar, and a little grated lemon-peel. Brown in the oven and serve cold.

RICE AND CHERRY PUDDING

Boil a cupful of well-washed rice with a pint of milk, a tablespoonful each of sugar and butter, and a pinch of salt. Put into a buttered baking-dish with alternate layers of canned cherries, pour the juice over, sprinkle with sugar, and bake in a moderate oven. Peaches or other fruits may be used.

RICE AND FRUIT PUDDING

Cook a cupful of washed rice until soft in milk to cover, sweetening and flavoring to taste. Take from the fire, cool, and mix with a cold boiled custard made of a cupful of milk and the beaten yolks of four eggs. Add half a package of gelatine which has been soaked and dissolved and fold in half a cupful of cream whipped solid. Mould in a border mould and fill the centre with canned apricots, peaches, cherries, or any other fruit.

SAGO PUDDING

Cook slowly for an hour two-thirds cupful of sago in a quart of salted milk. Cool, add the yolks of four eggs well-beaten with the whites of two, a tablespoonful of melted butter, four tablespoonfuls of sugar, and a cupful of milk. Add a teaspoonful of vanilla and bake for half an hour in a moderate oven. Cool, cover with meringue, and return to the oven until puffed and brown. Serve cold.

SNOW PUDDING

Heat in a double boiler two cupfuls of water, the juice of a lemon and half a cupful of sugar. Thicken with three small spoonfuls of cornstarch rubbed smooth with half a cupful of water. Cook for ten minutes, take from the fire and fold in the stiffly beaten whites of four eggs. Mould, chill, and serve with a boiled custard made of the yolks of the eggs cooked until thick with a pint of milk, and sweetened and flavored to taste.

SPICE PUDDING

Mix half a cupful each of molasses and chopped suet with the juice and grated rind of half a lemon, a teaspoonful of powdered cinnamon, and a pinch of powdered clove. Dissolve half a teaspoonful of soda in half a cupful of milk, mix, and sift in flour to make a stiff batter. Add half a cupful of mixed raisins and currants, turn into a buttered mould and steam for five hours. Serve with Wine Sauce or Hard Sauce.

SPONGE PUDDING

Butter a baking-dish and put into it two sponge cakes soaked in sherry. Pour over a cupful of milk beaten with two eggs and sweetened to taste. Bake in a slow oven, turn out and serve.

STRAWBERRY BATTER PUDDING

Mash a quart of strawberries slightly with two cupfuls of sugar. Make a batter of two beaten eggs, two tablespoonfuls of melted butter, a pinch of salt, a cupful of milk, and one and one-half cupfuls of flour sifted with a teaspoonful of baking-powder. Butter custard cups and fill two-thirds full with alternate layers of berries and batter, having batter on top. Steam for half an hour, and serve with Hard Sauce flavored with lemon or crushed and sweetened strawberries. Other fruits may be used in the same way.

TAPIOCA PUDDING

Soak a cupful of tapioca over night in water to cover. Drain and cook until transparent in a quart of milk with a pinch of salt. Add the yolks of five eggs well-beaten, sugar and flavoring to taste, take from the fire and fold in the stiffly beaten whites of the eggs. Pour into a buttered baking-dish, set it into a pan of boiling water and bake until it thickens, then remove it from the pan of hot water and bake until brown. Serve either hot or cold.

TAPIOCA CREAM PUDDING

Soak a cupful of tapioca over night in two cupfuls of cold water. Cook in a double boiler with a pinch of salt, six cupfuls of milk, and the grated rind of an orange, until the tapioca is soft. Add the yolks of three eggs beaten with the juice of the orange and one cupful of sugar. Take from the fire, turn into a buttered baking-dish, and cover with a meringue made of the beaten whites of the eggs and three tablespoonfuls of sugar. Add also a little grated orange peel. Spread over the pudding and bake for half an hour in a very slow oven. Serve cold.

PUDDING SAUCES

BROWN SUGAR SAUCE

Thicken a pint of boiling water with one tablespoonful of butter and one of flour cooked together. Add brown sugar, lemon-juice, and grated nutmeg or other flavor to taste, and serve.

FOAMING SAUCE

Cream half a cupful of butter with half a cupful of powdered sugar, add the juice and grated rind of a lemon, set the basin into a pan of boiling water, stir until it foams, and serve immediately.

FRUIT SAUCE

Mash fresh fruit with sugar to taste, let stand for three hours, and heat thoroughly before serving.

HARD SAUCE

Cream a tablespoonful of butter with two tablespoonfuls of sugar, flavor with wine and grated nutmeg, and chill on ice. Fruit juice may be used instead of wine.

SHORTCAKES

PEACH SHORTCAKE

Rub half a cupful of butter into one and one-half cupfuls of sifted flour. Add a pinch of salt and enough ice-water to make a smooth paste. Roll out, shape it into flat round cakes, and put together with butter between. Bake brown, tear apart while hot, and fill with fresh peaches crushed with sugar. Cover the peaches with the other cake, spread peaches on top and pile high with sweetened whipped cream. Strawberry, banana, blackberry, cherry, fig, blueberry, gooseberry, orange, and raspberry shortcakes may be made in the same way.

PRUNE SHORTCAKE

Stew a pound of prunes until soft, in water to cover, with half a cupful of sugar. When the prunes are soft, remove the stones and simmer for ten minutes longer. Make a biscuit crust, adding a little more shortening, and bake in two cakes with butter between. Split, spread with butter, fill with the prunes, cover the top with prunes, and serve hot with whipped cream.

STRAWBERRY SHORTCAKE

Sift a quart of flour with two teaspoonfuls of baking-powder and a pinch of salt. Work into it two tablespoonfuls of butter, add enough milk to make a soft dough, and bake in large pie-tins. Cool, split, spread with butter and crushed strawberries heavily sweetened. Pour crushed strawberries over the cake and serve.

FRUIT SOUFFLÉS

Drain any kind of preserved fruit and rub through a sieve enough to make a cupful. Add more sugar if required and fold in the stiffly beaten whites of eight eggs. Turn into a buttered baking-dish, bake for half an hour and serve immediately. Apples, apricots, bananas, prunes, cherries, chestnuts, cocoanut, figs, gooseberries, preserved ginger, peaches, pears, pineapples, quinces, raspberries, and strawberries may be used in the same way.

TARTS

APPLE TART

Line a deep pie-tin with pastry, fill half full of apple sauce, and cover with quartered apples cooked until soft in lemon syrup. Sprinkle with claret and powdered sugar, bake, and serve cold.

APPLE CREAM TART

Line a deep baking-dish with pastry and put in three cupfuls of peeled, cored, and quartered apples, the grated rind and juice of a lemon, three-fourths cupful of brown sugar, and a sprinkle of cinnamon or nutmeg. Bake until the apples are done, cool, and cover with whipped cream sweetened to taste and flavored with grated lemon peel.

APRICOT TART

Butter a pastry ring, line with paste and bake. Spread with marmalade, cover with apricots, sprinkle with sugar and maraschino, heat for a few minutes, and serve cold with the apricot syrup. Other fruits may be used in the same way.

CHERRY TART

Mix a cupful each of sugar and stoned cherries with one egg well-beaten with a teaspoonful of flour. Turn into a pie-tin lined with pastry, cover with narrow strips of crust, and bake. Other fruits may be used in the same way.

CHOCOLATE CREAM TART

Grate a square of chocolate into a pint of milk and bring to the boil, sweetening to taste. Thicken with one tablespoonful of flour rubbed smooth with a little cold milk, take from the fire, add a tablespoonful of butter and the yolks of four eggs well-beaten. Line patty-pans with pastry, fill with the cream, and bake. Take from the oven, cover with meringue, and brown.

FRUIT TART

Line a deep pie-tin with pastry and bake, take from the oven, fill with fresh or stewed and sweetened fruit, and cover with a meringue made of the whites of three eggs beaten to a stiff froth and three tablespoonfuls of powdered sugar. Bake until brown and serve either hot or cold. Peaches, pears, plums, rhubarb, or other fruit may be used.

GERMAN APPLE TART

Line a shallow baking-pan with pastry and fill with peeled, cored, and sliced apples. Sprinkle with cinnamon and powdered sugar and bake for forty minutes in a moderate oven.

GOOSEBERRY TART

Simmer a pint of gooseberries until soft in a thick syrup. Line a pie-tin with pastry and put on a border of the paste about an inch wide. Press down lightly, fill with the gooseberries and cross the tart with narrow twisted strips of paste, moistening with cold water at each end to make them adhere. Bake for twenty minutes in a hot oven and serve very cold with whipped cream.

GRAPE TART—I

Stem the grapes and cook in syrup until thick and soft, rub through a sieve and cool. Line patty-pans with pastry, fill with the grapes, and bake. Cover with meringue or whipped cream if desired.

GRAPE TART—II

Line a deep pie-tin with pastry, brush with thick syrup, and fill with white grapes. Sprinkle with six tablespoonfuls of powdered sugar and a wineglassful of white wine. Bake and serve either hot or cold. Other grapes may be used in the same way.

NEAPOLITAN TARTS
Roll rich pastry thin, cut into strips, bake in a quick oven and put together with jam or jelly between. Cover with frosting and serve cold.

PEACH TART
Roll rich pastry thin and bake three crusts in pie-tins. Cool, put together with crushed and sweetened peaches, chill and serve with whipped cream. Other fruits may be used in the same way.

PEACH TART MERINGUE
Line a border mould with pastry, fill half full with peach jam, bake, cool, cover with meringue, and return to the oven until puffed and brown. Fill the centre with whipped cream if desired. Other jams may be used in the same way.

PEACH CREAM TART
Line a deep pie-tin with good pastry and fill it two-thirds full with canned peaches that have been cooked for two or three minutes in boiling syrup. Cover with a rather thick crust and do not pinch down the edges. When cool, remove the top crust and fill with a cream made as follows: Boil a cupful of milk, and thicken with a tablespoonful of sugar mixed with a teaspoonful of cornstarch wet in cold milk. When smooth and thick, take from the fire, add the whites of two eggs beaten to a stiff froth, and a few drops of vanilla or almond extract. Cool, pour over the peaches, cover with the crust, sprinkle with powdered sugar, and serve.

PLUM TART—I
Line a deep tin with pastry, fill with preserved plums, cover with crust, brush with beaten egg, bake, sprinkle with powdered sugar, and serve cold.

PLUM TART—II
Line a deep baking-dish with pastry and bake. Fill half full of boiled rice cooked in milk and sweetened to taste and cover with pitted plums which have been cooked soft in thin syrup. Sprinkle with powdered sugar, dot with butter, bake, and serve hot.

RASPBERRY CREAM TART
Line a deep pie-tin with pastry, fill with raspberries, sprinkle with powdered sugar, and cover with crust but do not press down the edges. Bake in a moderate oven. Thicken a cupful of milk with a teaspoonful of cornstarch rubbed smooth with a little cold milk, add a tablespoonful of sugar, a few drops of vanilla, and the stiffly beaten whites of two eggs; cook until smooth and thick. Lift the top crust from the pie, pour in the custard, cover, sprinkle with powdered sugar, and serve cold.

RASPBERRY AND CURRANT TART

Line a deep pie-tin with pastry and fill with alternate layers of raspberries and currants, sprinkling each layer with sugar. Sprinkle with sugar, dot with butter, and bake. Cover with meringue and serve cold.

RHUBARB TARTS

Blanch and split half an ounce of bitter almonds. Cut one and one-half pounds of rhubarb into inch-lengths without peeling, add a pound of sugar, the almonds, and one lemon cut into bits. Cook together until thick, stirring occasionally. Line patty-pans with pastry, fill with the mixture, and bake in a moderate oven.

APPLES À LA NINON

Cook rice until soft in milk to cover, sweetening and flavoring to taste. Arrange upon the rice peeled and cored apples which have been cooked in syrup, reduce the syrup by rapid boiling, flavor to taste, add a little chopped candied fruit, pour over the rice and apples, and serve either hot or cold.

APPLE BROWNIES

Peel, core, and quarter five sour apples, put into a baking-dish with three tablespoonfuls of butter, and sugar and cinnamon to taste. Bake until tender and serve hot with cream.

APPLE FLUFF

Peel good cooking apples, cook until soft, and rub through a sieve. Sweeten to taste, adding a little butter and lemon-juice, spice, or wine to season. Fold in the stiffly beaten whites of two or three eggs and serve very cold.

APPLE PUFF

Sift a cupful of flour with a pinch of salt, add two cupfuls of milk mixed with three well-beaten eggs, and turn into a shallow buttered pan. Cover with peeled and sliced apples, dot with butter, sprinkle thickly with sugar, and add a little grated lemon peel or spice if desired. Bake for forty-five minutes and serve hot. Berries or other fruits may be used in the same way.

APPLE ROLL

Rub two tablespoonfuls of butter into three cupfuls of flour which has been sifted with a heaping teaspoonful of baking-powder and a pinch of salt. Mix to a soft dough with milk or water, roll into an oblong, spread with finely cut peeled apples, and sprinkle with sugar and spice. Roll up and put loosely into a pudding cloth which has been wrung dry in hot water and dredged with flour. Steam for two hours and serve with Hard Sauce.

APPLE SNOW

Cook peeled apples soft in a thin syrup to cover, and rub through a sieve enough to make a pint of pulp. Cool, add the unbeaten white of an egg, and beat with an egg-beater until very light. Serve cold with boiled custard or whipped cream. Other fruits may be used in the same way.

APPLE TRIFLE

Cook peeled, cored, and quartered apples until soft in thin syrup to cover, seasoning with spice. Drain, arrange in a serving-dish, and reduce the syrup half by rapid boiling. Pour over the apples, cool, and at serving-time cover with whipped cream sweetened and flavored to taste. Other fruits may be used in the same way.

BAKED BANANAS

Melt three tablespoonfuls of butter with three of lemon-juice and six of sugar. Peel six bananas and lay in a shallow buttered pan, far apart. Bake for half an hour, basting with the mixture in the bowl, and serve hot.

BAKED PEACHES

Peel large peaches, stick a few blanched almonds into each one, sprinkle with sugar, add a cup of water and bake, basting with the syrup. Serve very cold with the syrup poured over.

BAKED PEARS

Put a quart of peeled, cored, and quartered pears into an earthen baking-dish with half a cupful of sugar and a cupful of water. Cover tightly and bake for several hours in a moderate oven. Take up the pears, reduce the syrup by rapid boiling, pour over, chill, and serve with cream.

BAKED QUINCES

Peel and core four or five quinces and put a bit of butter into the core of each. Sprinkle with sugar, pour in a cupful of water, cover and bake for two hours, basting occasionally. Serve cold with sugar and cream.

BAKED RHUBARB

Cut unpeeled rhubarb into inch-lengths and pack closely in a bean-pot with alternate layers of brown sugar. Cover, bake for an hour, and serve cold.

BAKED BERRY ROLL

Sift two cupfuls of flour with two teaspoonfuls of baking-powder. Work into it a tablespoonful of butter and mix to soft dough with a cupful of milk. Roll into an oblong, cover with berries, sprinkle with sugar, roll up, fasten the edges and bake or steam, basting with syrup to which a little butter has been added. Serve hot with any preferred sauce.

BANANAS AND CURRANTS

Crush and sweeten red currants, mix with sliced bananas, and serve cold. White currants may also be used.

BANANAS WITH WHIPPED CREAM

Peel and slice six bananas into a serving-dish, sprinkle with sugar, and with either orange-juice, lemon-juice, or wine. Cover with whipped cream and serve immediately with cake.

BANANA FLOAT

Soak half a package of gelatine in cold water and dissolve in three cupfuls of boiling milk. Add a heaping cupful of sugar and cook for ten minutes. When cool but not stiff, stir in three bananas broken up with a fork. Mould, chill, and serve with whipped cream.

BANANA TRIFLE

Peel and mash through a sieve enough bananas to make a cupful of pulp. Add a cupful of cream and two tablespoonfuls of powdered sugar. Beat with an egg-beater until very light and serve cold in dessert glasses.

BLACKBERRY SPONGE

Soak half a package of gelatine in half a cupful of cold water, add two cupfuls of boiling water, half a cupful of sugar, and one cupful of blackberry juice. Stir until dissolved, then strain. When cool but not set, fold in the stiffly beaten whites of four eggs. Mould, chill, and serve with cream. The juice of other fruits may be used in the same way.

BOILED FROSTING

Boil two cupfuls of sugar for five minutes with one-fourth cupful of water, pour the boiling syrup in a thin stream upon the stiffly beaten whites of two eggs, and beat until thick. Flavor to taste.

CHOCOLATE TAPIOCA

Cook two tablespoonfuls of minute tapioca in milk to cover, using a double-boiler. Add the yolks of three eggs well-beaten, sugar to taste, and half a teaspoonful of vanilla. Cook until thick, and add half a cake of grated sweet chocolate. When quite smooth mould, chill, and serve with whipped cream.

CHOCOLATE CREAM FROSTING

Beat the white of an egg to a stiff froth, add two tablespoonfuls of cream, and enough confectioner's sugar to make it thick enough to spread. Melt half a cake of sweet chocolate in a double boiler with a teaspoonful of water, and pour over the cream frosting on the cake.

FLOATING ISLAND

Beat the whites of two eggs to a stiff froth and gradually beat into it a cupful of jelly or jam. Fill a serving dish with whipped cream sweetened and flavored to taste, and drop spoonfuls of the frothed jelly upon it. This may be served in dessert glasses.

FRENCH PANCAKES

Beat together four eggs beaten separately, one cupful of milk, half a cupful of flour, one tablespoonful of sugar, a pinch of salt, the grated rind of a lemon, and a teaspoonful of butter melted. Fry in small pancakes, turning once, spread with jelly, jam, or marmalade, roll up, sprinkle with powdered sugar which may be seasoned with spice, and serve immediately.

FRUIT ICING

Mix confectioner's sugar with enough cream to make it the consistency of thick paste. Flavor as desired adding chopped nuts, bananas, shredded pineapple, or other fruits.

FRUIT PUFFS

Beat three eggs separately, then add one cupful of milk, a pinch of salt, and enough flour sifted with a heaping teaspoonful of baking-powder to make a thin batter. Fill buttered custard cups, alternating with finely cut apples or other fruit sprinkled with sugar, and steam for an hour. Jam or preserves may be used in the same way. Serve hot with any preferred sauce or with cream and sugar.

FRUIT ROLL

Sift together two cupfuls of flour, two teaspoonfuls of baking powder, a teaspoonful of sugar, and half a teaspoonful of salt. Rub into it two tablespoonfuls of butter and add enough milk to make a dough that will roll. Roll into an oblong, keeping the dough thin, spread with softened butter, then with chopped fresh or preserved fruit or berries, sweetened to taste. Roll up, pinch the ends together, and steam for two hours, or bake until the dough is brown and crisp. Serve hot with any preferred sauce. Apples, apricots, blackberries, chestnuts, currants, figs, preserved ginger, plums, blueberries, oranges, peaches, pineapples, quinces, raspberries, and cherries may all be used in this way.

FRUIT TAPIOCA

Soak a cupful of tapioca over night in four cupfuls of cold water. Add a pinch of salt, and three-fourths cupful of sugar, and cook slowly in a double boiler until transparent, adding more water if necessary. Put into a buttered baking-dish in layers, alternating with fresh or canned fruit sweetened to taste. Have tapioca on top. Sprinkle with sugar, dot with butter, and bake for an hour. Serve either hot or cold with cream or any preferred sauce. Apples, apricots, blackberries, cherries, currants, figs, gooseberries, plums, blueberries, oranges, peaches, pears, pineapples, quinces, raspberries, and strawberries are all used in the same way. The less tart fruits require a little lemon-juice sprinkled on them. In making apple tapioca sprinkle each layer of apples with sugar and spice. A delicious pudding is made of strawberries and bananas sliced and combined with the tapioca.

GOOSEBERRY TRIFLE

Cook a quart of gooseberries to a pulp in water to cover, sweetening to taste. Put into a serving-dish, cool, cover with boiled custard, then with whipped cream. Other fruits may be used in the same way.

JELLIED APPLES

Peel, core, and quarter enough apples to make four cupfuls. Cook slowly until soft in syrup to cover, flavoring with a little lemon or spice. Add a package of gelatine which has been soaked and dissolved, mould, chill, and serve with boiled custard or whipped cream.

JELLIED PEACHES

Peel and split a dozen peaches and cook until soft in thin syrup to cover. Add half a package of soaked and dissolved gelatine and a tablespoonful of claret or maraschino. Mould, chill, and serve with whipped cream or custard. Other fruits may be used in the same way.

JUNKET

Warm a quart of milk, add a tablespoonful of rennet, cool, and serve with powdered sugar, grated nutmeg, and cream.

LEMON SPONGE

Boil the chopped peel of one and juice of six lemons in two cupfuls of water, strain and mix with two cupfuls of hot water in which a package of soaked gelatine has been dissolved. Sweeten to taste, and beat until it begins to set, then fold in the stiffly beaten whites of twelve eggs. Mould and chill. Half this recipe is sufficient for a small family.

MOONSHINE

Beat the whites of six eggs to a stiff froth and add gradually twelve tablespoonfuls of powdered sugar. Beat for twenty minutes, then add three large peaches peeled and cut into bits. Fill dessert glasses three-fourths full, chill, and fill with whipped cream sweetened to taste and flavored with vanilla. Other fruits may be used in the same way.

ORANGE SNOW

Make a pint of Orange Jelly, adding the juice of a lemon and a little grated peel. When cool but not set, fold in the stiffly beaten whites of four eggs. Mould, chill and serve with Boiled Custard. Lemon snow may be made in the same way.

PEACH TRIFLE

Make a boiled custard with the yolks of four eggs, one pint of milk, and two tablespoonfuls of sugar, cool, and flavor with a few drops each of almond and vanilla. Arrange slices of stale sponge cake in a serving-dish, moisten with custard, cover with crushed and sweetened peaches, pour over the custard, and cover with meringue flavored with almond, or with whipped cream.

PEACH DELIGHT

Peel and split ripe peaches and fill a baking-dish, sprinkling each layer with sugar. Dot with butter, add a cupful of water, and sprinkle with flour. Make a crust of one and one-half cupfuls of flour sifted with a pinch of salt and a teaspoonful of baking-powder, rubbing into it half a cupful of lard, and adding ice-water to mix. Cover the peaches, prick the crust, bake, and serve either hot or cold with cream.

PEACH SNOW-BALLS

Peel ripe peaches, roll in powdered sugar, then dip in boiled frosting, let dry for two minutes, and sprinkle with shredded cocoanut.

PINEAPPLE FLUFF

Mix canned grated pineapple with chopped nuts and quartered marshmallows, and fill dessert glasses half full. Cover with whipped cream sweetened and flavored to taste, and garnish with candied cherries or chopped nuts.

PINEAPPLE DESSERT

Select a large pineapple, cut off the top and scrape out the pulp with a large spoon. Mix with finely cut strawberries, cherries, and bananas. Sweeten to taste, fill the pineapple shell, put on the cover, and serve.

PINEAPPLE SPONGE

Grate a fresh pineapple, add a cupful of sugar, and simmer slowly for ten minutes. Add half a package of gelatine which has been soaked and dissolved in as little water as possible, and when cool but not set, fold in the stiffly beaten whites of four eggs. Serve with a custard made of a pint of milk sweetened to taste, flavored with vanilla, and thickened with the beaten yolks of four eggs. A can of grated pineapple may be used instead of the fresh fruit.

PLUM ROLL

Sift a quart of flour with a teaspoonful of salt, and three teaspoonfuls of baking-powder, rub in two tablespoonfuls of butter, and add enough milk to make a soft dough. Roll out, spread with one cupful of chopped raisins and half a cupful of chopped citron. Sprinkle with cinnamon and sugar, roll up, and steam for half an hour or more. Serve hot with Hard Sauce.

PRUNE SPONGE

Beat three eggs separately and mix. Add half a cupful of sugar, half a teaspoonful of vanilla, and three-fourths cupful of flour sifted with a teaspoonful of baking-powder. Soak and pit fifteen prunes, drain, chop fine, add half a cupful of sugar and the juice of half a lemon. Put the prunes in a buttered baking-dish, cover with the batter, and bake for twenty or twenty-five minutes.

QUINCE FLUFF

Cut up four or five quinces and boil until soft in water to cover, then peel, and rub through a sieve. Sweeten to taste, add the unbeaten whites of four eggs, and beat to a froth with an egg-beater. Serve immediately in dessert dishes.

QUINCE TRIFLE

Stew four quinces until soft, rub through a colander, and sweeten to taste. Turn into a glass dish and cover with a boiled custard made of one pint of milk, the yolks of three eggs, and two tablespoonfuls of sugar. Cover with a meringue and serve.

RICE BALLS WITH CUSTARD

Wash a cupful of rice and soak for an hour in cold water to cover. Drain and cook until soft in two and one-half cupfuls of milk, adding a teaspoonful of salt when the rice is nearly soft. Add sugar to taste and any preferred flavoring. Wet custard cups in cold water, fill with rice and chill. At serving time turn out on a platter, put a bit of red jelly on each ball of rice and surround with boiled custard.

RASPBERRY SPONGE

Bring to a boil two and one-half cupfuls of raspberry juice, sweetening to taste. Add half a package of soaked gelatine, and stir until dissolved. When cool but not set, fold in the stiffly beaten whites of three eggs, and beat until stiff. Mould, chill, and serve with whipped cream. Strawberry or currant juice may be used in the same way.

STRAWBERRY MERINGUE

Beat the whites of seven eggs to a stiff froth and add gradually a pinch of salt and seven tablespoonfuls of powdered sugar. Put into a buttered baking-dish in layers, spreading each layer thinly with melted strawberry jam. Bake in a moderate oven for twenty-five minutes and serve very cold with whipped cream. Other jams may be used in the same way.

STRAWBERRY SPONGE

Rub a quart of strawberries through a sieve, sweeten heavily, and add the juice of a lemon. Add half a package of gelatine which has been soaked and dissolved, and when cool but not set, fold in the stiffly beaten whites of four eggs. Mould, chill, and serve with sugar and cream or with whipped cream. Other fruits may be used in the same way.

STRAWBERRY TRIFLE

Fill dessert glasses half full of sponge cake and strawberry preserves. Cover with a meringue flavored with strawberry juice or with boiled custard or with whipped cream, and serve with a few preserved strawberries on top. Other fruits may be served in the same way.

SNOW-BALLS

Wet small square cloths in cold water and spread thinly with boiled rice. Put an apricot in the centre of each, having removed the stone. Draw the cloths together, tie securely, and steam for ten or fifteen minutes. Remove the cloths and serve with a sauce made from fruit syrup. Almost any other fruit may be used instead of apricots.

SWEET PANCAKES

Mix two tablespoonfuls of flour with a few drops of orange-flower water and a few grains of salt. Add the yolks of four eggs, well-beaten, and the whites of two. Fry by tablespoonfuls in butter, turning once, and sprinkling with sugar. Or, spread with jelly, roll up, and sprinkle with powdered sugar.

STEWED PEARS WITH RICE

Peel, split, and core four large pears and cook until tender with two cupfuls of claret and one cupful of sugar. Boil half a cupful of rice until soft in milk to cover, sweetening and flavoring to taste. Spread the rice in a serving-dish, arrange the pears upon it, reduce the syrup by rapid boiling, pour over, and serve ice cold. Other fruits may be used in the same way.

VANITIES

Beat two eggs very light, add a pinch of salt, and flour to roll. Roll as thin as possible, cut into fancy shapes and fry brown in deep fat. Sprinkle with powdered sugar and serve.

VIRGINIA PUFFS

Cream half a cupful of butter with a cupful of sugar, add the beaten yolks of four eggs, a teaspoonful of vanilla, and sift in a cupful of cornstarch and two teaspoonfuls of baking-powder, alternating with the stiffly beaten whites of the eggs. Bake in buttered gem-pans, hissing hot, in a quick oven. Serve with any preferred sauce.

The End

www.ingramcontent.com/pod-product-compliance
Lightning Source LLC
Chambersburg PA
CBHW072245310526
45795CB00011B/70

* 9 7 8 1 4 9 0 9 8 9 6 7 9 *